# Synchronicity Numbers

DISCOVER THE MEANING OF 11:11, 33 AND OTHER RECURRING NUMBERS

Anmarie Uber

Tuggle Publishing
FORT WAYNE, IN

Tuggle Publishing
tugglepublishing.com
anmarieuber.com

Cover Design by Juliette at Silky Cover Design
SynchronicityNumbers/AnmarieUber—1sted.

# Contents

*Dedicated to:* Andrew Tuggle, who suffered me bravely, while I struggled to write a book, the size of two full novels, in 2.5 months time. Thank you for your love, patience and tolerance.

*So many numbers...so little time.*

—ANMARIE UBER

# introduction

I have always been a person looking for the hidden meaning in life. Synchronicities, signs and omens have fascinated me for years, and in particular, number coincidences. The intensity of my search really amped up, in the late 1980s, when I started seeing 11:11, everywhere, and was wondering what it meant. Before long, I was noticing repetitious numbers, and digits in particular sequences, all the time. As the synchronicities increased, my life became a spiritual search for the truth, and along the way, my understanding of the Universe, and how it worked, developed, piece by piece. I was putting together the puzzle, with each psychic reading, mediumship session, channeling, meditation, healing etc. Gathering information over the years, has helped me come to an understanding, to some degree, of why we are here, what is going on, and where we are going after this. Oh yeah...and what these crazy number coincidences are trying to tell us.

About that, I believe that we live in a matrix-like hologram, and numbers are sign posts, marking where we are. I have found that, in addition to numbers and numerology, astrology can read the matrix, as well. I have researched a lot of the ancient meanings of these numbers, but did not expand, or go into that in this work. For starters, some of what is going on in their use is dangerous, and a lot of the number meanings can be quite in-depth, and much too large for the size of book I wanted to write, at this time. I decided to stick with the number's predictive meanings, and their connections to the planets in our solar system, as well as channeling through my guides. I prayed ahead of time, that whoever was supposed to read a particular number in this book, at some future date, would be guided to the correct interpretation for them. This guide, therefore, is for the future, and you, the reader. My Oversoul can see ahead, much farther and in more detail than I, myself. There were times when I was directed to let a number meaning stay, as is, because someone, at some point in the future was going to read it, and it would apply to them, at that moment. So, Spirit already knows when you are going to open this book, and what number you are going to pick, including all the variable alternatives that could change that scenario. I have left the book, as it is, even if I didn't quite agree that a certain number meaning should be applied, in some cases. With that said, I have left you with minimal, yet helpful instructions on how to use this book. It is for you, to allow yourself to be guided in its ultimate use.

**Guide to Using the Number Meanings 0 - 1000:** For clarity and insight, on your spiritual journey.

This book is not meant to be an interpretation of specific numbers in set numerology systems, but rather a guide to experiences along your life path, that occur at certain times. I liken this to an astrology chart, with its transits, progressions, challenges and blessings, that mark certain periods of time. The meanings of the numbers, herein, apply to their positioning on the matrix of the mind overlay. These are points on your journey through this construct.

1. If you are seeing a certain number repeatedly, then read that number meaning, paying close attention to whatever is on your mind, when you see this number.
2. This book is also an oracle. Quiet your mind. If you have an area of concern, focus on that, or ask in a general sense. Allow a number to come to you, and then read its meaning, for immediate guidance.
3. Each number has an affirmation at the end, to help you shift into the higher vibration of Grace, and thereby take advantage of the full energy of the number, or overcome any negative possibilities. Take your free will into your own hands, and not be at the mercy of the ego matrix.
4. For more difficult numbers, there is either a crystal, animal totem, herb/essential oil* or Guardian/Archangel to help with healing and support.

The crystals can be worn or carried with you. (If you do not have, or cannot find a particular crystal, then a stone of a similar color, or a stone that connects with you, will do fine as a replacement. Also, looking at a picture of the crystal will help attune you to its vibration.) The herbs or essential oils can be inhaled; it is suggested you research the best use for each of them. Animal Totems can be called upon, to bring support (the animal oversoul). There are many sites and books, if you would like to learn more about animal totems. Ask the Angels for support, through your thoughts, or in prayer. (Please specify, "Angel representing divine Source energy", as we live in a duality Universe, and just as "evil" is "live" backwards, so is there the malevolent counterpart to the benevolent Angels.)

5. Follow your own guides, when reading and interpreting these meanings. If you have trouble relating to, or understanding a number interpretation, try picking

another number, for more clarity, or ask someone close to you, for their opinion and insight. Sometimes our friends and loved ones know us better than we know ourselves, and see our lives much clearer, than we tend to see our own.

6. FINAL NOTE: I use Soul, Spirit, Source, etc. in these number descriptions, as well as discuss beliefs you may not share. Use what resonates with you, and leave the rest. Substitute whatever term best relates to your belief system. The idea is that we are talking about our true Source of Creation, which we are eventually returning to, and that is Love.

Many blessings, on your journey, with synchronicity numbers!

**With all herbs and essential oils, follow the recommended usages and cautions.*

*Disclaimer: The information in this book, is for entertainment purposes only. It is not meant to replace medical, legal, financial or any other advice that should come from a licensed professional.*

# chapter one:

# the numbers 0 - 1000

**0 - The Source.** The beginning and ending of all time. There is no "reality" to this number, because it is outside of time and space. It is outside the bounds of the artificial world. Therefore, it encompasses *all* in truth, because it brings all back to Source. There is nothing outside of Source. This number means it is time for you to meditate. Commune with your Angels, and ask for Source and Divine Love to fill you, at this time. You are needing to be centered and grounded. You are too caught up in the world, and need to get in touch with your inner self. The Holy Hosts are with you. Guidance is sure, and much needed. You are on track, if you make your spiritual life your focus. Say yes to any offers you receive. *As is the beginning, so is the end. I am all, and all is One. I am complete.*

**1 - Create.** The Source, beginning into life. Life made manifest through the unconscious mind into consciousness. Number one signifies a new start. It is a sign to take the lead, and show yourself what you can do. Tap into the creative intellect, and bring that into your work, focus, or life. Ideas take shape. All is well. This is a chance for you to start anew, and reap the reward of your own creations. This could be a project or business, or apply to the types of relationships you create, with your words, communications, and ability to give love. 1 also has to do with the responsibility of maintaining your boundaries, and loving yourself. *The creative Source flows through me daily, inspiring me to be all that I can be.*

**2 - The Mirror.** Two is balance of opposites. Now there is not just one, but the "other". The number 2 asks you to look for inner qualities that need balancing. What are you denying in yourself that is good, or not so desirable? You are not lacking. Lack is just an incorrect belief created by fear. Do not to seek confirmation in others. In other words, do not look outside of your self for what is within. If you look within first, all outside relationships will be healthy, in turn. In particular, two has to do with a pairing of opposites in partnerships, whether in your personal, or business life. Relationships can be healthy, if both individuals are whole in themselves. If this relates to business, make sure you are both bringing equal value to the table. In personal relationships, partnerships must have a balance of give and take. Put energy into your relationships, now. Its as simple as asking, "How can I love? How can I love myself, and this person in a more pure way? How can I give, without allowing myself to be depleted? If I am not in a partnership, is there some fear holding me back, or do I need more time to focus on myself?" *I am whole and free to be me with others. I give love freely, and therefore, I receive it in return.*

**3 - Connect.** This number is about creation. The union of the one and two, create a third. Three is a magic number, as it has the ability to create something out of nothing. Ideas become things. Thoughts manifest quicker...its as if the whole Universe has spotted you, and is ready to bring in what you ask. You are not invisible, but glaringly in the spotlight. You are affecting people with your presence, and they want what you have. You cannot hide from anything right now, including your problems, and must face them head on. They won't go away until you accept, and heal them, or solve the issue. Recognize the obstacle, and remove it. Often, this is fear-based. Three helps you connect to others in a dynamic way. It brings together groups, almost effortlessly. The message is to put yourself out there. Don't hide yourself away, or your ideas. Connect with others. Socialize. Make your presence known. If there is something you are afraid to reveal, now is the time to bring it out into the open. Often 3 can mean a "pregnancy" is going to be announced, whether that is an actual baby, or the beginning of a new project, or idea. It can also be a new way of thinking. If you are interested in speaking with your Angels and Spirit Guides, channeling should be clearer at this time, as well. *It is safe for me, to be me. I am always supported in my endeavors, and in being my true authentic self.*

4 - **Grounding.** The four stabilizes. Your life might need

some stability right now, or you may need to check the foundations of your dreams and personal life. Are things on solid ground? The four warns of unexpected experiences popping up, so be prepared for anything. These can be positive, or challenging, depending on what you have been thinking and manifesting in your life. Are you too controlling? Do you need to let go, and flow with Spirit? If you are holding the reins too tightly, or acting through fear, you will attract sudden changes. It is wise to make sure you are prepared for anything that can happen. This includes good things. Make sure you are open to receiving. Find a balance between control and allowing. New and unusual experiences, or people may be coming your way. Reconnecting with family, or spending time with close friends is a good idea. Take time to take care of others. Make sure all is on solid ground before assuming anything. Be practical, and pay attention to details. *I release all fear, and allow my good to come to me now, in a perfect way.*

**5 - The Current.** Five is an open number, and unlike the four,

which resists change, completely flows with what is happening. You are in the midst of many changes, and are transitioning. This may be a short time, or a long term feeling. The number 5 means things are moving forward. What you have sown, you will reap. The five suggests that things can move in your favor, if you stay positive, and allow the lessons, challenges and blessings to unfold in their own way. Stay strong in an inner knowing, that all will turn out as it is destined to be. Five is a sign that you can make anything happen in your life, and very quickly. Allow miracles to manifest themselves. Thank the Angels for bringing you what you need. *Miracles, find me now.*

**6 - Community Outreach.** Six is all about connections and

networking. Who do you know? 6 says to start asking others for help. Sometimes this can be difficult or uncomfortable. Ask your Angels or Spirit for help, and whoever is around you. The Angels may have sent someone who can act in their stead. Don't be afraid to allow others to assist you. In turn, who needs your help right now? Cultivate relationships in your life. Spend time in nature, either alone, or with others, and connect to the Mother Earth, and your relationship with her. Pay attention to your well-being, physically, emotionally and spiritually. Who do you need to connect with, and what do you need in your environment, to be at peace? 6 says it is time to find your inner calm, and deal with situations from this centered space. A visit from an old friend may be imminent. *All that I need comes to me now, and I accept my good with open arms.*

7 - **The Student.** The answer always lies within. All seeking and searching in the outer world always comes back to this. You may need some quiet time alone right now. If you cannot do this, then a form of it can be done, while in the presence of others, with quiet listening, acting as an observer to what is happening around you, or envisioning yourself acting in a play, realizing it is all a script...this helps you to detach from getting caught up in another person's issues or dramas, right now. With this method, you can then choose to emotionally react, or calmly respond. Spiritual studies are also highlighted, and you are encouraged to focus on this aspect of your life. Now is the time for studying what needs to be learned on a soul level, in order to move forward. You are making spiritual progress. Keep going. *I am calm, serene and listen for the Divine guidance, that is available to me in all situations.*

**8 - The Scales of Justice.** Eight is a sign of two things, either difficult karmic experiences are happening to you now, or you have a material windfall, or some type of abundance coming in. These play out very differently. If it is the former, you need to examine your feelings of lack, patterns that have happened to you, and how you block yourself. Also realize that karma can be outside of your control...except for your ability to not react to the experiences, and affirm that they are temporary, and therefore, not real (because all things change), and allow for the change. Turn it over into Spirit's hands. Only this can change your situation at this time...a sort of going with the flow. If you choose love over money, eventually all will be well, and you will not create new negative karma for the future. If, on the other hand, the 8 is representing abundance for you, cross your T's, dot your I's and prepare to receive the blessings coming your way. The money, or reward will come. *Abundance comes to me daily, in perfect order.*

**9 - Spiraling Up.** 9 is a number of infinity, although we think of the number 8, or 0 in this respect. 9 is about endings and repeats, being the last single number in the series. There is a life lesson that you are finishing up. What is going on in your life right now, that has been ongoing and difficult? It is coming to the end, or at least a segment of it is. Nine is also about travel. Are you going somewhere? Do you need a vacation? Take a break. Get some perspective on your life. Increase your education. *I see the Divine purpose in my life, playing itself out in perfect order. I forgive, release and let go of all that is holding me back.*

**10 - Opportunities.** The number 10 is about beginnings, like the one, but it involves a new beginning that is on a higher level of the spiral. You see things in a new perspective, and have more understanding about a situation, than you previously did. Ten is a beginning, a chance to start with a clean slate, and decide that you will do things differently this time. Are you sabotaging, or interfering with your own good? Are negative thoughts and beliefs, from old ways of doing things, creating negative results in your life? Its time to set yourself up to succeed, by deciding to choose positive thoughts, choose love instead of fear, and choose to understand, rather than react. What are your goals? Set them now, and clean the slate. *I am newly reborn in each moment. All is new to me. The past is gone. Anything is possible.*

**11 - Mission Accomplished.** This is a special number for lightworkers. The 11 is a doorway to other worlds. It represents the doorway into this world, and out. It means your soul has come here with a specific mission, and not a lot can be changed from your life script, because things are destined to play out in a specific way. You are on a set path. If you are seeing double elevens, such as 11:11 or 1:11, please read under these numbers. The eleven challenges you to become the best person you can be. This is not measured by worldly standards, but rather by how much you are able to detach from the world. Everything is transitory here, so none of us will be visiting long. Eleven asks you to face this fact, and realize what is truly important in life. This means forgiving those who have seemingly wronged you, and letting it go, because the next time you incarnate may be 10,000 years from now, or never again. Will this incident matter then? Find the higher ground. Master yourself. Master your attachment to fear. Ask the Angels for help with this. Your life is on a set life path, so you must master what has come to you, and what you experience. Eleven also warns you to watch what you say, or guard your words and stay silent right now. *My mission is clear. I am here to love and be loved. That is all.* Snow Quartz.

**12 - Surrender.** Twelve is a number of challenge. It is complete surrender. This is the most difficult challenge there is. It asks you to completely let go, and let flow. Allow all of your steps to be completely guided by Spirit. Anything else will throw you into the chaos of this illusion here, that we think of as "reality". Your life will be chaos, subject to another person's whims and desires. Plans will fall apart. You must let Spirit guide you around the obstacles, which means letting go of control and stepping back from the lead. When you step back, you can see who is in front of you. When you lead, everyone is behind you. Getting out of the lead position changes your perception of what is happening to you. You do not have to worry about where you are going, since you are no longer in charge. This gives you time to observe and see things as they really are. You can be led safely home. Compare this to walking in the desert on a scorching hot day. You are clueless, and have no idea how to survive in that environment. Anything can happen. A lot will happen, as you scrounge, looking for water or something you can eat. There will be more scarcity than sustenance. Or, you can get into the passing caravan (that you would have missed in your scrounging, and suffering and fatigue), and allow it to take you to the nearest town. You are given water and food, as you ride along, not having to worry about how you will get there. The caravan driver is from the town, and knows the way. Trust and surrender. *I let go, and let Source lead me through each day, as I observe my blessings, even if they are sometimes hiding themselves from me. As I am patient and trust, they always reveal themselves.* Guardian Angel Gadiel.

**13 - Release.** 13 is a marker post in life. It is a message of a

major event, scheduled to happen in your script. This usually signifies an ending of some sort, that is needed. You are experiencing endings at this time. These events, people, emotions, situations etc., have served their time or purpose. This needs to happen, in order for new growth to begin. A new start, new feelings, and new perspective. Thirteen asks you to take your power back, that you have given away to a situation, a fear, or to someone else. Feel the power of your true self fill you, and it will carry you through any fears, sorrow or reservations you may still hold about letting go. 13 asks you to choose the light. Use your power wisely. *I allow myself to release the past, accept what has happened, and move forward with grace.*

**14 - Communicate.** 14 means it is time to go your own direction. No matter how different, or unique your vision may be, you have to trust yourself, and what you know. It is a great time to get your thoughts down on paper, or verbalize your feelings. With 14, many good things will come from following your dreams. You must act on what you are envisioning, and take the first step. Stay true to what you feel intuitively, to be the correct direction. It is time to write the letter, make the call, speak your truth, begin a project, or write in your journal. *Creativity, honesty and divine clarity flow through me. I release all judgment, hesitation or fear, and act with confidence and purpose in the fulfillment of my dreams.*

**15 - Temptation and Entrapment.** This number has to do with desires of the flesh (meaning the material world), and how it controls you. Your temptations and desires - do they own you, or are you their master? This number requires you to find willpower for balance. Meaning, use your head. Use your higher mind to make decisions. Look at the long term. What is giving in to this situation going to cost you later? Observe your life situation right now. Does it have a basis in love? Are you connected to Spirit, your Source? You are a Divine Being, and cannot be trapped by the empty offerings of the ego, and a world of illusions. Things, other people, and anything else outside of you, is not going to bring you peace or real joy. Make your home within yourself first, and then everything outside of you doesn't control you, but rather is there for your entertainment. It is a passing pleasure, not a consuming desire, that will ultimately entrap you. Ask yourself what is enslaving, or trying to enslave you? *I cleanse* *myself of lower energies, and channel the Spirit of Divine Love and Truth.*

**16 - Resistance.** This number calls for you to take a look at

yourself. Are you being too controlling? Are you avoiding change? Is there something that needs to end, but you are resisting? Are you ignoring self-defeating behaviors? 16 could represent the disintegration of spiritual beliefs, that no longer ring true for you. The challenge here is to decide what is truly important. Can you let go? If you can't, life is going to let go for you. 16 is a warning that you are being given the choice first. This lesson will recur in different forms, until you learn it. 16 is a spiritual transition number. Its time to make a shift. This number is the opposite of burning bridges. 16 is the bridges getting burned for you, while you're still standing on them...you haven't crossed over. *I release and let go of that which no longer serves me, without fear. There is no lack in Spirit. All is well.* Marcasite.

**17 - Light of the World.** This number says you are reaching a

pinnacle, in the area in which you now serve. Your efforts are being rewarded, and you will reap some kind of benefit. You serve a higher mission in life, whether you are aware of this or not. The time is at hand, for you to become aware of this truth, and see results in the world. This is a number of light and love. It reaches all people through your efforts, such as the ripple effect. Shine your light, and cultivate love within yourself. The Angels are assisting you on your mission. You are a peace ambassador, here to assist humanity in rising to the next level. Trust in your divinity, and your purpose. Trust that everything you are doing is what you are supposed to be doing, no matter how grandiose, or ordinary. All things are in their place, and have their place. What is right in front of you now, is what is important. *I achieve all that I came here to do. Spirit is blessing me, and assisting me every step of the way. I release any doubts or fears that come up, that this is so.*

**18 - Old Karma.** 18 is a number of great responsibility. You may be feeling burdened and depressed. 18 is a call to look within yourself, and address the issues that are causing your turbulent state. Are you allowing negative thinking to create your reality? The advice is to forgive yourself, and release anger, frustration, hatred, and anything else that stirs you to discomfort. Negative emotions are signals, that karmic work needs to be done. They are not a signal for you to beat up on yourself, take that negativity out on others, etc. You are here to erase old karma, and forgive yourself. This is karma from past lives in particular, that is being repeated in this life. Bring your mind back to a state of acceptance, love, and release, and you will feel the strength again of this number's ability to accomplish anything...as long as you remove the mental barriers first. Remember that this may be an ongoing process, that needs time to get done, especially if 18 seems to be a lifelong number for you. *I release negative thoughts, and allow myself to experience peace now. I am a being of pure love and light. I am not the darkness of the past.*

**19 - Inner Child.** 19 is triumph over that which held you back. This number is a signal that an area of your life is turning in your favor. All will be accomplished as you envisioned. There are many blessings waiting for you, and much clarity is coming. Spend time with children, in nature or with animals. Get in touch with purity and innocence again. Breathe that into yourself. Pay attention and notice how much purity and innocence is in the world. There is just as much, as hate, greed and fear. It is your choice what you focus on. This should be a fresh new time for you, of increased mental clarity, fresh starts, and success. *I give thanks that I have a clear view of my future, and all things are in their perfect order.*

**20 - Move Forward.** 20 says it is time to reassess your past, and its hold over you. The past only defines you, if you let it. There is nothing holding you back, but old conditioning. Your Spirit is pure, regardless of what the ego wants you to think. Outside of this reality, is the true reality of Spirit, and your true home. Even outside of a vast, seemingly infinite Universe, is Spirit, which is beyond the limits of time and space. You are limitless. Decide this now. Allow Spirit to lead the way. Twenty says new doorways are opening to you, if you will only walk through. This is a chance to change your patterns and have a new experience. *I open to my true state of being, and allow it to lead me to that which is for my highest good, each and every day. The past no longer controls, or defines me.* Yellow Aragonite.

**21 - Persistence.** Triumph and victory are yours, if you will only stay in the game. It is coming. Your reward is finding its way to you, whether this is a happier state of being, a material blessing, or an accomplishment. 21 is a signal to keep going, and don't give up. Any difficulties are lessons you need, in order to accept your success. You will triumph eventually. This is also a time to pay attention to your intuition, as it will tell you when to act. The angels are with you. Notice any information you get at this time, whether it is from your angels and guides, or from an unlikely source around you. Everything is a message right now. And everything is speeded up. Hang in there! *My future is bright! I move forward with faith and confidence that all is well, and coming to me in its perfect timing.*

**22 - Dreamer.** You may be too caught up in daydreaming, and have your head in the clouds, relying solely on intuition or feelings, and ignoring what your logical/rational mind is trying to tell you. You may be restless, and prone to jump into situations without thinking. You need to ground yourself, and find balance. Make an effort to decide to see things as they really are. Pay attention to what is around you. Take off the blindfold, and face life without fear. Do a double take, before making a decision. This is a turning point in your life, that could mean the difference between a happy, or regretful change for the future. Don't lock yourself into anything, or sign anything permanent, until you have investigated thoroughly, and gotten a second opinion. *I have clear vision, and am aware of all possibilities. I see the truth in all situations, and act with wisdom and discernment.* Azeztulite.

**23 - Green Light.** Celebrate your good fortune. Help is on the way, good news, progress and good fortune. This number is pretty much unstoppable, except by you. Results are on the way, as well. Open to your good fortune. This is a "yes" for anything you are considering right now. It is time to take what you were intuitively given from Spirit in a vision or idea, and bring it into reality. All things are coming your way, and working out in your favor. If you are feeling positive about something, it is justified. *All good things are coming to me now. I am abundant and blessed.*

**24 - Abundance.** Doors are opening. There are new experiences coming, and many opportunities for assistance. 24 says you are on the right road to riches, meaning you will get what you are desiring, whether that be riches in a material worldly sense, or in the form of relationships, or spiritual gifts. Much is happening right now, and many people are coming in to assist you. Trust your gut instincts, and go with what feels right or correct. The Angels have been hearing your call, and successful resolution is on its way. Its time to celebrate even small victories or blessings, as they can lead to greater ones, if we stay in gratitude. *I am grateful for the many gifts and blessings coming my way. I am always in a constant state of abundance, and trust that I am being provided for, in whatever ways are needed. All is well and as it should be.*

**25 - Objectivity.** 25 says read the fine print. Look closely

before leaping. Opportunities are there, if you choose the correct ones. Use caution and common sense. Ask the Angels to bring what is correct, and you will have what is needed. Realize that the way your mind is conditioned to think, is not always real thinking. Use logic in a new way, without judgment. Think objectively, not how you were programmed to think. See from all sides, and look from a bird's eye viewpoint. All will be clear. *I take time to pause, and weigh my decisions. In this manner, I always choose wisely and correctly.*

**26 - Mixed Blessings.** Be awake and aware with this number.

It is a sign that you can have success, if you follow your own counsel. Step carefully. Ask the Angels for assistance. Realize that any hardships are lessons, and are helping to clear any karma residue that is still tied to your soul's journey. This karma may be a windfall, or a "winded fall", meaning you may be winded from falling but you'll get back up. Either way, this is a mixed blessing of success, but comes with a price. 26 usually represents major lessons, not minor ones. Sometimes these can involve choosing money/material success over love. Other times, it can be hard lessons learned through relationships. The key is to allow whatever it is going to be, and know that you will be helped in all things. *I choose joy and love. These are the only things that matter. Their energy brings in all good things. They are my natural state, and my spiritual heritage.* Zebra Stone.

27 - **Planted Seeds.** The Angels are announcing your success,

and bringing many things to a positive conclusion. Whatever you have started, will bear fruit. Whatever you have put your energy into, will yield results, and they are coming soon. This is a reward for a job well done. This may be a reward from progress in past lives, or efforts in this life. The Angelic Trumpets are sounding their call, and it is heard far and wide. There is much manifesting in your world. *Many blessings find their way to me in an endless stream. I accept my good, now.*

**28 - Settling In.** 28 is a sign that you are fighting against

something, that will not let you pass. There are obstacles in the way, and what you are trying to achieve is beyond your karmic destiny. It is not in your script, and even though you see it as life holding you back, you are actually trying to take the wrong path in a particular situation. The solution, here, is to let Spirit lead you. Any other attempt at what you are trying to accomplish may be blocked. There are certain things your soul signed up to experience, and forcing the issue, or things to go your way, will cause frustration. The more judgmental you become, the less progress you make, and you could end up in an angry spiral. Only the Creator can lead you around the obstacles. Forcing against it is fruitless. *I achieve success in all ventures, by letting go, and letting Source.* Purple Fluorite.

**29 - Trust You.** This is a number that contains a lot of

discord, and opposing energies. The people surrounding you have very different agendas from your own. You may have difficulty trusting other people at this time, or their opinions, actions and plans are not in alignment with yours. You do not see eye to eye, and anger, hurt feelings or betrayal may be the result. It is best to separate yourself, and make decisions that serve your best interests. 29 says to approach others with caution, and guard your feelings. Extricate yourself from any partnership, or connection that is upsetting to your inner peace. Following your intuition, rather than emotions will help you. *I am emotionally calm, balanced and safe. I trust my own inner vision, and protect myself and my creations. I open to a higher perception of my situation.* Green Fluorite.

**30 - Master of Fate.** This number is unstoppable, if the

individual is willing to use their wisdom to create what they want. Know that Spirit is telling you that you have everything you need to succeed. Whatever situation you are finding yourself in, know that you have the ability to change it, re-create it, or end it. You are a master in this particular situation, and can draw on experience, wisdom and know-how to make these alterations, as if out of thin air. Trust in yourself, and know that all will come about, if you are willing to utilize the gifts you have. *I know that I know. I am guided on my path, and am supplied always, with everything I need.*

**31 - Lighten Up.** This is a difficult energy. Ask yourself if you

are depressed. The energy around you feels heavy. You may need a healing session, and will need a change of scenery to get out of your funk, or to move things forward. You can stand alone, but this is not necessarily in your best interest right now. You may need to ask for help, and get out of your routine. Nature settings may be helpful with healing and lifting the dark cloud that has settled, but isolation is not recommended. Find a way to laugh, especially with others. Do not take things too seriously right now, or in your particular situation. If you lighten up, so will your load. *I allow myself to be filled with divine light and love. It strengthens every part of me. It is my Divine heritage, and natural state. Spirit is with me, and darkness cannot touch me.* Mother of Pearl.

32 - **Blessings Flow.** Thirty-two is a number of higher energies directing your path. It is a perfect blending of intuition and knowledge. Trust what you are getting at this time, and move forward. It is time to take the next step toward greatness. Rely on your inner knowing. You are divinely guided. Read 23, the mirror reversal of this number, as well. *Many blessings pour down on me. I am divinely guided to what is best for me, always.*

33 - **Manifesting.** This double number can suggest success in the extreme. Putting something out there in the world, yields results. Communication is strong, and at a high. Your ability to relate to others, communicate a sale, or bring comfort to a loved one is at its best. Your words cannot fail you. Speak your truth. Let love be in your words. This is a time to say what needs to be said. Go forward on a project. This is similar to number 32. You have mastered whatever it is you are working toward. Say the "word" or speak it forth - whatever you are wanting to manifest at this time. *I succeed in anything I set my mind to achieving. All things work in my favor. I count my many blessings.*

34 - **Trust Your Vision.** Certain actions have repercussions. This number is advising you to be careful what you say or

think, as it can yield results that are undesirable. There is a lesson to be learned here. You are in this situation for a reason. Learn the lesson, and you will be blessed. Ignore it, and you isolate yourself from the blessings. Any unusual ideas you are having at this time are part of these gifts, and should be noted, and acted on. Much can come about by acting on plans, especially if they are ahead of their time or future-oriented. Make sure you think everything through, all the way to the end. Set your goals, and do not let anyone tell you it cannot be done, just because they don't believe. Mend your fences, trust your visions, and accept that all is happening just as it is supposed to play out. I *allow myself to reach my potential. I trust my visions, and act accordingly, as I am guided.*

**35 - Suffering is not Required.** You have a karmic destiny, and your current situation is under this influence. You are being asked to forgive - an event, yourself, and others. Shed the miseries of the past. Do not bring the past forward into the present, and therefore the future. Do not give in to the temptation to dwell on past mistakes, heartaches, betrayals and the like. Do not give in to re-running the past in your head. To do so requires that you learn the lessons again, and suffer the same pattern. This is not necessary. You have the magic of the miracle, waiting for you to call on it, and it comes through forgiveness. When this is your focus, anything is possible with 35. *The Angels assist me in releasing the past and its hold over me. Spirit does not desire me to suffer, and I release this unconscious need, now. I step forward into a bright future.* Watermelon Tourmaline.

**36 - A Journey to Peace.** This is a powerful number, and it suggests you have reached a pinnacle in your worldly life or spiritual journey. It is an opportunity to move up to the next level. You can begin again, or find peace with what has gone before. This is perfect harmony, and unity. Life is coming to its peak. What could be done has been done. Either reap the rewards of a job well done, or find peace in knowing that the past is behind you. From here on out, it is up to you. The slate is clear. *My journey begins now. I have found my way. All situations are resolving themselves, and I am at peace.*

37 - **Friendly Assistance.** This number has a friendly energy

to it. You are being given the message that there is harmony. Your energy is in alignment with the situation. All things are a go. People are accommodating, and cooperative. They like you, and what you have to say. Relations are smoothed over, and everything is as it should be. It is a good time to rely on another person's assistance, ask for favors or get your way. Make sure what you are involved in, has your best interests at heart. Be a friend, to gain a friend. People may come out of the woodwork, to help, or to hang out. Welcome others into your circle. Let them know that they are valued and appreciated. *Assistance comes to me when I need it. I am open to receiving that which is for my highest good, and the good of those around me. All is well in my world.*

**38 - Going it Alone.** This number applies to a specific

situation in your life. It is a warning to tread carefully, when making plans with others. 38 warns of good ideas or intentions that get ruined by the input and involvement of other people. It is a time when you should either "do it alone", or possibly not be involved with this person. There may be advantages, but the cost could possibly be heartache, betrayal, suffering and loss. When acting alone, this number can bring worldly success, but one would be advised to question your deeper motives. If you focus on what is for the highest good of all, then it is okay to act...but again, alone. Otherwise, this number is advising to wait, and say "no". This may relate to a relationship, business idea, work or any situation in life. Also, be careful what you say...it is better not to speak your mind at this time. *I always act at the appropriate time. Spirit guides me to my good. I release the belief that I have to fight, sacrifice or acquiesce to others, to get what I need.* Praying Mantis Animal Totem.

39 - **Motivation to Manifest.** This number suggests that you

have all within you to succeed, by control of the mind and will. You need to view the situation from a different perspective. There can be much success here, if you are willing to give up what is in your way...obstacles, fear, lack of confidence...and realize these do not apply. They are beliefs of the mind. You actually have total control here. Tune into your core self, and its ability to change the future to your desires. Or rather, find first what it is that you truly desire. Motivation will be the key to you making this shift in consciousness. *I find my inner strength of mind, and act accordingly. All things are possible for me now.*

40 - **Stand Up to It.** Four is a karmic number, and its energy

is doubled here. 0 is a number of inclusion and exclusion. Whatever you are going through is karmic in nature, and has a heavy lesson tied to it. It means to use caution, but don't sit, and do nothing. Do not let fear keep you from doing what is necessary, or needed. There may be upset, so ask Spirit for comfort. You may need it, as this can be a difficult time. Remember, nothing lasts forever, so just get through it, so you can end the cycle. Future outcomes that are a byproduct of this effort, will be worth it in the long run. You are breaking through a lot of karma from several lives overlapping with this one. Do it now, without fear, so you don't have to keep doing it in the future. And don't isolate yourself, no matter how strong the desire. *I am safe, loved and whole. All lessons can come to me in Divine order, as Spirit assists me in releasing the past, and its illusory hold over me. I get out of my own way.* Camphor Essential Oil.

**41 - Raise Your Hands to Receive.** It is your time to shine.

Rely on yourself, and your own guidance. 41 is karmic reward! Play the lottery, do whatever you are inspired to do, relax and enjoy. This is a green light to go ahead with a venture, or a sign that the Angels are listening and bringing you blessings. You've earned it. Open your arms up, and lift them above your head in a pose of joyful reception. Let the higher energies fill you. All signs say "go"! Follow only your own wisdom. Other people's input is not helpful. *I trust myself. I open to the rewards for my efforts. Only good lies before me, and I am grateful!*

**42 - Heaven's Rewards.** Many blessings float down from

heaven to you. Relationships are beneficial and loving. Others come to assist you at this time. Know that your blessings are yours by right. They are karmic reward from when you gave to others in this life, or a previous one. The benefits are yours to enjoy. Create your surroundings/environment into a place that gives you support and upliftment. Spend time with children. Feng Shui your house. Anything and anyone, you need to assist you, is on the way. *I celebrate my many blessings, and give thanks.*

**43 - Power Struggles.** This is an ominous number, and warns

of deception and opposition. Things are not as they appear. 43 signals that it is a time for you to look at your misuse of power, as well as others using power over you. If you are involved in either of these situations, forgive yourself, and the other(s) involved. This is repetitive karma playing itself out. It has a spiritual lesson tied to it, that is crucial for you to learn...in order for you to not repeat the pattern, and to move forward on your spiritual evolution back to your true self. Power does not come from the world. It comes from the higher Spirit that is you, connected to Source. And Source is love. You are so much larger than the small personality you seem to be. Divine love heals all in this situation. *I see all with the eyes of Spirit. No lesser ego form can fool me. I am one with love.* Lavender Essential Oil.

**44 - Acceptance.** This is a serious number, of the doubling of the 4 and 8 energies. These are both karmic numbers, meaning experiences that one must go through on their path. This is not the time to take any risks, gamble or try your luck. Do not jump into anything, or blindly trust. It is a serious warning to be prepared. Your best course of action, is to sit tight, and let Spirit give you guidance on what is the next move, if any. Forgiveness is also a way to help heal karmic situations. Realize that whatever is going to happen, may come out of the blue, or be shocking or surprising. Try to remain calm. Turn to meditation for guidance. Spirit is always with you. *I accept that which is necessary, on my path home to Source. All is working out in my favor. I am always blessed, no matter what the seeming circumstances.* Red Coral.

**45 - Keep the Faith.** Karmic reward is coming to you now. There may be some minor upsets involved. Avoid negative emotions, such as anger, frustration and fear. All will be well, if you stay in a positive mind frame, and be open to accepting your good. You are reaping rewards for what you have sown, but by not trusting, you could delay or block what is trying to come to you. Remain calm and centered, and trust. Faith is what it is named for...**F**earing everything, **A**llowing Spirit anyway, **I**nitiating calm, **T**rusting in the guidance given, and **H**ealing yourself. This number is good news, so wake up, and be happy. You may get a sign or message from your guides, so stay alert! *Spirit delivers all that I need daily. I am safe, grounded and calm. All is well in my world.*

**46 - Unexpected Good.** This is a lucky number, so know that all is well. 46 a sign that the luck you are either receiving, or about to receive is karmic in nature. You must have clear, unselfish intentions in this situation. If they are selfish, or harmful towards another, you will alter your good karma. Trust and allow. Friendships are highlighted. Your life may be about to change unexpectedly for the better. *All good things come to me now. My good is just around the next corner. I honor it and give thanks for my blessings.*

**47 - Dragon's Head and Tail.** This number comes with many lessons. The 4 and 7 deal with past life talents, abilities and motivations that are ending, and the beginning of new ways of doing things, that will bring good fortune. 47 is related to the nodes in astrology. You need to do what is foreign to you. What you have not ever done, or don't feel naturally inclined to do. Going in this direction is usually where you will shine. Doing what is easy, is part of the past, and will not move you forward, to succeed. It is time to create a new you. Pay attention to what you say. Your words can get you in trouble, right now, as others are not sharing your best interests. It is time to tread carefully, on this path never chosen, because you will be learning along the way, how to tread it. Advice from others will not apply. Trying to walk it with others will lead to chaos and loss. This is your path alone. Your new destiny. The time is now. Get outside your old parameters and old karma. *I allow Spirit to lead me out of the desert, and into the waters of abundance.* Guardian Angel Mahasiah.

**48 - Vanquishing The Past.** This number brings hard

lessons. Your plans are being sacrificed for the desires of others. You may be asked to sacrifice, or you are the sacrifice. Since this is a karmic number, involving both 4 and 8, it is a sign that it represents repeated patterns from past lives, or this life, brought forward. This number also has a message, that it is time to throw out your beliefs about the *need* for sacrifice and suffering. This is old programming. You have the power here. You can change this situation. You have total control of the outcome, if you choose to take the reins. Use the power of your mind and your wisdom, and make the needed change now. It is merely a matter of will, and all follows, afterward. *I manifest exactly what I desire, through Spirit in a perfect way. All that is manifesting out of fear and old programming, is deleted and vanishes from sight. Only good can come of this situation.*

**49 - Fighting Yourself.** There are parts of yourself that you

need to bring together into harmony. Otherwise, you spend time fighting against yourself. There is potentially very chaotic energy with this number, and it must be handled with care. Much discord is unfolding, and could become worse, if you don't find your center, and realign. Clear out what doesn't serve...this includes things and people. It is time to buckle down and brave through it. 49 is giving a warning of possible turmoil. Getting organized, and calming your emotions will help you think clearly, and act accordingly in your best interests. Peace is your answer here. Peace of mind. Peaceful emotions. A peaceful disposition leads to structure, clarity and vision. Do not react in anger or negativity at this time. *I am calm, cool, centered and at peace with all things. None can sway me from the path toward my good.* Blue Tansy Essential Oil.

**50 - Showers of Abundance.** This number is a good sign.

Things are taking a turn for the better, and improving. 50 is a sign that you have achieved much, and more is coming. Celebrate your good fortune. The Angels have given you a special blessing. This applies to money, finances, business deals and swift change. You may be traveling or connecting with others from foreign shores. Know that all is well, and in alignment for your success. *Powerful abundance finds me now, in many ways, and in all ways. The time has come for my success in ________ (venture/goal/wish).*

**51 - Rushing to Nowhere.** This number can feel like "one

too many". Success comes easily and quickly, but are you taking on too much? Are you stepping on other people's toes that may become a problem later? It is time to take stock of your progress, your reasons for wanting what you want, and why. Is the direction you are headed in your best interest, or are you rushing forward, just because you can? Step back and take an objective look. Be careful of alienating or ignoring others. *There is no rush. Spirit is always supplying what I need in a perfect way, and in perfect timing for all involved. I take my time, so all things fall into place correctly.*

**52 - Accountable.** This number says to take positions of

power, seriously. Realize you have a spiritual responsibility for those who follow you, or your advice. There may be jealousies, or irrational thinking on the part of others. This is a positive number, if you take the precautions to protect yourself. *I trust in Spirit, to guide the way.*

**53 - Take Home Pay.** This can be a lucky number in material or financial terms. What is big, gets bigger. Expansion, growth and profits are coming. *I am blessed with abundance. I give thanks for my good.*

**54 - Energetic Breath.** 54 says it is time for some deep breathing work, to calm down ruffled emotions. Breathe in...breathe out. Release the tension. Practice yoga, or some beneficial exercise. Get out in nature, and notice what is around you. Stay still and in the moment. Go beyond the silence, and wait. Don't allow yourself to get distracted. Wait, until you start to see the beauty around you. Let it fill you. You are recharging at this time. Let it happen. Let the energy flow through you, naturally. See all negativity flowing out. You need to unplug right now, and get a break, so that you may come back fresh, and approach situations with new eyes, and a calmer demeanor. Using force will not work. *I am calm, centered and at peace. I soak in the beauty around me, and am at one with all.*

**55 - Make a Wish.** This is a magic number, where the spoken word will be done. What is your wish? The universe is backing it at this time. Everything is ready to line up and go in motion. It is for you to speak the words, or think the thought...so do so carefully. It is time for you to manifest what you want. Make a dream chart, or speak to your Angels about it. Decide what you are willing to do to have it, help it along or receive it properly. Your intentions must be pure, and with the best interest of all involved. Your blessings will be multiplied by ten. *I have all that I could dream or want, simply by asking for it. My good comes to me now, in a perfect way.*

**56 - Tossing And Turning.** This number has to do with a restless nature. It is not unlucky, but you can cause problems, if you are not coming from a relaxed and settled space. Read 54 for advice. Avoid speaking out of turn, and the magical movement of 56 can lead you toward your dreams. *I am love. I relax and let go.*

**57 - Objective Perspective.** This number tends to call things to a halt, for reflection and review. It is advised that you go within, and seek your inner truth. You must come from a place of clear intent, in order to succeed. Much wisdom is acquired by listening to the voice within. Trust in the wisdom of Source. 57 is a call to come forth, when the timing is correct, and all has fallen into place. You are watching and waiting in the meantime, for your time to act. *I examine that which is front of me. I trust that all falls into place, as is needed, and I release control.*

**58 - Dissolving the Past.** Endings, beginnings, openings, closings...the past is let go of, and you are set free. You have been given a chance to reunite with your soul, and begin again. If you have lost your way, it is now found. Mistakes fade away, and the new future is upon you. With 58, many things are possible now, that were not previously. 58 guides you forward, like the rudder of a ship, finding new shores to land on, new adventure, and the cessation of all that is no longer in alignment with you. *I accept my destiny, and open to the new winds of change, setting me free.*

**59 - Rejuvenation.** Channel the peace of nature. Like a fresh flowing stream, reaching toward you in its meandering, this number is flowing across your senses, and finding root in your soul. A fresh breeze of air may be coming into your life, enlivening you, and setting your soul afire. It is time to let your soul breathe, and open to the healing waters of Spirit, as the light of Love is manifesting in you now. This is a refreshment period, that reunites you with your true purpose for being. Allow your mind and body to heal. This is a fortunate number for the future. *I take time to heal myself, and have faith in the powers of renewal.*

**60 - Creative Spirit.** This is a beautiful number, representing a time of beauty. Circumstances are set for you to grow and flourish. Surround yourself with loved ones, pets, children and art. Let your creative juices flow. Create something beautiful and inspiring, or start a movement. 60 says whatever project you are working on right now, will be a success on many levels. You are inspired and filled with many ideas, that can lead the way to a finished result. Your life is like that of a butterfly, ready to take flight, after a period of change. Unfold your wings, and begin. *I am filled with the creative fire of Spirit. I bring beauty to all that I touch, and all bless me in return.*

**61 - The Aum.** This number gives visions of a monk meditating "Om". Your true genius lies in your center. 61 marks a time of channeling Divine Spirit into your creations. Write a poem, paint on a canvas, color in a coloring book...do something with your hands, that has no purpose, other than to let it out, and just be. You are learning to step aside, and let go of control. Your ego will lead you astray. Practice getting out of its influence, by getting in touch with the moment, and creating that which has no purpose, other than for enjoyment's sake. This is a time to stop and smell the roses. Stop running to catch up. Get off the hamster wheel. *I know that I have all the time in the world. I am patient, as I let go for awhile, and Let Life Flow. My only real purpose, is living this moment with joy.*

**62 - Logic Rules.** Life is a mixed bag, right now. Expect the good with the bad. You may be rewarded, but there will be a downside to the deal. The key to working with this energy, is to not identify yourself with your emotions. Finding a centered, logical approach will help. Coming up with creative ideas to solve problems, and getting input from professionals, will also help the ball roll in your favor. If you are reactionary, then all falls apart, and you get the worst of the energies directed at you. Stick to the rules, follow a plan, and stay logical. All will be well. *The Creator is my strength. I use my knowledge and ability to think. My ideas are clear, and I move forward with confidence.* Rosemary Essential Oil.

**63 - Blessed By Heaven.** You have brilliance at this time. Things move at lightning speed. All comes together, as if by magic. You can't lose. It is a time of enhanced and magnified luck, and blessings from heaven. You will say the right thing, do the right thing, and be in the right place with the right connections. The Universe is working in synchronicity with your goals. *I accept my visions as divinely inspired. Whatever is on the horizon, manifests instantly for me, in this moment. I have all that I need.*

**64 - Instant Karma.** Unexpected surprises. Are you ready? You will be receiving the exact complement of what you have sown. It can be wildly fantastic, or miserable. It is your choice, your intention and your life. How are you creating it? What vision are you putting out into the world, with your thinking? The results are manifesting. Karma is happening, as well as instant karma. Be careful what you say, or think. Everything is a direct reflection of your thought processes. *I examine my motives. I am capable of all things, and only choose that which is for my highest good.*

**65 - Restrained Freedom.** There is a tendency now, to rush

forward without thinking, because the energy feels so good. This includes saying whatever is on your mind, with no filter. Freedom, with a measure of restraint is called for here. You may be inspired with creative marketing ideas, or investment tips. Breakthroughs in all areas is imminent, but act with prudence. Tell no one of your plans, if that is an option, at this time. Don't show all your cards. Act with deliberateness. Restrain yourself. Now is the time to act, with carefully calculated steps. Pay attention. And keep quiet about it. *I am balanced and at peace with my choices. I act with calmness and confidence.*

**66 - The Path Less Chosen.** The double six is a sign that

things are changing. You are being given many choices, and are at a crossroads of sorts, or a doorway. You must choose the higher path. Let the past go. You are not going backwards. Choose wisely, follow the path of dreams and have courage, no matter how many setbacks you may have had, or who has told you that you cannot succeed. Let go of who or what has let you down, or crushed your Spirit. It is time to pick yourself up, and choose the path of hope, without the influence of the past, and its jaded jargon. Keep moving. Keep dreaming. The key to choosing is to allow Spirit to lead you. *I trust in the wisdom of Spirit, and release the trappings of the ego. I have faith in my dreams.*

**67 - Eternity.** This is the joining of beauty with Spirit. It is the conquering of the ego, and its hold on your existence. True beauty is found in Spirit. There are pieces of passing beauty on this plane of existence, which are only pale reflections of the true eternal Love. 67 signals that this is a time period where you are being opened up, and reminded that all is passing away in this life. It is transitory. Remember what is truly important, and lasts beyond the illusions of time. Let the small things lift you up, and bring your vibration to one of joy, so that true Spirit can flood your being. Let go of what you think is so important, or give it a secondary place to your spiritual path. You are here to learn, whatever it is that your soul is here to learn, from an eternal perspective. Where are you going after here? Have you mastered yourself? 67 is a sign that you are being woken up to what is truly important in life. *My way is clear, as all obstacles remove themselves. They were never there to begin with, as I move my mind from the smallness, to the Allness of Spirit.*

**68 - Together We Succeed.** This is a dynamic number, and one that can be unstoppable, especially in collaborations. There is a way around everything, and this number finds it. Your goals are within reach. Sign on the dotted line. Put something in writing. Money comes to you in a pleasant way. Materially your life gets better somehow. Blessings flow in, and fill your bank account, your health, your relationships, etc.68 represents combinations of people that help, working with groups, businesses that need to connect with customers, investments that include group relationships, friends, social groups and sharing. Give and receive, and the blessings flow. *I* *am open to working and sharing with others. My life is blessed by the people I am connected to, and a wealth of Love flows to me now.*

69 - **Make Merry.** This is a number of enjoyment, artistic outlets and amusements. There are many that can assist you, in what you are trying to accomplish. 69 gives a harmonious and festive atmosphere, and says it is time to let loose, or at least get some down time. *I have plenty of time for fun. I enjoy life.*

70 - **Alignment with Source.** This is a number of spiritual attainment and enlightenment. You may be needing alone time, or time to contemplate what has been happening. Your inner hermit is calling, and your inner voice. You seek the truth, and it is found through quiet contemplation, not activity or interaction. Remove the question, problem or person, and let the answer(s) come to you in the quiet. 70 is also related to the evolvement of spiritual consciousness. You are being called to higher levels of being, levels that are more in alignment with the true nature of your Spirit. *I quietly listen to my inner guidance. I am directed, and led in all things.*

71 - **The Karmic Wheel.** This is a number of spiritual lessons, learning and growth. Experiences are coming in the material world, that will put you through a karmic lesson/pattern that you have been repeating. It is time to learn this lesson and embrace its blessings, so you can let it go. *I accept with Grace, the blessings that Source has already set aside for me, in eternity.* Amber.

72 - **A Pause in Time.** If you have been angry at something or someone, now is the time for self-examination as to the root

cause of these emotions. Who, or what is disturbing your peace of mind? Is it you, yourself? If you are unaware of your anger, is it buried? You have the willpower to succeed, but the time for action may not be, as yet. Frustration can eat at you during this time, as you want to do what is on your mind, but cannot, or obstacles are blocking progress. Clearing your mind of the anger, and realizing that everything has its own timing, will help you to accept things as they are. Patience is called for, and understanding. This may be a time of disruptions in partnerships. Each party needs their alone time, whether they recognize it or not, and this needs to be honored. Getting near water may help calm you down, and encourage much needed contemplation. *I withhold the need to push for my way, and accept that there is a Divine timing for all things. I trust that everything is working out, in the best way possible for everyone concerned, and I am thankful for private time, to gain perspective and space.* Golden Ray Calcite.

73 - **One In A Million.** This number has to do with changes

for the better, that stem from your efforts and intentions. It is a number of great promise, and unexpected altercations, that bring in better circumstances. Anything is possible. *I anticipate only the good.*

74 - **At-one-ment.** This is a number of enhanced intuition,

spiritual connection to your Source, and sudden, unexpected gifts. It is a number that brings good fortune at some point in the near future. Call forth that which you need, and it will be given. *Abundance flows to me in perfect order.*

75 - **The Eye of the Storm.** New ideas come to you. New

thoughts, ways of doing things, and ideas for financial gain.

Act on what you are receiving, only if you have taken the time to look at all sides of the situation, and planned accordingly. There is much change happening right now, and it is a good time for a vacation. It will be an active one, with very little relaxation. Its almost as if you are swept up in the current. There are distractions and scattered energy at this time. New energies, new information, new locations, vistas, people, and stimulation from many avenues. Know that you are in the middle of a major wave of change, and things may not settle, exactly as you had planned. Write down your specific ideas, goals or plans, and save them for after you come out of this whirlwind period. *I am grounded, calm and my thoughts are serene. Everything is always taken care of in its perfect timing, and in a perfect way.*

76 - **Break Of Day.** This is a number of change, leading to

powerful transformation, in the areas of spirituality, health and family life. Blessings rain down upon you now, and what needs to be let go of, is ushered out gently. Your new life awaits. *Everything is working in my favor. I release and let go, to embrace the new.*

77 - **The Twins**. The double seven has a message of higher

energies seeking to manifest through you. You are being lifted up and out of yourself, into the true form of Spirit. This higher energy can help you achieve all of your goals, earthly, spiritual and otherwise. 77 represents the Divine relationship with oneself. The self can also be found as a reflection in others...in particular close relationships. This is also a message that you may be meeting a soul mate or someone of significance, very soon. This could be a friend, associate, partner, the birth of a child or twins or other souls that have a connection to you. It is a joining, or overlay of souls. If your mission here is of a higher nature, this can be a Twin Soul that comes into your life to bless you. "Twins" is definitely a theme right now, as things come in pairs. Everything is doubled. The blessings are doubled; the heartaches are doubled. Your focus or attention needs to be on those close to you...whom you have strong connections with...this includes both the difficult and pleasurable relationships. Use your energies unselfishly to benefit others, and things will change very quickly for the better. A major trip would also be beneficial at this time. Particularly over water. *My good sweeps in toward me now. Nothing can stop the blessings coming my way. I wish for others, as I wish for myself, and I rejoice, and am grateful.*

**78 - I Want.** There is a lot that drives you, to have what you want in life...the luxuries, the nice things. This wanting could be in relationships, wanting a nice, easy loving connection. Perhaps you think you need to buy your way into happiness? This number carries a lot of challenges with it. It is spiritual purpose warring with the material desires. It implies either a lot of hard work, or taking the easy road, just because you can...which may not be better in the long run. Don't avoid your lessons here. Overcome what it is you fear, and why you think you want these things, that you think you don't have. Is ego driving you, or your higher self? What is really best for you in the long run? It is okay to want to make your life easier or more pleasurable, but make sure it is not at the expense of someone else, or yourself. *I release and let go of the need for escape. My burdens are light, as Spirit helps me carry the load.* Dark Green Nephrite.

**79 - Uniformity.** This number implies balance in all things. It is ego drive, balanced by spiritual wisdom. This is a number of accomplishment, if one remains in balance. To fight against the self, can destroy what you are trying to create. It is a time for building up, or possibly re-building your life. It is a time for thinking things through to the finish, not rushing over details, or forcing issues. You begin with the foundation and add the bricks. Not too much on one side too soon, with no support, but in a balanced organized fashion. This is how you should build your life and your dreams at this time. Don't cut corners, and attend to all sides of the situation. *I create in a whole, balanced way. My life reflects this equanimity.*

**80 - Just Deserts (Deserves).** This is a number of monetary

success, and high positions of influence. 80 is a material reward number, and the beneficial karma of 80, may be from this life, or the previous. You will prosper. *I am in a constant flow of beneficial energy. All works in my favor.*

**81 - Me and My Opponent.** There is conflict within yourself.

You are fighting an inner battle, and must come to terms with reality. Fighting yourself, for the way things are, is pointless. Some things must be accepted as lessons your soul chose to go through. Fighting against them will make your problems worse. Focus on smiling and laughing more. You are in sore need of joy. Do something nice for yourself, to make you feel good, such as a massage, a relaxing bath or getting a new hair-style. Spend the money. You deserve it. *I understand that all things happen for a higher purpose. I trust the process of life.* Orange Essential Oil.

**82 - Doorways.** The weight of the world is on my shoulders.

This is the feeling from 82. There are heavy burdens on you, now. Half of what you want, is going to work out, but possibly at the cost of the other half, that may be just as important. This situation is karmic in nature, but fortunately not set in stone. You are being given options to choose different outcomes. It is best to use your intuition at this time, to understand the hidden nuances of what you are trying to accomplish. What can you unload that is no longer important? You have to choose, and there will be a loss, so decide what it is going to be and let go. *I make the best decision for everyone involved. The situation rights itself, and I accept my choices.* White Chalcedony.

**83 - Top Of The Heap.** You have incredible drive to be at the

top of the list, be first, or number one in some area of your life. This number speaks of worldly and financial success, but carries some of the energy of 82 before it...meaning something is going to be lost in the completion of your goal. *I act from a calm and centered space. I accept that all is for my highest good.* Ram Totem.

**84 - The Wise Student.** 84 harbors difficulty, estrangement

and possible loss. In any case, the warning here is to lay low, and avoid making major decisions right now. Realize that you are being taught many lessons at this time, and some of them may be uncomfortable, but the benefit will be immense. This too shall pass. *I am safe and whole, regardless of what is occurring outside of myself. All things renew themselves in time.* Wolf Totem.

**85 - Dynamic Potential.** This is a powerful number, of

energy that is unstoppable. You can accomplish much in the world, and circumstances can change, as if by magic. Be ready for transformations, as old forms move into new. *I am in touch with my own power, and use it wisely.*

**86 - Refined Taste.** This is a number of beauty and abundance. Communications skills are excellent, and your words hold sway. 86 is good luck in all undertakings. *I surround myself with beauty and love, which reflects my inner self.*

**87 - Evolvement.** This is a higher vibration of 78, and it is a number of completion. Completing the meanings and lessons in 78. Have you conquered the fears and issues from this number, to transform it into higher energy? The temptations with 87 will be stronger than 78, as well as the repercussions, if you haven't learned the lessons. This is a warning that dark side energy is again, trying to pull you in. *I align with my true nature, that is one with Spirit. I am eternal and untouchable. Fear is not the master here.* Gaspeite.

**88 - Gain and Loss.** Double Eight is a powerful number of rise or fall. Dark side energies are connected to, and do use this number in some of their dates and rituals (see final chapter). Good news is, Source energy is all there is in true reality, therefore, avoid dark energy, and use this as a selfless number in its expression. You have an impact right now, and if you use your influence for the good of all, you will be rewarded. If you try to horde or hide your good fortune, surplus or profit, you will suffer from loss. You must recognize your true power and learn its proper use. If you are an evolved soul, this number will be one of mastery, as you overcome the influences and temptations of lower energies. You will have mastered a significant level of soul growth, and the manifestations of this number can be huge, and beneficial on many levels. *I utilize my power wisely. I act with the interests of* *all involved. I willingly choose to become love, and act accordingly.* Poudretteite or Pink Tanzanite.

**89 - Super Hero.** 89 says you are seemingly prevented from taking action, or working toward goals. It is a time of back and forth, back and forth. This refining process does have a purpose. Spirit is not trying to prevent your progress, but rather develop you into the strength of your true inner nature. *I value every obstacle, as an opportunity for growth.* Elk Animal Totem.

**90 - Learning the Lesson.** You are ending a cycle of soul growth. You have come full circle with a particular lesson, and the time has come to finish up, and master it. You will be birthed into a new cycle, at the closing of this one. You are up another octave of the soul's progress, and completing the final phases of what was previously learned. It is time to finalize, put the endings on something, and let go. You have, or will be learning to master higher energies, and think in terms of oneness, wholeness and inclusion. Nothing is excluded from our lives, as all, affects all. It is here, that you are ready to take full responsibility for the attracting, contributing and creating of your current cycle. You realize that you are your own master. You no longer need the lesson, and can move on. *I own and recognize my willingness to participate in my journey of experiences. I release those now, that no longer serve me or the needs of those who depend on me.*

**91 - Single-Minded Purpose.** This is a strong number of focus, willpower and the determination to succeed. You have what it takes to reach your goals. All things are lining up for you. The Sun is shining on whatever you are thinking about. The Creator's grace is with you. Lead the way, and your dreams will follow. Let your Spirit shine. *I attract success.*

**92 - Sixth Sense.** This is a number of merging will power with intuition, This means learning to listen to, and trust what you get intuitively, before acting. This number may be very volatile, on an emotional level, and it is up to you, to channel this powerful energy in more meaningful ways. *I have all the information I need, to succeed.*

**93 - The Way Is Clear.** There are obstacles, but they are minor. This is a pause in time, while you are gaining clarity. Joy and prosperity are on their way. *I take time to give thanks, for my many gifts from Source.*

**94 - Plant the Garden.** You are in a planting time. Much growth has taken root, although you may not see it yet. Many things are in their early stages, and not yet showing results. Put your seeds into the ground, and plant how you want your future to be. What would you like to see change? What would you like to increase? You have the ability to create how the future will be. *All good things find me at the perfect time. I am patient, knowing that all is being prepared.* Horse Totem

**95 - Happy Surprises.** This is a number of magic and mystery. Many miracles are happening, as if out of the blue. Not much can stand in the way of your intentions. All is working in your favor. *Miracles find me now.*

**96 - Nothing but Blue Skies.** This is a fortunate number, promising new perspectives, growth and happiness. Your Angels are around you, lifting you up. All possibilities lie in front of you...rainbows, birds and fluffy clouds...which all speak of dreams coming true, freedom and hope. The rainbow is promises fulfilled, the birds are messengers of good news, and the cloud formations give signs of hope and prophecy. Look up. Things are looking up. *My Angels are always with me, assuring that I have all I need.*

97 - **Case Closed**. There are contracts and negotiations going on at this time. These may be of a legal nature, or between partners, co-workers, bosses, friends, associates, buyers and sellers, or any kind of deal-making, that calls for cooperation. They are coming to their conclusions, some successful, some not. This also applies to deals already made, and someone breaking the contract or agreement (whether written, verbal or unspoken). It may be you requiring a person to act a certain way, and they don't want to cooperate. It could be a spiritual contract with another person that your soul agreed to, when it incarnated here. Whatever the area, all of these contracts are coming to an end. The challenge is to learn from them, and move into a new phase. *I release all others from agreements that were made, and trust that Spirit brings to all parties involved, what is best for everyone.* Rabbit spirit totem.

**98 - Working Through It.** Many lessons are coming to the forefront, and some of them feel pretty hardcore. Tensions may mount at this time, and discord with others may be noted. Your intentions are in the right place, however, there are bleed-through lessons from past lives, disrupting what should be a smooth transition, or situation. Try to remain calm, focus on your objectives, and don't let emotions get in the way. It is not a time to push situations, no matter what the deadline or agenda. There are many gifts and blessings with

98, however some of them may not show up until later, after the emotionally-charged air has cleared. *I breathe deeply. I am at peace. The future takes care of itself.* Aragonite.

**99 - Gifts Given.** The completion of many cycles is occurring now. Either you are being bumped up to a higher plane of enlightenment, getting a raise, or someone is noticing that you have performed a job well done. Promotions, rewards, spiritual growth, and many other increases are at hand. It is a good time to donate to your favorite charity or cause, and giving back only brings in more of the wealth and resources that are coming your way. They come in many forms, not just material. Think of those less fortunate, at this time, and give to animal and family focused charities, or to anyone in need. Pay it forward, then open to receive the pay back. *I give freely and openly, understanding that we are all one in Spirit. My good flows to me in ever increasing amounts, allowing me to give more.*

**100 - Going Home.** This is a merging of the 1 and 10, up to a higher level. All of the double zero numbers (200, 300 etc.) signify a new cycle. It is a chance to begin again. It is a calling back to the One Spirit we are all a part of, and the journey home. This number means you have completed a level of working through karmic baggage...finished a pattern/theme that may have been with you many lifetimes. 100 means you are very close to the truth, on a particular matter. It is the ending and the beginning. It signifies accomplishment, even if this is only on the spiritual plane. You may have also switched dimensions of time, or to a parallel universe version of your script. This is a hole in the matrix, which allows you to change stories, or versions of your story, depending on your readiness and evolvement - if you've put in the work. There are other numbers that represent these holes, or doorways (other than the double zero numbers). Many on the spiritual side are watching your progress with approval and encouragement. Time and space can be bent, or manipulated when you see 100. These changes in time variables/dimensions, may not be noticeable to you, unless you are really paying attention to the subtleties. In essence, time has sped up, and many difficult lessons have become unnecessary for you to learn. *I am always guided and rewarded, as I make my way home to Spirit, which is my true purpose in being here.* Diamond.

**101 - Into the Looking Glass.** 101 says it is a time when you should remember that everything you are seeing, is a reflection of you. What you think, you create. Your partners, friends, associates etc. are all mirrors. Your world reflects you. 101 is also a number of equal partnerships. You may be with, or soon meeting someone who sees eye-to-eye with you. This could be a time when you meet a soulmate, or someone from your soul group. 101 is also a tunnel or passageway for you to open up to channeling your guidance, whether that be through words, visions, dreams, inspirations, sensations etc. You can be an open channel to your Angels and guidance at this time. This is also an open doorway, or portal to other dimensions, and you should check your surroundings, aura and energy field carefully for openings. Clear yourself of any attachments, or walk-ins who shouldn't be there. Professional help may be needed. Bless any openings or portals you see, and make sure that only higher energies are allowed in. *I am surrounded by Divine guidance, and I allow myself to create and attract, only that which is in alignment with my True Self.* Shattuckite.

**102 - It Takes Two.** This number signifies healthy

relationships, that create something through their joining. This could be two people who have a child, two business partners who start a business, etc. A lucky number overall. *I honor all of my relationships, and offer my gifts to the world.*

**103 - Building A Dream.** The communication lines are wide open. There is harmony, and stability, that comes with understanding, and being understood. Connected to 102, 103 says the creation begins to take root, with a solid foundation. *My life is harmonious and happy. I communicate with love.*

**104 - The Long Haul.** 104 is a lucky number for stability and growth. A great time to build anything up, or create long term plans. *I plan for the future, knowing that success is assured.*

**105 - Bed of Roses.** 105 a very fortunate number in financial sectors, health and relationships. Good luck and advancements. *I have good fortune in all endeavors. I am blessed.*

**106 - Birds Of A Feather.** This number has to do with meeting spiritual partners, kindred spirits and friends, who represent opposite traits in you. It also suggests that your physical health responds to spiritual healing, and alternative methods. *I am healthy in mind and body. My relationships reflect this.*

**107 - A Life of Purpose.** There are conflicting energies, at this time, about what you want in the world, and what your soul needs to grow. You have had many spiritual lessons, and a lot of the experiences and information that has come to you, is now culminating, and starting to make sense. You see why you have been through certain situations, or why things have happened. Realize you are better off now, because of it. The challenge with 107, is to allow life to take the lead, and understand that if certain things upset you, they are coming up for release, so let go, trust and try not to react. All things in this world continually change, but your purpose remains constant, even if you can't always see what that is. *I flow through life, with ease, and understand that I am cared for, and all things are always in their right place.* Iris, dried root.

**108 - Other Worlds.** With this number, I have visions of

Adam and Eve in the Garden of Eden. I feel this has ancient connections to older history that may have been lost...about how we were actually created. I also feel this number has connections to other worlds of beauty in the cosmos. 108 is a message that there is a grander scheme in everything. Trust that you are a part of something much bigger, than who you appear to be in this life. You are most likely a Star Seed, Indigo, Rainbow etc. that came from other worlds to see this one, and assist in its growth. Your light and love has brought this world to a higher plane of energy. *I honor my connections, and thank them for their assistance, seen and unseen, in my life.*

**109 - Cosmic Purpose.** This is a number of completion,

spiraling you into the next set of experiences and lessons. You have accomplished much. These may or may not have been worldly goals, as these are relatively unimportant, when viewed from the overall picture of the massive destiny of the entire cosmos. Your Spirit has much it will do beyond this Earth plane, and as with all the 9 numbers after 100, 109 is a progression of the soul's growth so far. Where you go from here, is largely due to your intentions. *I am a Spirit, seeming to occupy a body. My purpose is so much greater than even I can see. I submit to, and honor that which Spirit requires of me.*

**110 - Commitment to the Light.** This is a significant signpost on your journey in the Matrix. 110 is a combination of the original 1, the 11 doorway, and 10, your free will choice. After the first nine numbers 101 - 109, this is a turning point, of needing to make a choice to stay on the higher path. There will be temptations to lead you down darker avenues of the ego. You may be asked to make the choice, once again, to stay on the path of light. With 110, the doorway is open, and you can be pulled either way. 110 suggests you meditate, and ask for assistance and back-up, to clear your path, and willingly call upon the light of Spirit to fill you. Another meaning for this number, is it is time for you to make decisions. Be definite, commit. Commit to a project, a path, a person, a belief or an idea. Once you decide…and decide to stick with it (commit), the Universe can then bring it to you. *I am comfortable making decisions and committing to them. I trust that I am being guided to make the best choice for me in ___________situation, (or in all situations).* Gray banded agate.

**111 - The Gateway.** This is a powerful number, related to the 11:11, and you may be seeing it as 1:11, or 11:1. This is a sign that you have made your choice, from number 110, and have passed through a significant doorway, or entryway. It is a sign that you are a lightworker, who came here to make changes in the order of things. It is a sign that you are where you are supposed to be, on your path. It is also a sign that you are meeting up with others that are significant to your purpose here. 111 is related to soulmates, soul families, and Twin Flames. Many of these are all connected in the same purpose, whether or not they meet in this lifetime. This is also a doorway that is opened at specific times, for people to exit or enter this plane. There may be many people leaving the planet, as others attempt to come in. Both those with light and dark purposes are attempting to influence the masses, at this time, as both energies fight to enter the doorway. It is also signaling the new wave of light workers being born. Chances are you are already aware of your higher purpose, or are about to be. Keep in mind that 11, because it is a doorway, can be used by dark forces, as well as the light. Be careful in what type of energies you are spending your time. Re-assess yourself regularly, and re-align with your spiritual guidance. In a worldly sense, 111 means that all systems are a go, for whatever you were wanting to accomplish. There should be nothing that stands in the way of what you want. Aligning with others for a common goal is beneficial. *Those who are meant to be with me will come. I reunite with all, who assist me with my Divine Purpose, at the correct time.* Lemurian Seed Crystal.

**112 - Treasure Trove.** This is a number of divine revelations,

spiritual messages and anointings from heaven. There is much to be thankful for, with 112. The advice from Spirit is clear. Follow what you know. 112 overcomes all difficulties, and promises prosperity. *I am blessed by heaven. All is working in my favor, and I am divinely guided.*

**113 - Rain Maker.** This is a number of new beginnings, and

manifesting what you want. You have a lot of power to make things happen. This is a lucky number, and says you are in control of your destiny, at this time. *I use my power wisely, and enjoy my blessings.*

**114 - A Job Well Done.** 114 speaks of success, and getting

notoriety. Your efforts are being recognized, whether this be at a job, in a relationship, in business or any other situation.

Connections are being made, and you are seeing progress. This is a sign that you are being heard, and your efforts in the past have not been wasted. This is the Universe giving you a sign that you are doing well, and to continue. Keep the faith, enjoy this success, and never give up. Spirit is always with you. *I continue forward with confidence and faith, that all is happening for my highest good.*

**115 - Fun is the Agenda.** It is a good time to get out, into the company of family and friends. Socialize. Have some fun. You need to let loose. Free up your schedule, your mind and your time. Have a party, or attend a party. Mix with others, even if you are a homebody. 115 is calling you, to set aside that which has consumed your time, thoughts and energy, and join a class, gathering or something which takes you completely away from the normal routine and grind. If you make time, then things will adjust, and you will have the time. If you don't have the money for fun, plan to do it anyway, and the money will be there. *I allow the playfulness of my Spirit to shine through. I have plenty of time for fun and doing things I enjoy.*

**116 - A Grip too Tight.** 116 is a sign that you have to re-evaluate what you have built or created in your life, so far. There may be things that are not of the highest good for you, or that need to be altered or changed. There may be aspects that you are holding on to, that need to be let go of, or that you need to loosen your hold on. If you try to control things, they will backfire. This is a time of testing. The Universe is watching you, to see what you will decide. It is calling you, to release your grip, and allow things to be as they are. Forcing issues, or rigidity will only make you lose what you are trying to achieve. *I allow Divine forces to flow through my life, and put* *everything in its correct place. I trust that everything happens as it should, and let go of things I cannot control.* Condor Animal Totem.

**117 - A Heavier Load.** 117 is suggesting the energy of "one-too-many". You have taken on an extra load, or more than you are comfortable handling. Instead of enjoying the situation, it has become a burden. It is time to delegate, say no, create strong boundaries and be a little nicer to yourself. Not everything has to be done, or taken on by you. Unload, so you can heal, and enjoy your journey. *I am kind to myself. Source is handling the rest.* Lithium Light.

**118 - Aladdin's Lamp.** 118 is an unstoppable number, which means that whatever you are aiming for, is going to happen. It cannot *not* happen, unless you deliberately mess it up. Decide what you want...and you will get exactly what you request...so, as it is said, "Be careful what you wish for." The wisest course of action, is to ask for that which is best for all involved, because sometimes we unknowingly ask for things, and get what we don't really want. Or we ask for something that isn't what we thought it was going to be. Turning your desires over to Spirit, and asking for the best possible outcome, is recommended. *________, or something better comes to me now in a perfect way. I monitor my thoughts, careful to avoid negative thinking, which will bring in unwanted outcomes.*

**119 - Loose Lips.** There is a lot of support behind you. You can succeed with what you are trying to accomplish, but the warnings are to watch what you say in anger. This can ruin many plans, or destroy something that is precious to you. If you can keep your lips closed, and keep your anger or justification to yourself, then situations will continue on in a successful manner. Don't be your own worst enemy. Take your anger out in private, and tell no one. There is much to be joyful about with this number, as many blessings are flowing in. Just get out of your own way. Focus on what is good in the situation, and ignore the rest for now. *My live is Divinely guided. I allow all situations, even if I am uncomfortable with them. I flow with ease, and allow things to unfold as they will.*

**120 - Wisdom From the Past.** This is a number of

resurrection and redemption. What has been lost, will be found. Something old that has lost its value, is again useful. Look to the past for that which has been left behind, and reconsider its usefulness. Old or ancient knowledge becomes current, and is helpful to you now. Research the past, or the wisdom of those who have gone before you. Their messages or information for you still applies. Nothing is ever truly gone. If someone has left your life, they may be returning, or their legacy will be left behind. 120 signals gifts from the past. This includes spiritual knowledge that you have gained in past lives, benefiting you now. It may be a good time for a past life regression. Old patterns may be coming up, to be understood and released. *I recognize that all is cyclical, and honor the past and its lessons.*

**121 - Wealth Boost.** A number of rising to achievement, and

winning. Overcoming all odds. Money flow increases. *I am in the Divine flow of abundance.*

**122 - Green Pastures.** This is a number of high success. Good

fortune comes all at once, from somewhere unexpected. It represents windfalls, gifts, love, opportunities and winning.

You have overcome something karmic in the past, or in a past life, and a reward is on its way. It will be equivalent to the positive karma you created. Four leaf clovers, and the color green come through strong with this number, so it is most likely something you have done with love, or given from the heart. *Good luck and fortuitous circumstances wait for me around every corner. I deserve and accept them with love and appreciation.*

**123 - A Leap Forward.** Sequence numbers like this, in order,

signal fast movement ahead in your life, and in spiritual growth, offering opportunities to jump to a different path or script. You bypass certain lessons that you no longer need to learn, and move forward very quickly. This means that you have choices. You are at a crossroads, of sorts, with multiple choice options. You may have been headed down a karmic path "A", and now the Universe is telling you that you can choose "B", "C" or "D". This is a spiritual gift for you. *I exercise my free will options. I walk in the divine Creator's grace.*

**124 - Links in the Chain.** This is a very blessed number, that

deals with the expansiveness of the Universe. How everything relates to everything else. The Divine synchronicity of everything working together. This number is a message that harmony prevails. It is a sign, to know that your wishes have been heard, and your angels are working on delivering what you need. Have faith. You will get what is most needed in the situation. *I honor the interconnectedness of all things. My consciousness opens up to embrace all answers, as I accept the abundance of this vast Universe.*

**125 - Harmony.** This number is saying to explore the natural

world, to bring yourself back into balance...such as planting a garden, getting a few indoor plants, going swimming in a natural body of water, or taking a walk, or a hike out in nature. Breathe in what you see and experience. Breathe in nature's energy, its beauty, and feel how it speaks back to you. If you are in a city, create a natural environment with plants, crystals, air purifiers, colors and fresh fruits and vegetables. Surround yourself with things that have a positive energetic, or emotional impact on you. Decorate with natural furnishings, environmentally friendly paints and materials that are nature-based, and avoid pollutants. Clean up, and clear out your space, of anything negatively affecting your health or emotions. Enhancing your natural energy and aura will help you realign yourself with your own personal power. You will feel re-energized, and ready to take on the world. *I am a pure Divine being of light. I reconnect with my natural joyous state of balance.*

**126 - Finding the Self.** 126 is a number of discovery of self.

You are meant to be exploring you. Who are you? Have you been programmed by others, who told you how to be? It is time for you to define who you really are, and who you know yourself to be. It is a remaking of you. A rebirth of sorts. Who can you become? Are you playing out scenarios that are merely patterns of your interactions with others? Analyze why you are, where you are, at this particular point in your life. How did you get here? What experiences have led you here, and how can you do it differently next time? Where do you want to be, and what do you want from your life? Put these questions to Spirit for the answers. It is time to open up, to change the patterns and become your true self, not how others have defined you. *I open myself to the true inner light that resides within me. I am not a product of my environment.* White Sapphire.

**127 - Angels Wings.** You cannot fail. The Angels have your back. What you wish for will happen. All is in your favor, now. *I always have what I need. I am well protected.*

**128 - Stand Up.** There comes a time in your life, when you need to make a stand. Put a stop to something, or say your peace. This number is asking you to stand up for what you believe in, trust your inner guidance and what you know, and don't allow others to make you doubt yourself. Have confidence in your abilities and talents. You are capable. Don't allow anyone to make you feel otherwise, or tear you down. You know what you know, and that is what is important. 128 says to believe in yourself. Recognize that you are a Divine being and deserve to be treated with respect and love. Give this to others, and it will be reflected back to you. *I stand up for Truth. I honor myself, and know my own value.* Ruby.

**129 - Hush.** This is a time for quiet contemplation. All mysteries are being revealed to you. You will see that you are always being led. *I open myself to the insights being revealed to me now.* Purple Jade.

**130 - To Decide.** This number reflects someone who is comfortable in their own skin. It suggests security, and the ability to master any situation. Whatever you put your mind to, comes about. *I am at one with my true inner being. All is well in my world.*

**131 - Isolated Imaginings.** Magical things happen, when you take alone time, away from others. Much inspiration and creative ideas flow, and answers to problems appear. Take the time for yourself, to get to know you. *I am inspired by Spirit. Joy flows through me, now.*

**132 - Poised For Success.** This is a fortunate number of good luck and monetary gain. It advises you to rely on your own counsel, and act in accordance with what you know. *I live in wealth and abundance. I give thanks for my blessings.*

**133 - Use of Power.** It is a time for you to reconnect with your Angels, Spirit Guides and those higher beings that are with you from other realms. Listen with your inner ear, and receive the guidance they have for you. Happiness, joy and success, can be yours, if you will allow this energy to flow in. 133 says to create that which you desire for your life, through meditation, manifestation, visualization and other tools available for you, to create your outer reality. This is a lucky number. 133 is hijacked by dark forces, simply because it has incredible power to manifest joy and abundance. This is what Dark Side energies wish to prevent. Therefore, they target this number, and utilize it frequently, in rituals and harmful practices. This number is very powerful, because it deals with your ability to create, as a co-creator with Source energy. It is a recognition that you are more than who you seem to be. Therefore, trust in your ability, through Source, to create your reality. *I recognize my own Sovereignty, to create joy, abundance and happiness. I recognize that this is a natural state of being, and I call for these miracles now.* Blue Kyanite. Serendibite, if available.

**134 - Kicking Karma's Butt.** This number has to do with karmic conflicts, that lead to learning, and divine revelations.

Much understanding and growth can come from facing these conflicts. Trust in Spirit to guide you, so that the good energies of this number can assist you, in overcoming obstacles, and finding success. *I have courage to face what is in front of me. Source lights my way.* Archangel Jeremiel.

**135 - Push & Pull.** This number carries a warning of

difficulties and opposing energies. The advice here, is to take neutral ground in all things. Follow the advice from Spirit, and guide your thoughts toward positive thinking. What you are sending out, will come back. *I rely on Spirit, alone, to guide my steps. In this, I find success.* Yellow Rhodizite.

**136 - Universal Bounty.** 136 is a message of abundance and

happiness. This number is about announcements and messages. Messages about money and good news. It represents gifts. 136 says that success is guaranteed . *I receive the many gifts, that are coming to me now.*

**137 - Hopeful Horizons.** This number has to do with asking

the Universe for that which you need. It is time to get outside of your comfort zone, or outside the box, and take action that you would not normally take. Look for opportunities in places you would not normally look. Know that many opportunities are coming to you at this time, and the results are going to be better than you thought. *New opportunities find me now. I find stimulation, excitement and passion for my new life.*

**138 - Gavel of Justice.** This number has to do with legal

contracts, agreements, negotiations, verbal contracts or any rules, regulations or parameters that are set around a certain arrangement. Paperwork may need to be signed. Anything where you sign your name, or agree to something, is referred to here. This number says that whoever is justified in the situation, will be rewarded. *Divine Justice shines forth in my life. I step forward in confidence and Grace. All decisions are made for the highest good of all involved.* Crane Animal Totem.

**139 - Shame On Shame.** This number involves choices and

correct decisions. Which is the best path? This needs to be analyzed, and you need to take great care when choosing. It is suggested that you go over all the pros and cons, each detail, and all information to which you have access. Do you believe you need to suffer for something? Are you making choices based on guilt? The Path of Grace is always available to all. It is before you, as well as a new life. It is time for you to take up your journey, and let bygones be bygones. *I step forward onto A New Path of discovery, light, joy and freedom. I let go of old situations, thought patterns and belief in the ego.* Terraluminite.

**140 - Upsetting The Balance.** Spirit says you are journeying

in new directions, new paths and new ways of being. This means your choice has been made from number 139, and it is time to take the first step. It is important, when you are in the newer stages of anything, to walk slowly, and be aware of your thinking processes. Your relationships, your work life, your health, your family and home life and all situations are on a fresh clean slate. Therefore, it is best to stay in a positive mind frame. Create practices that allow you to do this. Stay in a state of optimism and positive anticipation, that things are different now. Things are going to be better than they were, and old mistakes are not going to be repeated. 140 speaks of starting again. How do you want your new relationship to be? How do you want your new life to be? *I repair and rebuild the past, with a step forward in Grace.*

**141 - May Flowers.** Your Spirit Guides and Angels are attempting to make clear contact with you, in order for them to guide you more specifically on your path. 141 brings you into the highest energy and space possible, in order to receive your blessings. The timing is spring into summer. *I receive the blessings of Divine Angels.*

**142 - Destiny's Way.** This a signpost, that you are on the right path. You are an advanced student. 142 has to do with relationships, love, romance, partnerships and passion. Pay attention to relationships, that have strong emotion connected to them. This is a sign that they are karmic in nature, and therefore, important. Honor these relationships, whether difficult, or rewarding. They are replays with the same soul, and represent repeated lessons that you are replaying over and over again, from lifetime to lifetime. 142 is saying that you are at an advanced stage of your spiritual growth. It is no longer necessary for you to continue these interactions, if they are hurtful or harmful, to one or both parties involved. You have to be the person that ends the conflict, and the repeating cycle. It is up to you then, to make this change in your destiny. *I release and let go of relationships that no longer serve me. I forgive the past, and end the harmful cycle.*

**143 - Inner Peace.** This number carries a warning for the future, regarding deceptions that can lead to tragedies. This number says to pay attention to the subtleties, nuances and hidden undercurrents, in other people's actions and words. If you harbor any doubts, ask your inner guidance to bring all situations into the light of day. *I see clearly and know the truth.* Sodalite.

**144 - Mousetrap.** This is a warning number, of extreme difficulties. Heavy karmic circumstances, manipulations and outright conflict, could be the order of the day, especially connected to family members. This could relate to losses and pain. The advice of 144, is to release all situations to Spirit, and stay neutral, when possible. Spirit can lead you out of the storm. *I am aligned with the my inner Spirit. I receive strength from Source.* Archangel Uriel.

**145 - Awakening.** You are here to serve a higher destiny. There are those working with you, from other worlds, and all are assisting with the common purpose here. They are lightworkers, and you will be joining with some of these, as is needed on your journey. You may be questioning why you have been led to, or are in specific situations or locations. Many of you have been put in specific locations, in order to raise the energy vibration of that area. Realize that your higher purpose in being here, necessitates this. Your soul and Spirit are well aware of what is needed, whether you realize your life purpose consciously, or not. 145 is calling for you to awaken to this purpose, and to attune to your guidance. All the things that you think you need, will be given, as is deemed appropriate for what you came here to do. *I have come to undertake a larger purpose. I am guided and directed at all times.*

**146 - Stake Your Claim.** This is a number of good fortune, and feeling secure. You are the decider of your fate. You can reject your luck, or accept it. Your choice. *I am thankful for all I have. The Creator holds nothing back from me. I accept his love.*

**147 - Ducks in a Row.** Organization is the key, to success.

Maintaining order helps you reach your goals, and attain peace of mind. Unruly or chaotic situations are controlling you, your reactions and emotions. This, in turn, controls your output. The productivity levels, of your day, decrease in direct relation to your preparedness to handle situations and problems, as they come up. If you are not organized, everything is more difficult. Organize your thoughts, files, home, work space, schedule, etc. *I slow down, and take the time to organize.*

**148 - A Molehill Into a Mountain.** There are many

disruptions happening right now, and 148 is a signal, that focus is needed. Interference come from everywhere, as well as the temptation to distract yourself. To overcome a lack of motivation, think in terms of creating discipline. It is not a question of whether you "don't feel like it", are "not in the mood" or "I don't know where to start". There are a million excuses your mind will tell you, to avoid action, and you will end up with little to nothing, in the end. Discipline is your answer. This means that you do whatever it is, on a regular basis, just like brushing your teeth. You schedule a time, don't think about it, just do it. Creating discipline means creating a habit. By doing what needs to be done every day, on a regular basis, you get results over time. And eventually, massive results. Start chipping away at it, and success will build on success. *My mind is disciplined, and focused on the task at hand. I will be rewarded for my commitment to action.*

**149 - Time to Spend Time.** 149 is giving you a message to tap

into your inner child, and do what brings you joy. Explore things you may have put to the wayside for "someday".

Someday, is now. It has already arrived, and may have arrived many times over. There is a fun hobby or project that needs your focus, such as woodworking, or hanging out with friends. If you feel you absolutely have no time, and find it impossible to allow enjoyment or play time into your life, then give yourself a definite date of when "someday" is. Put it on your calendar, and stick to it, no matter what. If you are really overworked or over-stressed, and don't know what you find fun anymore, ask a friend for help. And who knows, maybe your hobby will turn into something profitable. *I live a balanced life of work and play. I allow myself to be creative and have fun.*

**150 - Miraculous Intervention.** This is a number of all-around blessings, and goodwill. All is well. What you need to happen, can happen. *I am blessed by Spirit. All is working in my favor.*

**151 - Thought Before Action.** It is time for a "time out", prayer, meditation and silence. You need stillness now, to gain clarity on where you are headed, and what you are trying to accomplish. The drive to go full force into something is strong, but this number advises you to take a moment, and do some reflection. Sit in silence and calm your thoughts. Wait for clarity, and you may be amazed at how much information comes in, and what you may be re-thinking. This is a think before acting number. There is more to the story, or it can be accomplished more effectively, if you sit still...which may be the opposite of what you are feeling right now. This is a sign that you need to take that moment. *Divine clarity comes to me, when I silence my thoughts, and allow myself to be led by Spirit.*

**152 - Eyes Wide Open.** This number is a powerful one, from a worldly perspective, and says that you have a lot of initiative, drive, know-how and intuition backing you. Realize that when you go for something big, you will have some losses, or some who side against you. This is the nature of things. There is always the naysayer, or person who disagrees with what you have to say, or what you have decided to do. In this instance, it is best to listen to your intuition for guidance, which may seem buried, under your need to accomplish something in this situation. You have the opportunity to score big, and should aim high, but be aware of the pitfalls. *I trust my inner guidance, and let it take the lead in all undertakings.* Deer Totem.

**153 - Time Lines.** This number signals a slight pause for reflection, before continuing on with something, or someone. A lot of realizations are happening. It is a time to re-analyze, and go back into the past, to learn from mistakes and lessons. A lot of pieces of the larger puzzle are coming together, for you to move into a new phase of your life. Old behaviors or patterns are changing, and possibly you feel changed, or different. You see the long term, backwards and forwards into the future. It is as if Spirit is giving you a bird's eye view, or you need to take one. And remember, the Angels are saying that you have the right of refusal, meaning, you can and maybe should say "no" to certain situations at this time. *Life is cyclical. I see clearly where I have come from, and where I now want to go. My new future awaits me.* Green or Yellow Zincite.

**154 - Shake It Up.** Life is filled with adventure, and new experiences. Things may be getting exciting again, or you are in bad need of some stirring up. This is a good time to do something that you have never done before, or something you have always wanted to do. If it involves a relationship, there may be something you have wanted to say, or a different way or dynamic you have wanted to have, with this person. Make yourself over into something new, something more in alignment with your inner self...true to your visions, desires and dreams. Step out and do things differently. Get yourself into the space by taking a different route or form of transportation, than usual. Shake up your life. *My life is new and exciting. Everyday is an adventure, and I find enjoyment in living.*

**155 - Counsel.** Follow the path that leads to wisdom. Climb

the mountain, and talk to the wise sage that lives at the top. This number is telling you to seek out counsel, get a psychic reading, go to a rune master, seek advice from a church elder, see an astrologer or whomever you go to for spiritual guidance and wisdom. You need some outside perspective at this time, not because you are lost, but because it will shift you onto a different path, than the one you are currently taking, and with this change, you will trigger magic to happen. This is a time when great things can happen, but you need that nudge, to see it, and take advantage of it. It is also a time, when you will gain an outside perspective, which helps you see clearly. *I allow others to help me on my journey. I receive advice, of the highest wisdom, and act accordingly.*

**156 - Upgrade.** Repressed emotions could be making you ill,

or interfering with your happiness. 156 says that any health conditions should now be improving, or you should be making efforts to maintain or recover your health. Blessings are on their way. Know that life is looking up. *The Creator is with me, and sees me through all situations.*

**157 - Let It Shine.** You need more Sun. You need Vitamin D, cheering up, or some other kind of advantage the Sun has for you. Maybe you need to visit a locale that has more sunshine. Symbolically, you may need to adopt a more optimistic attitude about life. Feelings of optimism, and anticipating the good, will bring more good fortune to you. Life changes, as our perception changes. *I let Divine light shine through me, to others.*

**158 - The Blues.** This number has to do with the sky and wind...such as being up in the air, in an airplane on a trip, or going toward blue skies. Like the previous number, this suggests the blue bird of happiness, blue skies, and that which suggests joy and magic. It is saying that all things are possible. Grand things are possible, if you choose to aim for the stars. It also talks about having a connection to wind, weather and the air elementals - the sylphs. It may be good for you to get outside, and get some fresh air, get an air purifier, do some breathing exercises, such as yogic breathing, or bring a breath of fresh air into your life. You need to blow off some steam, or speak your mind. Maybe you need to paint a wall or two, a beautiful relaxing blue color. *I breathe in the beauty and magic of life, and let it permeate my being.*

**159 - Hands On.** This number talks about working with your hands. Do you have a skill that you are good at, such as pottery, construction, playing sports etc.? Do you type quickly, do accounting or write books/articles? Maybe you are good at massage, or have a loving touch with your children. 159 says you need to put your hands in the dirt, and get gardening, or get hands-on, to help heal a situation, or solve a problem. Get in there and do the work, and make contact with others through physical means. Your loving touch is needed. *My efforts are always rewarded. I utilize my unique gifts to help all, and am helped in return.*

**160 - Holy Mission.** This is a number of aligning with your Divine Purpose. You are here to spread a special message, and give your own unique gift to the world. 160 is good luck and finding your purpose, or living it. *I have a place and a purpose here. I am Divinely blessed.*

**161 - Sound Vibrations.** This is a sign to listen to your inner voice. Notice around you, what is actually being said, not what you hear. 161 says to get outside and listen to the birds, the crickets buzzing...listen to natural sounds. Your inner ear, or clairaudience is heightened with this number. Notice vibrations, and their connections to higher energies. Pay attention to how certain sounds are raising or lowering your energy. Some scatter your energy or thoughts, and create chaos. Find some quiet, and listen to natural harmonious sounds, that are soothing, uplifting and healing for your energy field. Classical music, sounds of nature, your own heartbeat, a cat purring etc. Eliminate noise. *I find healing, peace and spiritual connection, through harmonious sound. I open to my inner guidance, and listen with new ears.*

**162 - A Friend Indeed.** This number has to do with betrayals in friendships, and hurt feelings. Sensitivities run high, and there can be loss and pain. Understand what you truly value, and only allow that into your life. Think first of filling your needs, and loving yourself. Then your peaceful presence will be a blessing to others. You will realize, that you were not at the mercy of anyone else. You are a free individual, and can move forward into a happy future, with or without anyone else's approval. *I trust in Spirit. All is provided, and I move into happiness.* Armadillo Animal Totem.

**163 - Out in the Open.** This number is highlighting issues with your reputation, and the face that you put out to the world. How do others see you? How are you presenting yourself? This includes business, work, socially and in family life. It is a message to be concerned with how you appear, your motives, your trustworthiness, and influence. It may be a sign that in the business or career sector, you could succeed on a very large scale, but in general, it means that you are in the spotlight, and to prepare for that. You cannot hide. All is brought out into the open. *I am an open channel for Spirit. I realize that my only purpose, here, is to be of service. I allow Spirit to work through me in all my endeavors.*

**164 - Group Effort.** This is a positive number calling for leadership, in groups, associations, at work, or in any setting where you are connected to others socially, outside the home. You may be the organizer, or need to take a more active part in groups that you are associated with, or 164 may be calling you to join a group. You have ideas that could benefit others, and need to share them. You may have a cause you care about or an addiction, or problem, and 164 is suggesting possibly starting an action group, to lead the way to change, in areas that you care about...for yourself and others. 164 is also telling you to be choosy and careful when selecting friends into your close circle. There may be some gossiping. 164 does say that it is important for you to be involved with others, and have a support circle of friends. *I am part of a larger family. We are all united in Spirit, and each part has its place in the Whole.*

**165 - Animal Nature.** Animal energy is highlighted with this number. Do you have a pet? Does it need more care, or a vet check up? 165 says you need to be around animal energy at this time. This includes taking a class, or reading a book about exploring your spiritual animal totems, adopting a pet, volunteering or visiting an animal shelter or sanctuary, or spending time in the back yard observing squirrels, deer or wildlife native to your area. Animals carry a purity, that is lacking in human/ego motivations and interactions. Animals only kill for food, or protection. They do not kill for sport or boredom. Most are affectionate to those they know will not harm them. They live in harmony with the Earth, and each other, keeping the sacred balance. It is wise for you to be around their energy now, for healing or learning purposes, and to make a connection. Maybe you want to take this to the next level, and go vegetarian, vegan or become a supporter of an animal rescue association. *I am at one with all creatures.* A great book to read about connecting and communicating with animals, is "Life Without Limits", by Peter Calhoun.

**166 - Color My World.** This number speaks of needing more color in your life, for healing purposes and its positive effect on your psyche. The advice is, to seek out some color therapy, utilize crystals and their color vibrations, work with the aura or chakras, and wear, decorate and surround yourself with colors that bring you into a more balanced state. Wear colors that give you confidence, that are attuned with you, or have a soothing energy. Carry colored crystals, that are in harmony with your Chaldean Numerology Day Number (see my book, "5 Numbers of Destiny"), and astrology chart. Which planets rule your numerology and astrology charts? Utilize the colors associated with these. *I live a colorful, healthy and happy life.*

**167 - Budding Prosperity.** This is a number of big changes, that lead to positive expansion and growth. The correct energies are coming in, at this time, to create change for the better. Increase and luck is highlighted with this number. *Life gets better and better. All is working in my favor.*

**168 - Players.** This number warns you to be cautious about situations or people that you invest time, money or energy in, and to analyze your own motivations and actions, as well. It tells you to pay attention to your inner conscience, that inner voice that warns you away from certain things, that are not in your best interest. It is not a time for judgment, but rather being aware of who, or what you are involved with, and why. *My eyes see clearly, all that needs to be seen and understood in ______ situation.* Purpurite.

**169 - Road Signs.** This is a time for U-Turns, turn-arounds, and re-dos. The direction you are headed, is either the wrong way, or what you have created so far, has to be re-done. There is a more direct route, or better way to get where you are going, or to get what you want out of a situation. If doors are closing, or the way seems blocked, try a different approach, or a completely different direction. It may also feel like a one step forward, two steps back cycle. It is time to find another way. Once you find it, good fortune follows. *I am always Divinely guided by Spirit, in all situations.*

**170 - Crossovers.** 170 has to do with the other side, contact with those who have crossed over, and remembering the dead, and their gifts. A loved one, friend or someone from the heavenly realms is trying to reach you, and make themselves known to you. 170 could mean the imminent or upcoming death of a loved one...usually someone you expect to die...such as a relative that has been terminally ill, for some time. Know that any who pass, will do so peacefully. Even if the death seems difficult, they will find instant peace on the Other Side. Their soul understands, on some level, what is happening, and will not need the adjustment period when they cross over. This number also states, that you have achieved a very high level of spiritual development, and awareness of other levels/states of being...the visible and the invisible. *I honor those who have gone before me, and acknowledge that we are still together in Spirit.* Blue Tourmaline.

171 - **To the Drawing Board.** Spiritual lessons are coming to the forefront, and cannot be ignored. Suffering and adversity, may be the order of the day, but it is vital that you work through these challenges. You can be bumped up to a higher level of understanding and evolvement, when these tests are passed. Ask for guidance and assistance, during troublesome times. *I have the ability to move out of fear, and into love. I cannot be held back from my good.* Fuschite.

172 - **Failure Is Not An Option.** Things are looking up, with 172, and cannot fail. Even if things don't appear to be going your way, they will be soon. You will be receiving assistance from the Universe, that will have long term positive effects. The number 1, is connected to this number, meaning 1 day, month, week or year. The timing of when this situation either turns around, or gets even better will be in this 1 energy. This assistance will be in the form of a blessing or gift, will come all at once, and will influence the future. *I trust that all things are being taken care of, and I wait for my good.*

**173 - The Choice to Choose.** Opportunities abound with this number. Know that there are many choices available to you, and that they are all good options. It is a time of luck for you, because you have several roads before you, and there is no bad choice. Everyone is a connection, and the word is out that you are here, and available for these opportunities to come to you. The Universe is delivering on what you have previously asked for, or thought about. This is a good time to do gratitude work, because your good is on its way. *I give thanks that I am supported and guided toward my good.*

**174 - Expanded Mind.** Good luck on many levels, is connected to 174. You may possibly be reaching a level of enlightenment about something. Viewpoints are opening up, and the treasures of the Universe are yours for the taking. Allow these shifts in your energy, to happen now. *I am abundant, and have access to all the information I need.*

**175 - A Penny Saved.** This number is about securing your funds, your back up and your bottom line. Whether this be in a relationship, your finances or some other situation, the advice here is to do what brings you security in the long run. Think in the bigger picture, or long term goals. Instant gratification, or making choices based on the present moment, will not ultimately give you what you want. Change is always imminent, and the only thing that is sure. Make certain that what you are deciding, can weather the storm of change, if your present situation should not stay as is. It would be wise to build up savings, have a back up plan or take a conservative stance on whatever you are considering. *I make wise decisions for me, and those that depend on me.*

**176 - Sound Frequencies.** This number is calling you to spend some time singing, toning, chanting, or expressing yourself through the voice. Maybe this means taking up acting, letting loose in the shower or practicing public speaking. Join a group that teaches how to speak, take voice lessons, or learn how to speak professionally and successfully, using the tone of your voice. Notice how you say things to others. Let inhibitions go, and try singing in public. Also, meditation with chanting sounds is very beneficial for balancing out your energy fields at this time. Use your voice in positive ways. 176 says, "Express yourself!" *I freely express joy, now.*

**177 - Into the Night.** 177 is signaling a time, when you are working out a lot, through dreaming and your sleep. This number is talking about night time...dreams, visions, astral travel and all things you do while you sleep. If you are having disturbing dreams, you may need protection around your bed, while you sleep. Your guides may be giving you extra training while you sleep, in the form of dream symbolism and travel, to certain learning locations. Many of your dreams are past-life recall, and issues/fears that have been on your mind of late. Some of it may be predictive symbolism, but 177 says that you are in a "working through" phase at the moment. Therefore, many of your daily stressors, are being worked out through your dreams, so that you are better able to handle them, and function in your waking life. Spirit is also speaking to you, through the dreams, with messages. A regular sleep schedule will help, tremendously. *I remember my dreams, clearly, upon awakening, and understand their messages.* Fresh Spearmint leaves around the bed.

**178 - Making Headway.** This number has to do with dangers and pitfalls. If one follows the way of ego desires, one is lost. This is a test, to see what you will choose. Are you more interested in material gain, or spiritual advancement? Choosing the former, will lead to a fall, as the material world is castles made in sand. This karmic situation is pulling you in, as if you are a magnet. Know that eventually, you will be learn that only Spirit can bring peace, and hope for a secure future. *I trust in Spirit alone. My permanent good finds me now.* Rat Animal Totem.

**179 - Good Vibrations.** This number suggests going on a vision quest, of sorts. Finding alone time, to connect with your guides, has benefits. 179 can relate to shamanistic work...either seeing a shaman, or developing your shaman skills of journeying. 179 also talks about divine rhythms, and the possibility of joining a drumming circle. Rhythm and beat are closely connected to 179, and you should listen to some stimulating drum, bass or heavy rhythm music, and move your body to the beat. Spiritual journeying may be needed (by you or a trained shaman), to receive the answers, clarity or results for which you are looking. *I am one with the rhythm of life. My heart beats in harmony with the Earth and all of life.* White Sage leaves.

**180 - The Voice For Spirit.** You are a blessing, and a channel for the good. You have an important message for someone, or can help them find answers. It may be a time for you to channel your guidance, or explore the world of channeling. There is a purer energy working through you at this time, and 180 says that you have attained a high level of spiritual growth. You are still being tested, but definite progress, toward becoming who you truly are, has been made. *I am a voice for Spirit. All truth, wisdom and answers flow through me effortlessly.* Clear Quartz, wrapped in Copper, with any Red gemstone.

**181 - Those In Need.** If there are family members that are elderly, or ill, they may need your care at this time. This number has to do with care-taking and tending to the ill, or the needy. This may be children needing your attention, or someone who requires help. 181 also says you may be overloaded, and may not have the energy or time to give. This number carries a lot of stress, but also the drive and charisma of success. It is up to you. Try to manage your load the best you can. People are relying on you now, because they have confidence in you. *My load is light, and I am able to carry it with ease.* Rosewood Essential Oil.

**182 - Much To Learn.** Be open to learning. This is a number of going back to school, to learn something that is in your interest, or benefit. If you are not planning on getting additional schooling, maybe you are learning from someone around you, literally, or in the form of experience. This number says there is more to learn. If you have been thinking about going to school, have a desire to learn something new, or improve a skill, now is the time. The money will come. *All the knowledge I need, comes to me now, and I accomplish all things.* Archangel Raphael.

**183 - Physical Body.** This number is talking about needing some body work. A massage, a healing session, reflexology, acupuncture, or a flotation tank session would be beneficial. Pay particular attention to your body at this time, and what it is trying to communicate to you. Do you need a break? Do you have aches and pains? Do you need more sleep? Maybe you need an energetic removal. In any case, your physical self needs tending to, and this may be as simple as stretching every day, or going to see a doctor. This number may be warning you, before something happens, so take care of yourself. Even pampering has its purpose, as it helps to reduce stress. *I care for myself, and enjoy vibrant health.* Inhale Hops, dried flowers.

**184 - Coming Together.** This is a number of joinings, such as

family get-togethers, marriages, visiting relatives, forming friendships, merging a business etc. Anything that comes together, relates to 184. When things come together, the past is rewritten. This is also a number of new beginnings, and taking the risks of commitment. The message is to examine the merger or union, and make sure that all is as it should be, before making the leap. The commitment should feel good, as you are joining yourself fully to something, and should want to be there, or in the situation. *I am part of a greater whole. Spirit guides me in all my commitments.*

**185 - Silver Spoon.** There is nothing stopping you, with 185.

You are meant to succeed, and have been given all that is necessary, to guarantee this. Manifest what you want, and know that the fruits of your labors, bring more blessings. *I am gifted with abundance. I celebrate my good fortune.*

**186 - Dangerous Friends.** This number is connected to 168.

There may be selfish motives here, or someone is draining you. A "using" type energy is at play. It would be a time to form alliances very carefully, and determine what the underlying agenda is, before committing, or taking any action.

*I trust that I am guided to those, with my best interests at heart. Everyone in my energy field, is for my highest good.* Eye Agate.

**187 - Healthy Connections.** Your partnerships need

attention. If this is related to your personal life, it may be time to spruce things up with romance, caring deeds, or acts of service, that make your partner feel needed, loved and appreciated. This could also mean that it may be time to end a relationship, or news is coming, that this pairing needs to be seriously re-evaluated. If the partnership is business or work-related, it may be time to cut ties, or observe what is going on. Is this association to your benefit? Can this person be trusted? In any case, this number says to pay attention, and watch for upsets or problems. It is time to expend some energy fixing the situation, or cut it loose. *I attract Divine partnerships, that are healthy, holy and for the highest good of all.* Dumortierite.

**188 - Wishes Granted.** This is a number of high success, and

worldly gain. It has to do with big business proposals, executive decision-making and growth in all sectors of business. It definitely represents monetary increase, or a means to make this happen. In general, 188 says your goals are being realized, in a better way than you thought. Your will to create this particular situation has a big impact, and results will follow. Make sure your intentions are in line with what you really want, and that this *is* what you really want. Worldly goals come with some kind of price...usually the cost of something more valuable than money. *I ask for that which is for the best, for all involved, and celebrate my good fortune.* Toad animal totem.

**189 - A High Cost.** This number is connected to the one

before it. Read 188. 189 relates to the lessons, or price tag that came with 188. In a world of duality, conflict always arises with any goal or dream, if it has a purely material basis. Realize that the conflict or obstacles that may come up now, are the cost of receiving something (in 188), that you recently wished for, or may have wished for a long time ago. Forgive anything that is upsetting. There is good with the bad, so focus on what is good in your life, and what you have. *I am responsible for all that I create, and can therefore alter a difficult situation to a more glorified state, by deciding to wish for that which Spirit wills for me.* Wulfenite.

**190 - The Real Deal.** You now have access to a situation, that may have been unreachable for you. Spirit is also enabling you to become a better person, in terms of choices and spiritual growth. You are becoming more of your true self. Rewards flow through, when we work with Spirit, and align ourselves with who we truly are. *I welcome my rewards from Spirit, and am grateful for the many gifts that find me now.*

**191 - Change For The Better.** This number suggests a change in circumstances. Positive growth, better love relationships, and an increase in income are possible. *I give thanks for the good, coming to me now.*

**192 - Think It Through.** This number says, even though situations can be frustrating, take time to think before action or speech. In general, this number says that you should be able to acquire that which you need or want. Contemplation brings good results. *I act from a centered place of wisdom. All is revealed to me.*

**193 - Mommy Dearest.** This number has to do with issues

from your childhood...in particular your mother figure. What was her upbringing style, and how did it affect you? Was your birth mother in your life, or was she absent? If you were adopted, how do you relate to your mother? It is in recognizing what we were taught in youth, that allows us to understand and make new, or better choices, now. Perhaps you had an excellent mother figure and want to be just like her. 193 asks you to examine your own mothering styles. (Remember this relates to feminine energy, and not necessarily being of the female sex. You may have had a father who provided the nurturing you needed.) How are you treating your own children, pets or yourself? Nurturing is a basic need. If you were denied this, than now is the time to find ways to care for yourself, or those who rely on you. *I care for, and love myself. This is a basic right and need, as I am a child of Source. In turn I give love and care freely, openly and easily to others as well.* Turtle Animal Totem.

**194 - A Promise Broken.** This number speaks of promises

and agreements. Has there been an agreement made, that is being breached, or is someone not living up to their end of the bargain? This can be related to agreements or promises you made with yourself. Did you wish to be at a certain place in life, when you reached a particular age, and either you don't feel you are there, or maybe you have completed or surpassed that vision? This number has promise, in that, it says you will reach what you have sought to attain, by having faith. It is your own self and fears that have influenced the choices you have made, or not made, up to this point. In essence, you have created what you thought about, perhaps reliving the past and bringing it into your future. If promises with yourself, or others are being broken, realize that you can recreate a new contract or agreement, in the future. Life is always bringing you, what directly reflects your own thoughts. *I desire to keep all promises. I turn them over to Spirit, and follow what I am guided to do in each moment.* Allspice Essential Oil.

**195 - Recess.** This is a number of good luck, pleasure and overall enjoyment of life. Take time to revel in amusements. Create a happier life. *I am filled with playful energy, and have time to enjoy my life.*

**196 - Boosted Up.** Harmony is occurring, with 196. A lot of energies are building up in your life, to jettison you up to a whole new level of living. Things are falling into place and aligning with your higher good. What has been needed, is finding its way to you. Your life seems amplified, or sped up, and if you are exploring your spiritual nature, you have accelerated your growth. *Higher energies work through me now, setting the stage for accelerated growth and evolution.*

**197 - Necessary Removal.** This number has to do with other people, and how they support, or interfere with your destiny. Who are you surrounding yourself with, and have they been in your life a long time, or only recently? Are they acting out repeated patterns, or reflecting the same attitudes and problems of other people from your past? This is a time to clear the way, and this may include letting go of people that are no longer healthy for you to associate with, who are not serving your best interests. Those who harm you, or do not wish the best for you, do not belong in your energy field, or your life. Sometimes it can be difficult to deny those who may be family members or a spouse, but if you are to move into more positive energies, you have to be willing to stand up to those who would slow you down, or block you. 197 also emphasizes that it is very important to honor and hold on to those who offer unconditional love, or some kind of support, that allows you to continue forward on your path. *I forgive anyone, who is not here for my highest good. I bless them, and let their energy go.* White Jade

**198 - Showing the Way.** 198 has to do with higher truths, and the Angels and Guides who are connected to these. It is suggested that you make an effort to connect with them, as they have many important messages and truths to impart. You are moving up into higher levels of being...vibratory frequencies...and there is much you need to know, in order to flow with the shifts that are occurring, at this time in your life. You are asked to explore books, meditations, channeling methods, getting a reading, using crystals or anything else that can assist you in reaching and connecting with your higher guidance. *I am Divinely guided. I connect with my guides, and know what I am to do.* Angelite.

**199 - Instant Gratification.** This number has to do with visions, dreams and manifesting. 199 is a message to be careful what you are thinking about, because you are in an instant manifestation stage, where results can be immediate. This includes long-term goals, that have been taking a long time to come to fruition. Things are working in your favor, and you have a direct channel to Spirit. What you think, happens, so watch your thoughts carefully, so you will manifest what you want to see happen, in the best way. If you are getting visions, inspirations or nudges from Spirit, follow what you have been given. *This, or something better comes to me now, in a perfect way.*

**200 - Two Sides of The Mirror.** 200 signifies the beginning of a new cycle. This can be in the area of relationships, money or anything that comes in pairs. This number goes along with 199...what you think about, instantly manifests back to you. Your thoughts act as a mirror, bringing in the exact equivalent. 200 also has a direct relationship to a large group of Angels, who are in charge of keeping you on your path. (There is also an opposite duality, that seeks to distract you from your path.) 200 asks you what you see, in the mirror of your creations? This is a chance for you to create a whole new reality for yourself, spiritually, or in any area. *I call on Source, to bring me clarity and wisdom.*

**201 - Ambitions Realized.** 201 is a number of personal power, energy and abundance. All is lined up for you to take the lead and succeed. What do you want to do with your life? What are your goals? 201 says the time is now, to create that which you desire. *I attain my goals and dreams.*

**202 - Two Paths.** This number has to do with dualities, and opposing choices. You are being given a choice, to choose the "right", over the "wrong". This number represents doorways for both the light and dark to enter. Which path are you going to choose? The higher path of Self, leading back to Spirit, or the lower path of temptation, and eventual misery and pain? The tempting path, many times brings in our desires, but almost always traps us, in the end, and creates many more lifetimes to live, working out these unwise choices of the ego-self. When you realize you are Divine Spirit, this higher choice may have to be made repeatedly, because the lower energies will continue to interfere. Especially if you are making progress. Choosing the dark path, is like making a decision that feels great now, but long term, it has a high price. It brings you misery and imprisonment. This place of illusions and escapes, will never make you happy. A return to who you really are, relieves the emptiness inside, and brings the peace for which you are searching. 202 is also a message that you will be meeting a partner, who is the equivalent of the choice you have made, and who has made the same choice. This person will bring an increase in your peace of mind, or an amplification of the dark path. *I always choose wisely, because I allow Spirit to choose for me.*

**203 - Midas Touch.** 203 says a project or goal you are

working on, or wishing for, could come to a swift conclusion. This number puts a positive spin on anything it touches, and if you are using your communication skills properly, you should have no problem seeing satisfying results. Whatever you set out to accomplish, will be bigger than you thought, and farther-reaching. Go big, and aim for the stars. It is a signal to go forward, say "Yes", and sign on the dotted line. The situation moves quickly, and assistance comes in, when needed. *I am gifted with all that I need and want.*

**204 - Match Made In Heaven.** This is a number of "no holds

barred". Success is yours for the asking. Relationships are in harmony. Divine pairings can happen, at this time. *I am blessed with harmony and happiness.*

**205 - Dream A Little Dream.** This number is about dreams,

visions and plans for the future. It is saying that you can make anything happen, if you will dream it, and set a plan in motion. Ask for the Angel's assistance, to align your vision with Spirit, so that all aspects are in harmony, and do not cause upset, or loss for others. You can have what you want, but others do not have to suffer, in order for you to get your needs met. Envision what you want, release it to Spirit, and practice affirming daily. Keep the vision in your mind, of positive end results. 205 also says that you are in tune with Spirit, and are receiving guidance. *All of my dreams come true in a perfect way, for all involved.*

**206 - Healthy Karma.** This is a number representing your

everyday life. 206, is a sign of lessons being learned in your everyday world. Who are you interacting with, and what are the karmic lessons with these people? Also, you may have challenging karma coming in the areas of health and work. 206 is a signal to pay careful attention to diet, your emotions (and their impact on your health), and whether or not you are getting enough proper exercise. Making positive changes, now, is necessary. Be aware of your performance in relationships with others, in the home and at work. Begin to make healing changes now, to avoid the challenges of karma that may be coming in these areas. *I accept that all that happens to me, is a direct reflection of my choices, past and present.* Obsidian.

**207 - Divine Revelations.** This number is about direction,

and the drive and willpower to get where you are going. If you will make a definite choice, and focus on one path, you will achieve what you are setting out to do. You have the grit and determination, to cause change and reach goals. This is also a spiritual number. If you have made a commitment to a spiritual path, know that you are Divinely guided. When you are given inspiration or direction, it is time to take action. Whatever you are passionate about, will come to pass, whether this is something personal, or a more worldly humanitarian cause. Spirit is backing you now. You will have the energy to succeed. *I am an alive, energetic being of light. All paths before me are open.*

**208 - Reflective Image.** This number is about self-care, self-image, and love/lack of love, for self. Are you treating yourself with respect, or are you allowing yourself and others to degrade you? This is the number of being a doormat, or at the mercy of something, and feelings of inferiority. We all have these areas in our life, although some like to believe they don't have these insecurities. It is time to work on you...accepting your appearance and body image, forgiving yourself, and acknowledging that you are a Child of the One True Creator. All beings deserve respect and love. This number has to do with power plays, superiority and inferiority complexes, and the denial of truth. Always look in the mirror first, and begin there. *I love me. I am worthy and lovable.* Clary Sage Essential Oil.

**209 - See Saw.** This is a number of opposite energies, trying to unite. Willpower, and passive acquiescence are both are needed for you to succeed, and you must decide which to use when. Acting at appropriate times, in appropriate ways leads to accomplishment and victory. This is a lucky number of good energies. *I assess situations with ease, and act accordingly.*

**210 - Unlimited Being.** This is a powerful number. It means you have reached a certain level of advancement, and asks that you surrender in a specific situation, so that correct decisions will be made. This number has so much expansiveness and substance, that it requires the individual to let go, and let

Spirit lead. *I am gifted with abundance, and find joy in sharing this with others.*

**211 - Prepared To Succeed.** A situation that seems to have been stagnating, is going to change, seemingly overnight. You need to stay grounded, if you are to handle this energy. All systems need to be in place, and you need to be ready to proceed, as the change occurs...and whatever it brings. Whether this is a positive or unfortunate turn of events, is up to you, and how you handle yourself, prior and leading up to it. Prepare. 211 can be likened to an online business, that puts out major advertising efforts to sell a product, and hasn't even stocked the product yet, or hired employees to pack and ship the item. A positive change is coming, and it will be what is needed, no matter what the seeming outcome. *I am grounded, organized and ready for anything Spirit sends my way. All situations work out for the very best.*

**212 - Common Ground.** This number has to do with having common goals with others. There is harmony, especially if there is communication. All eyes are on the same prize, and all heads are thinking in the same direction. This number speaks of harmonious pairings, and magical outcomes that come from people working together. Everything is a "go". Two heads are better than one, meaning that input from all parties, is the most beneficial for success. Be willing to listen and communicate your needs or desires. *I value the opinions of others, as spokespersons, or mouthpieces for Spirit. All necessary information reaches me now.* Lemon Chrysoprase.

**213 - Redefining.** This number has to do with endings and new beginnings, in the areas of love and money. It says that you have learned, or been taught a lesson, so that you don't make the same mistake again. 213 has redefined your values, and you are starting anew, and reborn. What has been in the past, is no more. You learned what you didn't want, so that you can know what you truly want. 213 means positive changes for the future with finances or love life. *I welcome my abundant new life, filled with happiness, hope and changes for the better.*

**214 - Gifts Granted.** This is a very fortunate number, and

relates to people who are very reclusive, studious and serious-minded. 214 brings things to successful conclusions. Life goes in cycles, and you will receive the rewards from this number, either sooner or later...but you will get them. It may be asking you to take a situation more seriously, do some research or spend some time alone, receiving inspiration and answers on how to proceed. Go on what you know, through your own efforts, and do not rely on other people's advice. *I listen to my inner voice, trust what I know, and follow my instincts.*

**215 - Tainted Victory**. This number has to do with

interference, particularly in romantic partnerships, such as a third party or relative who causes problems for a couple. Is someone trying to throw a stone in your path, or make things more difficult? There are possible betrayals, and someone is not telling you the truth. It may be someone doing something behind your back, or even you, lying to yourself. Either way, not all is lost. You will still reach your goal in the situation, but with a little tarnish. Bless those that would seek to harm or undermine you, and you will be blessed, by the law of return. *Nothing can keep me from my good.* Petrified Wood...although this stone may be under conservation protection. Substitute with any fossilized stone.

**216 - As Within So Without.** The Universe is telling you, that you just need one small shift in yourself, to see massive change in your outer world. Remember that everything is created within, by your thoughts. This is the cause. Everything outside of yourself is the effect. If you are looking to make changes, or have an influence, working in the outside world (the effect), will have little effect! You must go to the cause, which is within yourself. What is at the root, or heart of your problem? Explore this. What thoughts are you thinking? Now, progress will be made. Your effects will simply appear in direct proportion to changes in the cause. *My life begins with me. I choose to think happy thoughts, my world changes to reflect this.*

**217 - Magnified Instinct.** My current word count in this book is 37, 737, as of the writing of "217". 3s and 7s have to do with Jupiter and Neptune, meaning, your dreams and visions are expanding and manifesting into reality. This is a number of good fortune. It says to follow your instincts, because they are correct. Now is the time to act. Go with whatever you feel in your gut to be true. 217 also represents a connection to all people, as they play an important role as helpers. Friends come to the forefront to assist. Do what you know to be right, and trust that knowing, even if it seems foreign or strange to you. Go with your gut! *I trust my self, and my instincts. I always choose wisely, and make decisions with ease.*

**218 - Solo Goal.** This is a number that comes with cautions, relating to hardship and defeat. 218 comes with great difficulties, caused by anger, acting rashly and speaking out, when some things are better left unsaid. But all is not lost with this number. It can have violent tendencies, if one doesn't rein in their negative feelings. Begin to actively think positive, and go on your own advice and counsel. Work alone, and keep a single-minded focus, as it is more likely that you will get a positive outcome, if you only expect it in one area. Other areas will suffer, so narrow down what you will accept, if you go forward with your goal, realizing that you will not get everything you want. *I am at peace with all of my life. I allow Spirit to take charge of my thoughts.* Brown Jasper.

**219 - Forthcoming.** Your goals and dreams are expanding.

What you are putting out into the Universe is building, and getting ready to manifest, or return benefits to you. Situations are lining up for your benefit. Your job now, is to wait patiently for the delivery, or the sign to take action. *I am divinely guided to my good. All is being readied for my success.*

**220 - First Rate.** New psychic centers are opening up.

Especially your 3rd eye. Light is flooding your cells, and your vibratory rate is increasing. You are accessing more parts of your brain. There are memories from other lifetimes, coming to the surface, as well as spiritual kinships forming. Emotional currents run high. Prepare to grow from a cellular level up. You are uniting with your true Source. Good fortune comes in an instant. *I celebrate my luck, as my energy aligns with Source.*

**221 - Precise Perceptions.** 221 is telling you that you are very

balanced. Your judgment, thoughts and intuition are in alignment, and correct. Your thinking is clear, and quick. It is a lucky time to act on impulse and decide quickly. Go with instantaneous responses, ideas, impressions and visions. Sometimes your answer comes in a quick flash. Pay attention, and you will know exactly what you are to do next. *My thoughts and emotions are clear. My intuition guides me in each moment, and my actions are precise.*

**222 - Moon Magic.** This is a magical number, that opens

portals to other dimensions, or allows other entities to come through. You may be noticing paranormal activity in your home, or somewhere you frequent. You may need a clearing. It is also a sign that you are wide open intuitively, as well. Energies are heightened, and vibratory levels are raised, making it easier to see the other side, or things we couldn't normally see. Its as if you have on x-ray glasses. 222 also signals that this is a time to take care of yourself, and make sure your needs are being met. Pay attention to the lunar cycles, as they may be affecting you, or others at this time. Hormones may be raging, or psychic abilities are on super alert. A lot of sensory input is coming, from this dimension and others, so hold on for the ride. *I find a centered space of calm, in every moment.*

**223 - Purpose To Prosper.** This is a number that represents

success, in a spiritual and worldly sense. It indicates new frontiers in your spiritual view points, and philosophies. You are gaining knowledge and understanding, and your spiritual purpose is in front of you, waiting for you to explore it. You have assistance on all levels, progress, success and good news. *I fulfill my purpose, and many rewards come with it.*

**224 - Lessons Learned.** This is a sign that you have recently,

or are currently in the middle of a major life lesson. This is usually karmic in nature, and one you have encountered before. Therefore, it may represent a pattern you have been continually repeating, and now finally understand. There may be payment for the lesson, but you are overcoming the hardship, and moving forward. 224 says there is a positive ending to the situation at hand, and eventual success in relationships. *I forgive the past, and welcome the future.* Yellow Jasper.

**225 - Flood of Good Fortune.** You have extreme abilities in reasoning and distinction. You can separate the thorns from the flowers. There is literally nothing standing in your way, as your ability to see to the heart of any situation is very developed. Success has found you, through your own previous trials and efforts. *I am in a Divine space of understanding and clarity.*

**226 - Comedy And Tragedy.** 226 is all about relationships, learning to have healthy ones, and letting go of addictive behaviors. 226 says it is possible that you are becoming engaged, or married. This number is also a signal that you have learned from previous marriages, relationships or friendships, and have decided that you will pick a better choice this time, or may prefer to be alone. The key is, that peace of mind is extremely valuable to you now. Drama is not welcome. If you are involved with someone, you are the determining factor on whether this relationship or marriage will last. In a more general sense, you must enter into any relationship with others, with the motive to love the other person. Selfish agendas will backfire on you. Being a martyr will also backfire, or any old relationship patterns and roles. *All of my relations with others are happy, holy and healthy. I am blessed.* Staurolite.

**227 - Faery Tales.** This is a powerful number of harmony and getting what you want. At times, you may have to speak up and ask for your needs to be met, but this number is a sign that the Universe is looking out for you, and has your back. So does everyone else. All are in your life for a purpose, and your wishes and dreams are coming true now. This number promises good luck, and strokes of good luck, lucky streaks and leprechauns leading you to the pot at the end of the rainbow. 227 is connected to 226. If you have been working on those issues, and carrying around your Staurolite stone, then the fairies and elementals can begin working with you, and leading you to your good. This number is one of general success. *Life is as I have made it, and my rewards are coming, now.*

**228 - Shared Burdens.** 228 is a warning that heavy payments are due. This may be in a literal sense, such as taxes, or a major bill, but it can also represent karmic payments. What you put out, has come around. This numbers says, if you have been doing things for the wrong reasons, there is a price to pay. If you are taking on another person's responsibilities, your own life will suffer. Meaning you have taken on their karma. The only thing you will get from doing this, is losing yourself. It is time for you to draw a line in the sand, either with yourself, or with someone else. *I release myself from guilt, and taking on the burdens of others. I take responsibility for my own life.* Water Buffalo Animal Totem.

**229 - Winner And Loser.** This number can represent arguments in the home, discord and in some cases, violent circumstances. This number says to be careful in situations in which you have found yourself. There may be betrayals, heartache and loss. On the positive side, anything that comes up with this number is the final crisis, or climax, and endings can happen, that need to happen. The negative side of this number, usually has to do with misuse or abuse of power. Either you are misusing or denying your own, or someone holds their power over your head. If this has to do with a situation, then how is it controlling you or your behavior? You are not a victim, and neither is anyone else, yours. *I respect myself, and others, and I extricate myself out of situations that don't reflect honor and love.* Pyrite.

**230 - All Possibilities.** This is a number of self-mastery,

where anything can happen. You are being asked to re-examine your life, and decide exactly what it is you want, and where you want to go. Take time to contemplate, and then put it out there to your Angels. Know that it will come true. 230 says anything is possible, including miracles. Perhaps your Angels and Guides want to work with you more, and teach you how to work with higher energies. Heaven and Earth moves to assist you. *I accept the miracles, coming to me now, as natural manifestations of Spirit energy. I am clear about what is right for me.*

**231 - Possibilities And Impossibilities.** Like 230, this

number has a lot of energy behind it. It is a number of power and manifestation. And this power of manifestation lies in you...whether you allow something, or block it. There is help from loved ones. If you operate out of a space of love, many things can happen for you. This is a number of miracles, teleportation, bi-location, spontaneous healing, and interdimensional soul travel. As with 230, all things are possible for you now. *I am capable of performing miracles. The impossible becomes possible.*

**232 - Good News.** This is high vibratory number, especially in a spiritual sense. There is some announcement coming, usually in a relationship, or good news reaching you. A lot of wisdom and awareness is yours now. You are grounded and clear, and many things can happen. Everything you need to know, should be coming to you loud and clear. This is a very lucky number. *I am in a Divine Space, to receive all I need. Everything is being taken care of, and I relax and trust Spirit.*

**233 - Keeping Quiet.** This number says that you must work alone, and act on what you know. Do not rely on other people's advice, or include them in your plans, or you will bring on difficulties and pain. Keep your plans to yourself. It is crucial not to share anything, at this time, so zip your lip. You can tell others, only after you have results, or have accomplished what you set out to do. If you are not careful, their thoughts will destroy your plan, while it is still in the beginning stages of creation. *I am silence. All things happen in this space.* Bobcat Animal Totem.

**234 - No Way Through.** This number carries a great deal of angst, and frustration. This is the epitome of 2 steps forward, 1 step back. Sometimes ten steps back. The problem is, if you are rushing, or trying to force something to happen, it gets shut down. Ideally, the key is to let Spirit lead the way. If you are being blocked in a certain direction, perhaps it is the wrong direction, the wrong timing, or there is some aspect you are not considering. Take some time for contemplation, before acting or deciding on anything. Then, things will flow in their natural way. *I relax, and let go of control. All things find me, in their Divine Timing.* Peppermint Leaves.

**235 - The Choice Is Yours.** 225 is a number full of choices.

There are usually only two choices, if you narrow them all down. This number represents good choices, and bad choices. If you are ignoring your logic, and your instincts, you may make the bad choice. If it is for someone else, and not necessarily the right choice for you, don't do it. If it is a choice that will harm others in some way, then say no. Choose the wise path, and your results can be wonderful. *I listen to my inner wisdom, and choose accordingly.* Lemon Essential Oil.

**236 - Divine Helpers.** This is a number of positive support.

Others will uplift you during this time. There is encouragement, and people have your back. It is important to be grateful, for what you do have, and to express this gratitude to others. They need to know that you appreciate them, and recognize what they give. You also have support from ancestors and Spirit Guides. There are many around you, lifting you up, whether seen or unseen. It is time, to also support yourself, with positive words, that acknowledge your true beauty as Spirit, and as a Sovereign Being. *I celebrate that I am part of a larger family of the Earth and Spirit. I am supported and loved.*

**237 - Snowball Effect.** Jupiter, the planet of luck, is bringing

your dreams into being. Spirit is aligning your personal goals, with the overall picture of what is best for all. When the timing is right for everyone, your dreams will manifest. They are not limited, so dream big, and wait for the delivery. *I want for nothing. My dreams manifest in their perfect way, at the perfect time.*

**238 - The Bigger Picture.** This number speaks of old habits, and of taking things for granted. If things have come easily, 238 says the situation may not be so malleable, this time around. There is a lesson you did not learn, and it is coming up now, for you to be aware. How do you sabotage yourself, or others? Do you take others, or yourself for granted? 238 says that it is time to get realistic, and examine your motives. Examine yourself, and be prepared that not everything may work out...but remember that what happens in this world, is tied into the overall Universal, or even Cosmological purpose. Release yourself of personal agendas, as higher purposes are at work. Efforts now, are rewarded later. *I accept that I am a Universal Being, with a responsibility to the whole. I accept what happens, as a part of a larger plan.* Pink Kunzite.

**239 - Undoing The Illusory Self.** With 239, the message is clear. You are being given an opportunity to master a situation that you are currently in. This is mastery over the control this situation has on you, as well as overcoming psychological patterns and energetic aspects of your personality, or imprinted self. This relates to the persona you have become, through outside influence, experience and the like. Releasing these masks, is the first step toward uncovering and acknowledging who you really are. Your mind is very powerful, so use its ability to create your world, and see the results. The phrase, "You can do anything you set your mind to", is the key to unlocking this mastery. *I am a Divine being, and so much more than I have been taught to be. I am limitless.*

**240 - Solitary Refinement.** In general, this number promises success and fulfillment. Loneliness or the feelings of being alone in the world can be alleviated. A partnership, pet or a good friend forms a connection with you now. *I am fulfilled. I find comfort and safety, despite what is going on in the world.*

Marjoram Essential Oil.

**241 - Move With The Groove.** This is a number of high creativity. Inspirations can come to you, and creative dances, or pastime entertainments can liven, or stir your soul. It is time to let the waves of creativity move through you. What new ideas or joys are coming to you, by opening to this energy? It is a time for dreaming, believing and celebrating, for no other reason than your own enjoyment. You need this. *I allow creative energies to flow through me, bringing me back in balance. I allow joy to move in me, regardless of whatever else is happening in my life.*

**242 - Stop The Madness.** This number is talking about blocks that are keeping you separated, or apart from something. A lot of times, this signals a relationship, where two people cannot come together, because of a third party, money issues or something in the way. If so, this relationship has past life ties, and is repeating a pattern. 242 can also signify legal issues, or something in the fine print that prevents a situation from moving forward as planned. It can also represent the desires of your ego-self, at war with your Spiritual Self. Whatever area this number is symbolizing for you, know that you are in this, in order to address a fear, and break a cycle. Not to accomplish anything in the situation itself, but rather to look closer at what is karmically going on. This situation may be causing a lot of pain and anguish, but try to remember that you, and the others involved, have done this before in many lifetimes. The time to break this cycle is now. For advice, pick another number and read its meaning. *I am limitless. Karma cannot hold me, if I am willing to understand and release, that which seemingly holds me back.* Rose.

**243 - Middle Ground.** This is a number of taking sides.

Someone is siding with you, while others are siding against you. Or you and a partner, colleague, friend etc., do not see eye-to-eye. 243 comes with a warning, regarding animosity and disagreements, that lead to destructive ends. Because this world is a duality, whenever you take a side on an issue, you automatically create, or give power to an opposite viewpoint. Just like creating a vacuum, requires that it has to be filled. Instead, choose to take the middle stance of seeing both sides (even if you don't agree), or at the very least, listening to and respecting the other side. Peace can be found. If this is something minor, then there are no worries. If this represents a situation of major importance to your life, then definitely take the middle ground for peace. It is the only way to "win", and avoid the destructive possibilities with this number. *I strive for peace, and respect all viewpoints.* Apple or Hyacinth blossom, fresh. Or Cumin, dried seeds.

**244 - Factual Evidence.** This number is about clear

intentions. It is a warning that situations can "go south", if you are not following your own knowing, or wisdom. Look carefully at what others are doing, and listen to what they are saying. Do the actions match the words? Are they telling the truth? What is their agenda? Go deep. Examine everything, before saying yes, and make sure it is a "sure thing". Success can be had, by acting on your own advice, or on what is known...facts. Have physical proof in front of you, of motives and agendas, before joining forces with anyone. Acting alone is in your best interest. *I am in touch with my inner truth. I pay attention to subtle cues, and act with confidence.* Weasel Animal Totem.

**245 - The Classroom.** 945 has to do with travel and public speaking. Either you are being called to speak or teach publicly, or maybe you are traveling to hear or learn from someone else. This number represents students, teachers and in particular communication. Spiritually, 245 asks, "What are you here to learn?" Teachers learn from their students, and learn the material, by teaching it. Are you a role model or teacher for children? Teaching with love, is the main goal of this number. 245 also represents traveling with the mind, which again is related to learning, and opening to new information. Keep your mind stimulated. *I am love, and impart this love to others.*

**246 - Leap Frog.** This is a succession of even numbers, which means a natural progression toward success. There is a slight pause, as you re-evaluate how far you have come, and where you are going. The next even number in this series is "8", which can be karmic in nature. The idea of this break in time, is for you to forgive and release the past, so that the next step is a positive direction for you. Much will be determined by your own intentions, but in general, 246 is a leap forward, toward success. *I create a life filled with love. Everything else follows from this.*

**247 - Metamorphosis.** Major changes are coming, for the better. Your life is getting ready to drastically shift, and new experiences are replacing the old. Good luck and good fortune come with 247. *I am ready for my good.*

**248 - Burning Away The Old.** This number is calling for you to cleanse your space, so you can focus your thoughts, and do what needs to be done. Burn sage, white copal or frankincense resin, and clear your aura, and your home. Open a window to let the negative out. Let the fresh air in. Call in the nature spirits, to bless your space with love and protection. Realize that what you desire, will come, but there will be difficulties to contend with, as well. There are changes that you cannot predict. On the positive side, this number brings material wealth and accomplishment. Keep your energies clear, and yourself in a balanced space, so that you can handle any losses or suffering that may accompany the rewards. Realize these are karmic in nature. *I make progress toward my dreams, and forgive the rest.* Chrysocolla.

**249 - Undesirable Energies.** Follow the advice for the

previous number, as there may be dark energies in your space, or around you. Are you in company with someone negative, and picking up, either their negativity, or an actual entity attachment? Clear your space and yourself. Are you being led into a tempting situation, or distracting yourself with temptations? Sometimes we may feel like running or escaping from life, but this number is saying this is not a good idea. 249 also advises you to protect yourself from unwanted energies; some suggestions would be to wear frankincense oil, carry sugilite or black tourmaline, or use visualizations. Break free from your self-imposed prison, and step into the light. I *am a light being. Nothing, and no one can convince me otherwise. I choose the light.* Chiastolite.

**250 - Measuring Worth.** 250, is a very positive sign. It

signals success, from careful observation, and from the use of your psychic senses. It means you have been paying attention, have gathered and learned what you need to know, and now have everything you need to succeed. This number is also saying that your ability to assess a situation, or pare it down to the truth underneath, is strong. Trust your instincts and what you know. *I have everything I need to succeed.*

**251 - Price Tags.** This number carries a lot of promise for success, but it comes with a fee. Other people can benefit you, at this time. Perhaps an inheritance, or money is coming in from someone else. Legal issues reach a positive conclusion...you will be satisfied, but you will not win everything. This number also signals strong psychic ability that was developed in past lives. A job in a related field, or as a medium is a possibility. 251 can also point to soulmates who have a lesson to teach you. If you can both learn the lesson, than this could move on to be a beneficial relationship. *I am success.* Tanzanite.

**252 - Opposites Attract.** This is a blending of opposites. This number is telling you that two people or things could come together, to create magic, and a more balanced whole. Two people could work together, and bring complementary abilities, or skills that the other does not have. This number also says that you could be meeting someone who is your opposite, and fireworks are about to start. *I welcome in whatever is needed.*

**253 - What About Love?** 253 is a number about love, and being loved. It calls for you to examine what you love, and why. Who you love, and how you can love better. Are you calling something love, that is really just perceived need, or dysfunction? This number asks you to explore unconditional love. Divine Love. This means no conditions, which would require you to include everything. It does not ask you to be a victim to someone, who is abusing you, while you give unconditional love in return. You are to love yourself, as well. Some people you may have to love from a distance, or in a Universal sense. This is your challenge, and your blessing, for as you love, so is it returned to you. *I am Divine Love. I can be nothing else.* Archangel Chamuel.

**254 - Divine Child.** This number talks about children who

are fighting, or misbehaving. Are these your own children, or does it symbolize adults in your life, who are still small children inside? This number asks you to examine your connection to your inner child. How are you still acting as a child in your adult life? Do you feel out of control, or imprisoned in your life, or current situation? When you think back on them, are your past childhood scenarios, still upsetting to you as an adult? Ultimately, we are children of Source. Therefore, we are unlimited, but have been placed in a world, where dark forces have sought to trap us, and keep us down. Deny this now. Reclaim your sovereignty as a Child of the One True Creator, whose will is at one with Source. You are Spirit. Nothing can trap, or limit you, except your willingness to take on, and believe that it can. *I free my mind of the past, and all mind programming. I am, in Truth, free.* Archangel Zaphiel.

**255 - Vision For The Future.** This is a number of prophecies

and visions. Many things are coming to pass. Much information is coming your way. This is the time to tune in, listen to your Guides, and observe what is going on. What did you sense would happen? What is going on in the world at large, that others may have predicted? What can you do to make changes for the better, for yourself, the Earth, and everything on it? This is the time to gather that information, and contemplate what exactly is happening around you. Perhaps its time for you to contribute, by sending some positive energy into the world. Realize that you can influence your situation, by surrendering to the Divine, and allowing that energy to flow through you. *I am divinely guided. My healing intentions are felt by all.*

**256 - Supreme Balance.** This is a powerful number of

harmony and magnificence. All things are balanced with 256. One must be careful not to let one side of the nature take precedence, or you will lose this harmony. It is a number of windfalls, good fortune and overcoming difficulties. 256 will overcome all hindrances, or blocks. *The Divine Creator is my supply, and my strength.*

**257 - Prepare Ye The Way.** This number says it is not a time

for action, yet, but rather a time to make preparations. Get ready for your good. Prepare the road ahead. 257 is a beneficent number of many blessings. *I await my good, and prepare the way.*

**258 - Secret Deceptions**. This number can be a difficult one,

as it may speak of infidelities, or partners who are not acting in trustworthy ways. This could be business, personal or any type of partnership. Another interpretation of this number, is you not being faithful to yourself. You could be lying to yourself, or not admitting or wanting to face the truth. Or you could be doing things that are against your best interests. Examine closely what is going on with those close to you, as well as your own motives and self-treatment. *I face myself and others, with honesty and truth.* Emu Animal Totem.

**259 - Through New Eyes.** This is not an unfortunate number, however anger or rash decisions can meet with undesirable ends. Overall, this number is connected to spiritual vision, beliefs and perception. Your understanding of life, the afterlife, and other mysteries is changing. Your spiritual foundation is being strengthened. *I understand the way, and what I am here to do.*

**260 - Compassionate Burnout.** You are an attractive magnet, to everyone you meet. People of any age want to be around your energy. This can be a good thing, but if you are empathic, this can be a nightmare for you. People could suck you dry. Also, 260 warns of being aware of other people's influence on, or over you. Don't give up yourself to others...even loved ones. If you are making choices, or following the desires of anyone other than yourself, you will be led off your path. Put up some boundaries, so that people know their place with you. If you are becoming depleted, or buried by other people's dramas, and energies, don't be afraid to say "no". *I am entitled to my own space.* Charoite.

**261 - Charmed.** This is a number of fulfillment and good times, good friends and positive relationships. You may be feeling motivated to have fun, take a vacation or start something new. *I am blessed with a happy life.*

**262 -Spin The Wheel.** This can be a number of good fortune, and possibly winning in small games of chance, such as door prizes, small lotteries, slot machines, scratch offs or raffles. Usually this number is related to relationships, and "winning" a person. This relationship may have felt out of reach for you, or there were difficulties. The lesson, here, is you do not need anyone outside of yourself, and the "winning over" of another, simply means that you had to convince, or earn this person's respect, attention or approval. In some situations, the relationship may not turn out as you thought. Pulling back, and standing in your own power, will garner you the respect you may be seeking. This number does, however, favor balanced relationships, that can be loving, harmonious and beneficial. *I am naturally lucky. All things that are necessary for my path will find me.* Rainbow Quartz.

**263 - Mighty Words.** Your words carry weight. It is a time to speak, but with care. Others are drawn to you, and swayed by what you have to say. 260 is connected to this number, as people are attracted to you, but this energy is amplified. Therefore, 263 carries a lot of responsibility. What you say, does one of two things: Makes other people follow your advice to the letter, or gets you into trouble if you are too outspoken. So, be careful what you express, as you are in a sense, responsible for your message. It is always wise to let Spirit speak through you, with love. At times, it may be necessary to keep quiet, and communicate in unspoken ways...through action or thoughts. *I am an open voice for Spirit.*

**264 - Soul Group.** 264 has to do with relationships with family members, and loved ones, or those you live with...these are connected to deep past life connections, where you lived many lives together. Some of these are part of your soul group, and are joined in purpose, to work through issues, in order to go home together. 264 has to do with understanding the unity and harmony in all things, and how we are connected. *I am part of the greater whole. All is happening as it should be.*

**265 - Killing It.** Powerful energies are available to you now.

You can overcome just about anything, that seems to be holding you back. Luck and good fortune come with 265. *I use my power wisely, for the good of all.*

**266 - News Flash.** 266 is extremely magnetic, and you have an

attunement to, and an attraction with others. If you are a writer or speaker, your words say volumes. What you communicate carries emotion and caring. Others want to be around you, or know what you know. You can make anything happen with this number. Get out and deliver your message, no matter how large or small, someone needs to hear it, and you need to say it. *I speak my truth with Love.*

**267 - Serendipity.** This is an amazing number of successful

relationships, enjoyment of life, and assistance from others. Everything seems to be going your way. Fortuitous circumstances find their way to you. *I am in the right place, at the right time.*

**268 - Let It Go.** This number speaks of drastic changes that

can happen overnight. It is a sign of difficulties, loneliness and isolating oneself. It is similar to the boss, who has little contact with his/her employees. Maybe you push others away. 268 forces you to address who you are, and what you are doing. The ego has taken over. Change is imminent. *I loose and let go of everything, trusting that I will have what I need.* Tangerine Quartz.

**269 - Anyone Listening?** This is a number of disruptions, that lead to abandonment. You have many goals and dreams, but also much interference. You may feel that nothing is working, and obstacles are thrown in your path. It can be a time where you feel you are left alone, to fend for yourself. It may even be that your Spirit Guides and Angels have gone silent, and don't seem to be listening, or helping. This is a major transition time for you. The feelings of abandonment can lead to anger and despair. You are being taught about the darker side of life, during this time. You are being strengthened, so that you learn to recognize and rely on your own power, thereby, overcoming layers of your fear. You are not truly abandoned, and there will be gifts that come from this period of trials. *I trust in myself. This is a time for me to step into my own power, and in turn, be strengthened.* Copper.

**270 - Heaven's Blessings.** This number comes in as a blast of energy! Good news. There is an abundant life waiting for you. You are in alignment with Spirit, and can channel in whatever you need. Know that doors are opening, and whatever you are involved in, can succeed. Abundance applies to a loving partnership, money, spiritual wisdom, having what you need, a fulfilling career, supportive family and friends, etc. 270 says this is a sign from the heavens to free yourself, and open to your good. *I am a Divine Child of the Universe. All things are available to me, now.*

**271 - Hand Slap.** There are delays to plans, and may be disruptions or endings, if you are holding on too tightly to desired outcomes. Releasing control, can help avoid these pitfalls, and get the ball rolling a little faster. Whatever the situation, on a higher spiritual level, you are being tested, and cleansed of fear, in order to move beyond the blocks. Success is certain, but delayed, if one focuses on fear. *I release fear and the need for illusory control. All is working out in my favor.* Atacamite.

**272 - The Way Home.** You are a leader in the spiritual and

psychic realms, and could lead the way for others. You are master of psychic clarity, and the abilities of harmonious communion with Spirit and your Guides. 272 is a sign, that you have the wisdom, guidance and ability to solve or resolve any situation. You are in a leadership position here, for helping to keep others on their path. This number also means the joining of spiritual partners or friendships, with common viewpoints, and origins. This is a lucky number. *I light the way for others, so that we may all return home.*

**273 - Captivated.** There is something holding your attention.

You are divinely focused and clear. Spiritual truth and guidance is open to you now. Take time to tune in, and tune out the outside world. Whatever you are focused on, will be revealed and given. *Spirit holds my attention, and reveals all to me, at the perfect time.*

**274 - Immense Transformation.** Another powerhouse

number, related to 265 and 256, 274 says, there is nothing you cannot do. If you are coming from a truly centered and spiritual place, you are a powerhouse of energy and creation. You can make things, as they need to be. Keep in mind, that as you create, so do you let go of that which no longer serves, or is no longer in alignment with who you currently are, or where you are going. This is a number of radical transformation, so be prepared, that these changes are going to be massive, or all encompassing. Whatever is in the way of where you need to go, will be removed. This includes dark side energies. *I align with my power to move forward on my path.*

**275 - Ascended Mastery.** This number is of a higher order,

and has seeming magical properties associated with it. The gifts of foresight, prediction and enhanced psychic abilities is highlighted here, as well as higher abilities of teleportation, telepathy, accessing the Soul Star Chakra and spontaneous healing. You can access these abilities, or experience their benefits. The higher elects are working with you and your issue, at this time. Jeshua and other ascended masters have achieved these levels. The answers could be coming, in writings or books. My advice, is to be your own Master, and not worship these false "gods". *I open to the solutions, as I acknowledge that I am much more, than I appear to be.*

**276 - The Call of the Dark.** This is a warning of misuse of

power, and its consequences. The ego wants control. Therefore, the wrong choices are being made, and whomever is involved, is letting ego desires, fear and temptation rule. The draw to darkness is strong, and hides itself in many forms, masked as insecurity that seeks power, however meaningless and empty this worldly power may be. Giving oneself over to the Creator and His Will, is the only way to avoid the coming destruction of this number. 276 could also be relating to a time, when others make their passage home. Either way, this is a very disruptive number. *I choose the light. I recognize my true being, as part of the Divine Spirit, and therefore, release and dissolve fear, as it is not who I am.* Tibetan Black Quartz.

277 - **Eventual Triumph.** This number says you are heading toward success. Some endings may need to occur, in order for the new energies to come in. *I accept my good fortune, now.*

278 - **Identify with Spirit.** This number is a warning sign that there is conflict between your spiritual nature, and your ego-self. It could also be a warning of others, who pretend to be spiritual gurus or teachers, when in fact they are just after your money, or their own notoriety. 278 if reminding you, that you have the spiritual answers and truth within you, and any outside solutions, suggestion, temptations or teachings will be misleading. Remember your higher truth, and why your soul came here. Get in touch with your origins, pre-dating Earth incarnations. You have a higher purpose, and your inner self remembers. *I am love, peace and joy. I am the higher qualities of my true nature, and I share these with others. We are all blessed, in turn.* Azeztulite with a vein of amethyst in it, or Azeztulite used with a deep violet Amethyst stone.

279 - **Alignment with the Light.** This is a high number of accomplishment. You are aware of your spiritual purpose, or about to be, as was spoken of with number 278. Your spiritual purpose (Spirit's purpose) is the answer. Avoiding rushing, as well as practicing a higher form of forgiveness, is beneficial. You are being given what you need, and have asked for, so stay centered on your higher purpose. If someone is asking for love, give it. *I am a Diving Being of Christ energy. I fulfill my purpose gladly, and with an open heart.*

280 - **Build Your Foundation.** This is a message to store up your resources, and build up foundations. 280 speaks of reversals of fortune or circumstances, and a mix of heartache

and hardship, with reward. You don't know what you are getting with this number, so be prepared. And be prepared to revisit former issues, efforts, projects or relationships, because Spirit is saying you are missing the meanings, patterns and lessons. 280 is success and failure in one, meaning payment for what succeeds. Learn the repeating lesson here, so this number can fade out of your energy field. *I am aware of all aspects of________ situation, and release the soul template that is holding me back.* Rhodizite.

**281 - My Way.** This is a number of conflicting energies. The

key to overcoming the clash, competition, chaos and tug-of-war with this number, is to amplify its strengths, which are moving to the beat of your own drummer, choosing what is right and correct for you only, and wearing the color yellow, especially yellows with a hint of green. Stick to your own inner knowing, and move on, silently and unaccompanied. Do not speak of your plans to others. *I follow my inner path, and move forward, knowing that I know.* Yellow-Green Apatite.

**282 - The Hand that Feeds.** This number shows a lot of

difficulties. It deals with relationships that have heavy karma, and possibly two relationships in particular. This number must be taken from a spiritual perspective, because that is the only way to overcome the problems and issues, that 282 is speaking about. In this relationship scenario, there is one dominant party, and one passive party. In other words, one person is the ruler or makes the rules, and the other has to abide by the first person's wishes. This number shows an unhealthy balance in a relationship, and if you are the victim in this scenario, it is for you to understand that you need to detach, and observe what is happening carefully, from a removed viewpoint. It is in this space, that you are then able to receive guidance from Spirit, and know the correct action to take. Realize that these games we play with each other, are merely repeats of cycles from the past, and from past lives. They in no way, reflect one person's superiority over the other. We are all equal beings in Spirit. It is for you to take the perspective suggested, so that you may choose to end this cycle, and release the other person from this pattern, as well. *I honor the divinity that is present in all, including myself.* Black Alabaster.

**283 - Earth.** 283 is a number that correlates with Mother

Earth. It is a number that requires grounding and stability. It is time for you to prepare yourself for many changes. This means creating stability, in order to handle these changes. A strong foundation, will enable you to weather any storm. Be informed, that these changes are not necessarily unfortunate in nature, but can *feel* devastating. Therefore, this number is saying prepare yourself, and keep in tune with the Earth. This may require you to go put your hands in the dirt, sit on the ground outside, or simply meditate, and join your heart with the Earth's heart. This affinity with the Earth, will help you move through the changes quickly and easily. In a grounded space, you will understand much better, what is occurring. Know that the riches of the Earth, await you, when this period is over. *I am a child of the Earth, and a child of Spirit. I am safe.* Moss Agate.

**284 - Blinders On.** 284 is a message about communication

difficulties. There can be misunderstandings, with this number, and warnings of unfortunate associations with others, who are not beneficial for you. This number can speak of many types of catastrophes, and says that these difficulties occur, when you are not listening to your inner self. When you are ignoring the warnings you were getting about a particular situation, a particular person or anything that does not feel right, or play out with ease…meaning there have been many obstacles or blocks on this particular path...it is up to you to recognize these warnings, and eliminate these destructive situations from your life. Your feelings and emotions will be your guide. Pursue anything that gives you a calm and centered peace. In being willing to detach, from those things that are harmful for your highest good, you will find that this number brings in much success. Especially with life-purpose and finances. *I am a divine being of Christ. I choose only that, which is in alignment with my true self.* White Shell.

**285 - Hanging On.** This is a high warning number. Like the

number before it, 285 involves many difficulties. If you have not solved, or removed the situations from 284, then 285 can possibly be the result. It is advised to read 284 first, as 285 is a suffering of the influences from 284. Understand that any difficult consequences at this time, represent things that need to leave your life anyway. In some cases, 285 can relate to individuals passing on from this existence, or possibly you passing on through and out of a difficult situation. *I call in my Angels for support. I am lifted up in love, and my good is revealed to me. I am at peace.* Astrophyllite.

**286 -Inside The Mirror.** 286 can be very difficult indeed. It

can be related to dealing with a major loss, or reflect losing your childlike nature. It is a time when spiritual values and beliefs are challenged. Your viewpoint or perception of life seems skewed. Note that this is passing, and that the lessons inherent in this number, are karmic in nature. If you're going through a difficult time, call on your Angels for help. In other cases, this number indicates, viewing oneself from an outside perspective. It is as if you are inside a mirror looking back at yourself. In this way, you can evaluate, how you affect others, and why. This self-analysis, will enable you to make the necessary changes to enrich your future life. *My Soul is supporting, guiding and comforting me, with a loving embrace.* Tektite.

**287 - Put Through The Paces.** This number is saying that everything is ultimately happening for a reason. There is a purpose for the pain. It is for you to overcome the seeming pain, by seeing the spiritual truth behind it. Heal the wounds of the past, and move forward into the future. You cannot do this, if darkness remains around you. Therefore, it is advised that you release all things that would lead you astray, or cause harm. 287 is a reward for a job well done. There is peace at the end of this. There is enlightenment and understanding, when this number is mastered. *I choose the higher path at all times. I walk in the light, and the darkness dissolves.* Celestite.

**288 - Double Trouble.** 288 is message to you, that karma is being doubled at this time. This means, either, that you have two past lives simultaneously bleeding through this one, or you are dealing with a double dose of difficulty in a particular situation. Either way, it is advised that you stay centered, and tune into guidance for what is your next move. Act only on the advice given from Spirit. The message is to forgive all parties involved, any situations that seem difficult or painful, and above all stay removed, detached and centered. *I am Divine power. My will is at one with the Divine will. I act from a place of* *power.* Golden Obsidian (Gold Sheen Obsidian).

**289 - A+.** This number has many messages for you. It means that you have overcome or mastered a situation, and are about to receive a final test. This test is not to torture you, but to test your will and your commitment to the growth which has taken place. 289 also suggests, that success is yours. That you will pass this test, because you have been through many difficulties in your life. You have overcome much karma, and have continually striven to evolve. You have stuck to your path, and will now see the results of your tenacity. 289 says that many new spiritual understandings and truths will be revealed to you now. Many of your former questions to Spirit will be answered. And you have succeeded in moving on to a new level of self mastery. Know that success will be yours. *I am the light. I have no other identity, then that which is aligned with Source.* Seraphinite.

**290 - Only One Real Choice.** You're being given a choice to make: Choose wisely with your heart, or continue with a situation that is detrimental to your future. You are choosing between a loving situation, and unloving situation. Sometimes the decision means loving yourself, as opposed to being in a circumstance that would represent guilt, suffering and coercion. Meditation, and getting yourself into a space that is in alignment with higher energy, can help you see clearly in this situation. *I am love. All of my actions and decisions, reflect this.* Mookaite Jasper.

**291 - Drive To Succeed.** You have the initiative and know-how, to make what you want, happen. Your vision and approach is unique. What you have to offer, is very individualized and memorable. An auspicious number. *I know my value. I have much to offer.*

**292 - Ready, Set, Stop.** This is a number of stops and starts. It suggests delays, interruptions and pauses. Eventually you will get where you are going, but there are some things that need to be let go. These delays are possibly coming up, because you are resisting releasing what has already served its purpose. There is dead weight, or issues that are bogging you down, and keeping you from reaching a resolution. What you are aiming for, is in sight. Let the past go. *I shed what I no longer need, so that I can move forward again.* Blue Opal.

**293 - Dream Weaver.** This number has to do with groups and communities of people. 293 means that whatever you are working on, is going to require a group effort. This means accepting help from others. If this is career or job related, you will need the assistance of others to complete the work project, but you should remain the creator of the original vision. If you are in a personal relationship, this means you will need the effort of the other person, for things to work, but you must take the lead. Good luck and blessings follow. *I move forward toward my dreams, and allow others to assist me in their realization.*

**294 - Chaotic Cloudbursts.** 294 indicates many starts and stops, and changes in direction. Some of these are due to interference from other people, a clashing of interests, anger or emotional outbursts, and betrayals of trust. If you are involved in the chaotic energy of this number, you are asked to sit peacefully, and quietly meditate. Notice if you have negative thoughts while you sit. Negative thoughts signify negative energy attached to you, and you may need a cleansing. Meditating with your guides, will help you to see clearly. *I am peace. I maintain calm, as Spirit guides me through the storm.* Novaculite.

**295 - Magic Formula.** This is an auspicious number, in the areas of creative projects, love affairs, writing and teaching. What you have begun, will succeed. *I manifest that which I need, now.*

**296 - Imprisoned.** This number is a signal that you are being sacrificed for the plans of others. You may be a pawn in their scheme to get what they want. If this is relating to a situation, instead of a person, then the circumstances do not work in your favor. The odds are not against you, but have been *set* against you. 366 is saying to choose yourself first. Don't give yourself over to another person's plans, or give up your dignity, ethics or conscience to satisfy the whims of anything, or anyone else. *I am all I need. I respect and value myself.* Eagle Animal totem.

**297 - Over the Moon.** 297 is saying that the cycles of the moon, are affecting you at this time. You are extra sensitive to the moon phases. If you are a Cancer Sun sign, this influence will be even more amplified. 297 is telling you to pay attention to what phase the moon is in, and act accordingly. If it is a new moon, it is a time for you to put out a new idea, send out a prayer, or start a new project or relationship. If the moon is waxing, and in an opposite astrology sign to your Sun Sign, it means to halt all forward movement. If it is in the same sign as your Sun, it is a green light for you to move forward. If it is a full moon, you should continue forward. A waning moon is a time to let go of, clear out and end things that have served their purpose. 297 says your psychic senses are heightened. You may be extra sensitive, extra emotional and should pay attention to all subtle and finely tuned vibrations or psychic impressions. Trust your gut. *I am in harmony with the universe. I flow with the seasons, changes and shifts.* Green Moonstone.

**298 - The Final Push.** This is a sign that you are very close to

achieving, that which you wanted to accomplish. You are in that "last-push" phase. It's like climbing up a cliff. You're almost to the top, and you just have to get around a couple slippery areas, find a grip and pull yourself up. This number suggests success. It says that you will get where you are going. Stay focused on the goal, and know that Spirit is with you. You are surrounded at this time, by Angels of higher levels, and enlightened beings, who are there to assist you with these final steps. Therefore, whatever you are trying to achieve, don't give up. *I reach my goals with ease.* Citrine. (Real citrine, not the heated amethyst variety.) Firefly Animal Totem.

**299 - A Higher Awareness.** 299 is a number of

enlightenment, connected to Buddha. If you are on a spiritual journey, you're getting very near to reaching enlightenment, if not actually reaching it, in this lifetime. In relation to a more mundane earthly experience, this number is saying that you will be enlightened with the details needed, so that you may continue forward, with what you're trying to accomplish. 299 is a very high-energy number. It is like the dark, just before the dawn. Many blessings are on their way to you, spiritually, emotionally and materially. *My spirit is open, and I clearly receive all guidance necessary, for me to complete my mission here.*

Nirvana Quartz.

**300 - The Trinity.** 300 is a merging together, of all the selves into the one self. It is a number of divine mastery, of this plane, and of spiritual growth. It is the attaining of what was sought, from the number 298, and 299. These manifest in 300, a new level of enlightenment and growth. You are poised to succeed, whether that be in the material world, or on your spiritual path. Many things are possible now. All is increased, and gets bigger. *I welcome my good. All possibilities lie before me.*

**301 - Lightning Strikes.** This is a number of good fortune. It signals things that come from out of the blue, that are for your benefit. This number states that what you are wanting, can be manifested quite swiftly. The waiting period is over. What you are looking to accomplish, in any particular circumstance, will be resolved in a very sudden manner. In some cases, this may seem detrimental, but will be beneficial in the long run. Overall this number is a sign of happy events. *My good is before me. All that I need, has been delivered.*

**302 - Abundantly Speaking.** This number is a grand slam of success. You cannot fail. The answer is yes. The Angels of Abundance are working with you. They are willing and ready, to bring that which you require, and that which you request. All things are possible here, so it would be wise for you to think clearly, calmly and deeply about exactly what it is that you want for your life. This clarity is necessary, because you will get exactly what you're asking for. *I am abundance. I have all that I need.*

**303 - All Is Good.** This is a near-perfect number. Know that you are spiritually mentally, emotionally, and physically in alignment with your guidance, your spiritual path and your purpose. Nothing can stand in your way, with this number. 303 is a magic doorway for you, to enter into a completely new way of being. In essence, a new life. 303 says to call it forth. It is already yours. *Only good lies before me.*

**304 - Buddha's Delight.** This is a number of high spiritual energy, growth and reaching the heights of an ecstatic experience. If you are meditating, or trying to reach enlightenment, 304 is a message that you are going to break through many barriers, and have an experience of true bliss. This number also refers to breakthroughs in everyday life, especially in areas where we have felt blocked in the past. Barriers are crossed, and we are no longer held back. It is a time to celebrate your good fortune. What you have been trying to move past, is now leaving. 304 also relates to the sale of houses or property, especially if it has been up for sale for quite some time. *I experience many breakthroughs, and my life is filled with miracles.*

**305 - Moolah.** 305 is a high energy money number. It says that games of chance, or high-risk speculations will pay off. This says to go with your gut feeling, even if the situation seems illogical. If you feel a strong push in any direction, then that is the direction to go. Regardless of circumstances, 305 says to move toward your goal, and take the risk. This relates in particular with stocks and investments, or anything relating to finance. *I'm abundantly wealthy.*

**306 - Better Than This?** This is yet another extremely powerful number in the 300 series. The message here is ultimate success. This is a high spiritual powerhouse number, that can accomplish and deliver in the extreme. Go ahead and make a wish upon a star, dream a dream, and pursue a goal. You have a lucky clover in your back pocket. *I am in an endless flow of divine abundance.*

**307 - Epiphany.** This is a number of divine wisdom. All that

you have been seeking, is coming to a cohesive whole. All previous studies have not been wasted, and are merging together into truths. Any situation you are currently in, will be revealing Divine Truth to you. You will know that which was previously hidden, that which was previously misunderstood, and that which was misrepresented. All will be out in the open. You will feel relief with this number, and a sense of joining with the all that is. *I am at one with the Divine. All is one.*

**308 - Elect To Correct.** This is a number of halts,

impediments and issues that stop the flow. What should be easy, has become difficult. A mistake has been made, and must be rectified. Are you the one that made the error? Or was it someone else? This needs to be resolved, in order for harmony to be regained. This situation calls for corrections in perception and viewpoint, and for words spoken, that should not have been spoken. Rectify these errors, and success is yours. *I return to love, as my true nature.* Alligator Totem.

**309 - Charioteer.** This is a number of great success, but only

if you stand by your beliefs. If you get drawn into the dramas, opinions or demands of others, your vision is lost. The end is no longer in sight. You remain stuck, in a limbo -like state, unable to move forward. It is simply, for you to realize, that you have created this situation, by allowing another to lead. Take back the reins, and direct your life toward what is right for you, alone. *I surrender guilt, and my need to be needed. I am my own master, and the only master of my fate.* Lapis Lazuli.

**310 - Name Of The Game.** 310 says it's time to purify your intent. Analyze your intentions, and understand what your true motivations are. Stabilize your life, by clarifying your reasons "why". Why do you want a certain thing, or a certain person? Why are you doing, what you are doing? Knowing what you are about, will help you solidify and create a positive foundation, that brings you rewards. Just as we purify our environment and our bodies, so must you cleanse your intentions. With 310 you will get exactly what you put out. What you are building, creating, or desiring will reflect this. If your intentions are pure, you will have a strong foundation, strong reputation, and a lot of support. *My intentions and desires are pure. I act for the highest good of all.* Juniper Berry Essential Oil.

**311 - Stargate.** This number is connected to all those who came to Earth, with a higher mission. This includes Star Seeds, Indigos, Crystals, Rainbows, etc. Do you resonate with one of these spiritual identities? A higher counsel is overseeing the activities and progress here, of these beings from other places. 311 is about higher purpose, and raising the vibration of self, to a 5th dimensional level. In turn, what you perceive outside of yourself, will change to a fifth dimensional level. Many changes can happen, and miracles can become the norm. 311 relates to your life purpose, and soul mission here. It asks you to get in touch with yourself, know what is important to you on a deep level, and ask yourself why you think you are here. Know that you are already on your path, if you're asking these questions. If you feel you are not on your life path, simply ask your Guides to redirect you. *I accept and honor my true mission and purpose.*

**312 - Divine Creation.** Many beautiful things can flow with this number, and many expressions of Spirit can come forth. These can be artistic or creative works, channeling, healing energies, inspirations, etc. The message here is to work with this flow, and surrender to it, letting it work through you. For those who are highly creative, this should be a very productive time. *Divine creative energies flow through me, and my true nature is revealed in my creations.*

**313 - Higher Vibrations.** This number speaks of higher octaves of frequency. Your vibration is being raised, through experiences of difficulty, and overcoming these hardships. You may feel drawn, or have been on a spiritual quest, or search for information. There may have been many wrong turns, or challenging lessons. You may have come across a lot of misinformation. Something in you, has made you aware of when you are hearing truth, and this has led you to a more finely tuned and focused path. You are very close to higher truths, that most of the world has missed. Your energy is matching that truth, and your vibratory level is speeding up. You should be noticing changes in the way you think, feel, and react to the world, and are opening to abilities that would normally seem impossible. An increase in telepathy and other psychic abilities is a possibility. In a more mundane sense, you are able to see through to the truth of a matter. You are correct, and should trust your own judgments and conclusions. *I am one with truth.*

**314 - Pixie Dust.** 314 is a strong number, relating to the forces of nature and your ability to work in harmony with these natural elements. It would be a good idea for you to explore the nature elementals, as spoken of by Paracelsus, Peter Calhoun and many other Masters who worked with these forces. It is time for you to step into your own power, align yourself with the natural forces and create your world. *I am a powerful being of light and love. I work with all, toward the common good.*

**315 - Gangsta Ganja.** 315 is related to the number 314, but there is the temptation of being drawn into activities that are not in your best interest. These relate to using plant substances, that draw in the darker energies. These are plants that deal with mind alteration, and hallucinogenic properties. Some of these plants have benefits, when used in other ways, but when used for escape, a high, or pleasure activities, they prove to be spiritually detrimental, indeed. Many consider these plants to be safe, but this is not necessarily true. 315 warns of overindulgence, misusing spiritual power for personal gain, and the like. You risk attachments of dark entities, and your space being compromised. If one's intentions are pure, this can be an extremely powerful number, for uniting higher forces with the earthly plane, for the good of all. On a more mundane level, 315 warns of misusing substances, addiction and other escape methods, from issues of your early childhood and possible abuse. 315 does support, however, those seeking counseling or assistance with their problem. This can relate to any problem, in addition to those listed, so 315 says to purify your intentions, and seek healing. *I am one with all. I do not need to escape, because I am already, truly free.* Dream quartz.

**316 - A New World.** 316 speaks about the breakdown of our society, and its restrictions. A new world is coming, a new way of being, and the old ways are being flushed out. Greed, selfishness, control, lack of respect for the environment, lack of respect for animals and all life, and a lack of awareness of higher truths, are attitudes on the way out. You are part of the movement to bring in this higher energy world. Realize that situations around you may be crumbling, or things might feel slightly out of control. There seems to be one sudden change after another. Understand that this is the breakdown, before the birth. In a more ordinary understanding, 316 relates to upsets, or a tearing down of what was the norm, but this is laying the path for something better. Allow change to happen, and you will see great results. *I am part of the movement for change. What has gone before, can be no longer. Love is all there is.*

**317 - Words Of Love.** 317 signals a misuse of words. It is a reminder that your words are extremely powerful, and that you must watch what you say, think, and how you express yourself. Love is the ultimate power, the ultimate expression and is all there is. If you can communicate in loving ways with others, and bring love into all of your conversations, movements, motivations and creations, you will see great success, and results that last. Your message will be felt and heard by many, for a long time to come. *I speak with love. I am love.* Rainbow Mayanite.

**318 - Cleaning House.** It is time to get organized. Clear out the closets, storage units, your work office, files, email accounts, and anywhere else that needs organization, and clearing out of clutter. A clear environment, reflects a clear mind. Organization and structure, assist in organized thinking, and productivity. *I am healthy, happy, whole and complete.*

**319 - Timelines Joining.** Your vision is clear. You see into the past, the future, other worlds, dimensions and beyond. You have the gift of sight. 319 asks you to recognize the enormity of your Spirit, and your far-reaching vision. You are so much more, than this existence. You are existing simultaneously in other realities and dimensions, and in other timelines. These other aspects of yourself, are blocked off from your awareness. 319 says you are being given the gift to see. On a more mundane level, 319 speaks of being able to see to the heart of the matter, or the hidden truths. All secrets and unspoken truths, will be revealed. This number is also encouraging you to be honest, and speak your truth. *I see clearly, and I am aware of my magnificence.*

**320 - Fairy Godparents.** 320 carries the message of success in all ventures, and karmic rewards. It is a number of movement, and group support. People want to back you, and whatever it is you are trying to accomplish. You can move up the ladder at work, get the relationship you want, find ways to improve your home life, and succeed in any venture. *I accept my good, now.*

**321 - Countdown To Accomplishment.** New business ideas, avenues for expression and healthy changes, are related to 321. Success is coming, because you did not give up. You are recognized and rewarded. *I achieve my desires. I am one with the energy of luck and abundance.*

**322 - Reach For The Sky.** This is a fortunate number, as long as you are not naive about your circumstances, but even then all will work out in the end. Faith, and a fresh approach to situations and people will be rewarded. *I am an innocent child of Spirit.*

**323 - Strike It Rich.** Monetary reward, and success come with 323. Physical results, help and advancement follows. *My bank account is overflowing with income. My goals are easily achieved.*

**324 - Self Possessed.** This is a number of mixed blessings. You are going to get the good with the bad. Whatever you're trying to accomplish, you will get a mix of people assisting you, and those that try to hinder, or block you. This number is asking you to push forward, using your intuition combined with logic, making smart decisions based on security and stability. Highly energized emotions such as anger, frustration and impatience, will feed more energy to the people who are blocking your progress. Making calm, heart-centered decisions is wise, if you are to succeed with what you desire. *I am the calm at the center of the storm. I am confident and know my way.* Scapolite.

**325 - A Long Road Of Lessons.** If you are reading this description, you are an old soul. You have seen it all, and most likely experienced it all, in this life and in previous lifetimes. You've learned much through this growth, and have defined your ethics from it. You've also defined what you will tolerate and what you will not tolerate. Mindfulness sets you apart from the ordinary, and lights your path ahead. Things are clear, and well-defined. You know what you must do, and who you must do it with, in what way, and why. 325 is a number of success in all endeavors. Your desires find you now, after a long, lonely and painful path. *I am wisdom. I achieve all that I desire, because my will is at one with the creator.*

**326 Courage to Walk Away.** 326 is a sign that you are about to be entangled in a situation that will be difficult to escape. Whatever path you are walking, is more complicated than it appears, or you may be ignoring the signs that you were given - to turn around, or go the other way. If you continue on in the direction you are headed, your plans or goals could be lost. It will take some effort to relinquish the situation's hold on you. The direction you *should* be headed, is the exact opposite. *I am a child of the Universe. It is my divine right to be happy and free.* Larimar.

327 - **In The Cards.** This is a positive number of success and accomplishment. Listen to the call of the Angels. They are guiding your steps. All is well. *I accomplish many miracles.*

**328** - **Hazardous Ground.** This is a number that can be filled with frustration, and warns of possible despair. It is a difficult number, and Spirit is asking you to call upon Archangel Raphael, of Divine Healing. For success, one must trust the intuition, and emotional clues. If you rely on knowledge, rational thought, or ego desires, the situation could fall apart in your hands. The reason for this, is 328 requires a delicate tip-toeing around the land mines, in order to avoid an explosion. This can only be done, when being led by intuition and Spirit. Otherwise, 328 warns of possible drastic endings. As mentioned, these can be avoided, by following the advice of this number. *I am awake and aware of my intuitive nudges, and I acknowledge their importance.* Yellow Selenite.

**329 - Well-Being.** You are reaching the pinnacle of your

goals. What you have envisioned, comes quickly, now. *The past is gone, and my future unfolds in brilliant displays of abundance.*

**330 - Toward Perfection.** This is a sign that you are reaching

a high level of mastery in your life. Your light body is merging with your physical body. Your cells are being reawakened, and you are being lifted up to higher levels of awareness. It may be wise for you to call on those ascendant beings, who are connected to you. A master is coming to give you a sign, whether this be appearing in physical form, or downloading information to you. 330 is a definite number of triumph and victory in any setting, or venture. You must walk in the light, if you are to access all of the power that is behind this number. *I am the master of myself. I have access to all information now, as needed.*

**331 - Channeled Truths.** This is a number of spiritual

insights and deep connections to truth. You have the answers, at this time, and should consult your guidance for further instruction. *I am divinely connected to my inner guide. All answers are available to me, now.*

**332 - Hidden Agendas**. 332, is a number of advancement. It is

also a warning, in dealings with others. Someone may not be as they appear, or have your best interests at heart. If you were thinking of doing business with, or joining with someone else, the message is to keep your eyes open. This number recommends you are better off following your own advice, or doing business alone. 332 highlights communications and things that are hidden. Some achievement and profit could be made with this number, however, any gains should be acquired with caution. *I am a vessel of clarity and truth.* Aulmauracite.

**333 - Limitless Light.** 333 is a number that connects you to the Divine. You are at a very elevated level of spiritual advancement and mastery. Because you are at this high vibrational state, this makes you a target, so to speak, for lower energy vibrations. It would be wise, therefore, for you to learn how to protect your energy field, your personal space and where you sleep. It is not so much that you need protection, as much as you cannot be vigilant 24 hours a day, to keep dark forces at bay. The possibility for them to target you, is extremely high, because they are against the advancement of revelations, about our divine nature. And it is this Divine nature, that you are to shine forth, now. Be the light that others need to see, in order to assist them on their journey. 333 is divine communication with Spirit, Angels, Spirit Guides and any other high vibrational beings that have come to assist you at this time, for the evolution of the planet. 333 is perfect communication. What you say carries weight, and reaches the ears of those who can assist you. Much is accomplished with this number, and what you focus on expands, in enormous ways, beyond what you can imagine. This is expansion in the extreme. Therefore it is a beautiful time, for those who are here to assist others, to shine their light. *I am a Divine being of light. I fulfill my mission.*

**334 - A Powerful Mind.** This is a powerful number, of highly developed mental faculties. It suggests that you should trust what you know. You have learned lessons needed, and therefore can act accordingly. It would be wise for you to act, in accordance with the Divine, if you wish for the situation to play out correctly, and not have repercussions later down the road. 334 is good luck and wisdom. *I am wisdom. I am in alignment with Divine force.*

**335 - On Close Inspection.** This number asks you to stop,

and look carefully, at the direction you are headed, or the negative avenues your thoughts may be taking. It would be wise for you to come up with a mantra, or some type of meditative affirmation, that you can repeat, to encourage positive thinking. This is also a good time, to refrain from saying what is on your mind. Unfiltered speaking, will destroy the possible benefits and rewards of this number. The advice here, is, to keep quiet, evaluate, or reevaluate, and take action, only after a full analysis. *I see clearly, and act accordingly.* Fennel Essential Oil.

**336 - Slingshot.** Energy is building behind you, ready to

catapult you forward. Before this happens, you are being given a pause, to consider your options. This is a number of good fortune, and making amends. *The way is clear. I am blessed with many gifts, seen and unseen. I glorify the oneness of all beings.*

**337 - Purple Majesty.** This is a number of intentions and new

beginnings. What you intend, will occur. What needs to fall away, will be removed, in order for the new energies to enter. 337 is a number of expansiveness and growth, on material and spiritual levels. *I am transformed in the light. All who see me, see love.*

**338 - Grand Slam.** This number says that whatever you are aiming to achieve, is going to go through the roof. Meaning, that your plans are going to be met with high success. You can accomplish exactly what you are setting out to do, if you stick to the plan. If it relates to a personal matter, know that you are the one in charge, and all goes in your favor. Use your power wisely, though, as this is a karmic scenario, so you will want to avoid replaying old patterns. Bringing love into the situation, and having an agenda that has a basis in love, is the best route for you to take. *I act for the highest good of all. I am responsible for my influence on others, and therefore I choose to be love.*

**339 - Five Stars.** 339 is connected to 338, in the sense that this is the enjoyment of the reward. It says all things work in your favor. *I am joy, and I share it with others.*

**340 - Eagle Eye.** 340 is an excellent number, of a finely tuned mind, and attention to detail. Nothing gets by your inspection. Know that your attention, or lack thereof, will determine outcomes. Overall, this number relates to a success, well earned. *I see clearly. All is revealed to me.*

**341 - Transported.** This is a number of karmic reward. You are being given the keys to the kingdom. You can do no wrong. High success and advancement are very possible. Timing is spring or fall. *I am blessed with vast abundance. I open my doors for its arrival.*

**342 - What It Takes.** You may be feeling scattered, and unable to focus. There seems to be too much going on, you are being interfered with, or you can't clear your thoughts, to know what to do next. Maybe the situation seems unsolvable or volatile. 342 asked you to begin to prioritize what is most important, first. One step at a time, one day at a time, one thing at a time. As you ground yourself in the present moment, you will see that step-by-step, you reach your goals and desires. The present moment is all there is. *I breathe in this moment, and am fully aware.* Bastnaesite.

**343 - Two-Faced.** 343 is asking you to look at the duality in yourself. This represents two opposing choices. The decision to follow what you know is right, and the choice to follow the ego. If you follow the ego, your plans can be ruined. This also relates to others who may be showing you two different faces. In a situation, there can be two sides, or pros and cons. 343 is telling you to pay attention and choose the correct path. *I see behind the mask of duality, and understand the truth.* Aegirine

**344 - Can't Buy Me Love.** This can be an oppressive number, with the theme of choosing money over love. If this is relating to a partnership that you find yourself involved in, one or both parties are determining which holds more value for them, love or money. In other words, they are determining whether a person can offer them love, or the money can offer them love. We see the want of money, as greed, but greed doesn't really exist. Underlying the seeming greed, is a fear of the loss of love, and the belief in lack. The individual thinks that something is lacking in their life, and that money, or a relationship can provide this. This could be marrying for love, or entering into an agreement for the benefit of financial gain. These kind of relationships come with an expectation or a cost. This is the complete opposite of unconditional love. If you find yourself in this situation, it may be better to pass this by. This could also relate to a work situation. In general, this number talks about the deeper issues, of lack, fear and the deep inner belief, that we are denied love. *I experience Divine love within myself. My outer life, reflects this.* Pink Topaz.

**345 - Mountain Climber.** This number speaks of reaching

the pinnacle or top of the peak. It is a precarious place to be, because one false step, can lead you slipping down the other side, or back down from where you came. It also suggests being king of the mountain, and having to guard that space, from others who would climb and take it from you. This is a metaphor for jealousy, competition and believing that we have to fight for the same space, the same person, and the belief that there is not enough for everyone, to go around. If you find yourself aiming for something that has a lot of competition involved, know that the achievement of this goal will require you to fight to keep it. It would be better for you to go your own path, and choose a goal where you can make your own rules, where the stakes are not this high. There is enough to go around for everyone, therefore you do not need to fight your way to the top, or crush another in order to have what you want. If the scenario is happening in your life, it is time for you to step back and reevaluate your beliefs. Success, that one has to continually fight to keep, is a prison. *I choose the path that is mine alone.* Sandstone.

**346 - Grab Bag.** You can create change and growth, in

anything to which you set your mind. You have the ability to create something new, or rise from the ashes, no matter what the circumstances. Good fortune bestows many lucky opportunities on you. *I create my life, the way I want.*

**347 - Over The Next Rise.** Your future awaits. It is coming up over the next hill. You can begin to see it on the horizon. What you need, finds you now. Good fortune is sure. *A lucky future finds me now.*

**348 - Protection.** 348 can suggest, being under attack. This can be on a spiritual level, having dark forces or entities in your vicinity, or being around a person who has this type of energy. This could also relate to being put on the spot, or judged by someone. The message is to protect yourself. This can mean cutting off contact with a person, who has dark energy, addictions or anything else that is affecting you, and bringing you down. Whether this be in your personal life, or work, it is best to put up a spiritual and physical barrier around yourself. This may mean caring protective stones, or sealing off your personal space, as well as not allowing this person to have your attention. If this is happening at work, know that someone may want to stab you in the back, or just has bad energy. Put up your barriers, around yourself, and then bless them, so that the negativity is removed from you. You are no longer a magnet, or target for this energy. *I am a divine child of the light. I am blessed, and all are blessed by me.* Moldavite.

**349 - Grief and Loss.** You may be grieving the loss of someone, or something. Either this is coming, or you have been carrying it for a long time. Sadness can build up in the body, mind and spirit, and create toxins. If you've been holding in your emotions, now is the time for you to safely release them. Holding on to something, can keep you stuck in the past. Letting go does not mean that you forget the situation, or the person, it simply means that you put it to the side, so that it is no longer dominating your energy field. Grieve appropriately, but realize that you must go on living. *I am at one with my feelings. I allow them to flow, and move toward healing now.* Green Taralite.

**350 - Dreams of the Impossible.** This number has a magical quality, and suggests that you are in a phase of growth, miracles and new experiences. Many things are being introduced into your life. Open to the new, different and unusual. Explore, to open your consciousness to the new wave of energies entering the planet, at this time. If you consider something to be outlandish, or "crazy", that is your sign to read about it, or do it. What you learn now, will further your growth and evolution. There are messages and blessings in everything right now, all around you, from your Angels and nature spirits. Open up that inner magical child-self, and let the possibilities of what is impossible, begin. Remember, there are no limits. *I know that anything is possible in my imagination, and therefore can be possible in my reality.*

**351 - Trailblazing.** This number speaks to the innovator and the engineer. Those creative souls, who are here to make a difference. You are the pioneer who carves out a new path. Trust your ideas. Don't follow what others have done, or at the very least, contribute your unique spin to something. You are in charge of what happens, and are the answer. Only you can take it where it needs to go. *I have unique abilities and ideas that are important, for the overall good of all involved.* Carnelian.

**352 - Heights Of Glory.** A number of success, high honors, high placement in business, social stratospheres, or being held in high esteem by those close to you. If you are honest, and treat others well, there will be no problems accomplishing what you desire. *I can reach my dreams, now.*

**353 - Dream Job.** Make money, doing what you love. Do what you are good at, and follow your dreams. Any other way of bringing in an income, will be burdensome, with limits and problems attached to it. Decide now, that you are going to believe in yourself, and start with step one. If a situation has you worried about the financial aspects, ask yourself if you really enjoy being connected to that arrangement. Let go of control, and open the doors to money now, by calling in your Angels, and letting them bring you what you need. *I accept prosperity now, in all forms. I can make money, doing what I love.* Peridot.

**354 - Obsessive Replays.** Are you seeing health issues pop up? Are there unusual things wrong, that you can't explain? Did you give in to something you should not have? Making choices, or avoiding making them, can take a heavy toll on our nervous system. Especially long term worry, or obsessing over mistakes from the past. To avoid possible health challenges, forgive yourself, and take steps to either extricate yourself from the consequences of your decision, or make a new choice. *I forgive myself for previous mistakes. I now have clarity, and choose wisely.* Bloodstone.

**355 - The Power To Decide.** What will your future be? It lies in your hands. You have great power to manifest, and must use it wisely. What you envision, becomes reality. *I attract all that I need, and find joy in the pleasures of living.*

**356 - Group Energy.** This is a number of joining with others, to achieve a common goal. Much success can come from networking, and connecting with those who can help you manifest your dreams. Referrals, affiliations, assistance and beneficial plugs from others, help you achieve your goals. *I have a positive network of supportive friends, business associates, and peers. All is accomplished, through my many connections.*

**357 - Head To The Beach.** 357 says you are in sore need of a vacation, some playtime, or a distraction from the daily grind. Amusement parks, a beach by the ocean, or anything enjoyable that takes your mind off of life's stresses, is recommended. 357 is a number of pleasant experiences and diversions that give you a chance to recharge. *I enjoy my life, and remember that playtime is as important as work.*

**358 - The Transformer.** The number 358, is related to power and influence over others. The power spoken of, is the ability to transform situations. You may be noticing that your entry into another person's life, has changed their circumstances in some way. Maybe their situation was torn down, in order to be rebuilt. This number also relates to yourself, and the tearing down of old belief systems, that do not serve you any longer. You are here to harness, and understand how to tear down gently. If you are wielding your power too harshly, or resisting the dismantling, then it will be done for you. 358 warns that these changes could be sudden, damaging, or drastic. Therefore, learn how to handle your power, and your natural influence over others. *My power comes from Source. My will is His will.* Tiger's Eye.

**359 - Remaking Success.** 359 can mean having hopes that are not realistic. 359 is *not* saying that you cannot achieve what you hope or wish for, but simply that what you are currently thinking about, is not what is called for in your present situation. It is time to ground yourself, and see things as they really are, before taking action or telling others. Rethink, re-plan and redo. *My higher mind, logic and emotions are joined as one.* Sagenite Agate.

**360 - Angelic Forces.** This is a number of high achievement and growth. It is a sign that the Angels, in particular the Cherubim and Seraphim, are supporting and guiding you. Your requests have been heard by heaven, and are coming to completion. This is a done deal, so celebrate the good news. Victory is yours. *With the Angels of Divine Creation at my back, I am victorious.*

**361 - The Heart's Desire**. 361 is a sign that you will be able to bring your heart's desires and dreams into the world. Listen carefully to what is in your heart center. Tune in, and get in touch with who you really are, and what you are here to do. If something feels good, you are on the right track. Doing what you love, and what is meant for you to do, is why you are here. It is time for you to bring your creations into reality. If this number is relating to a relationship, know that this needs to be a heart-felt connection. If not, you will be meeting someone that you share this connection with, soon. *My heart speaks to me, and I follow.*

**362 - True Colors.** There is a situation, or a person around you, hiding something. If it is a person, maybe you are having to share them with someone else, or something else. They only give you part of their time, attention and loyalty. If you remain tied to this individual, you will suffer to some extent. If the reverse is true, and you are not being fully honest, it is time to own up to what is really going on, and your true agendas. Let go, so that something or someone better can come in, now. *I am open and honest, and attract the same to myself.* Goshenite.

363 - **Bewitched.** This number cannot fail. 363 is success and harmony in all things. What you are thinking about, can grow bigger. Your spiritual vision is being expanded. You are like a magnet, with incredible attraction for others, as well as attracting in what you need. An auspicious number. *I am a magnet for my good.*

364 - **Spellbound.** Divine partnerships are entering your life. You have the ability to see anything through to its finish. You can make or transform your life, to what you need. Like 363, you are electrical, and magnetic, and others notice your sizzle. *I am a Divine Being of light and love.*

365 - **Hidden Help.** There is much assistance coming to you, from unknown sources. If you are having problems in a specific situation, know that help is on the way. You may have no idea where it is coming from, nor could you imagine how, but coming, it is. This number says to act on faith, and continue. What you are wanting to create, or do, will be possible. *I trust that I am supplied with what I need, when I need it.*

366 - **Pennies From Heaven.** Everything in the physical realm, is yours. Material abundance, good luck, and assistance from the heavenly hosts. What you need, has been gifted to

you. Accept your good fortune now. *My gifts are many, and my burdens light. The Angels carry me around all obstacles.*

367 - **Halting the Madness.** Situations may be ending, or put on hold, in order for things to be put in their correct places. All is lining up for the win, if you are willing to cooperate with the higher will of Spirit. *I follow my internal guidance. I am always led to joy.*

368 - **Going Big.** There is money or gain, in putting your ideas out into the world. Being in the public eye, and releasing a creative work, or just letting another person know how you feel, can be beneficial and rewarding. Getting your ideas down on paper, or going through with something that you were afraid to do, is asked for, with this number. You will have success. *I have confidence in myself. I let my inner creativity flow out into the world.*

369 - **Ideal Symmetry.** This number has a perfect flow of harmony and unity. The only thing that can stop the benefits of this number, is indulging in negative thinking. Know that you are poised to win. 369 says that things may seem too good to be true, and you may resist your good fortune, by sabotaging yourself. Don't do this. Celebrate and enjoy this cycle. If you are involved with other people, you are a win for them, as well. *I deserve prosperity, in all areas of my life. I accept it now, as my Divine birthright.*

370 - **The Power To Unite.** Your decisions can determine a situation. You are in control of your future, and if you act from the wisdom of Spirit, all will work out favorably. *Luck is*

*on my side. I trust in a higher wisdom.*

**371 - Climbing the Ladder.** This number has a cold, hard energy. There is a ruthlessness that goes along with any gains. It seems that to progress, one must step on toes, back stab and do whatever is necessary, as the situation requires. If you are in this position, of being forced to be ruthless, it will be a struggle to get where you need to go. It would be better to re-evaluate whether you really want to be in this situation, at all. If it means hurting others to get what you want, it is wise to remember that you get back what you give. 371 may also be relating to a situation that will require "tough love", in order to help another person. Or, it may require you to give a "hard no", meaning it will be difficult to refuse, but overall more in alignment with who you are in the long run, if you do refuse. *I see clearly. I am able to say no to anything that requires me to abandon my integrity, as a Child of Source.* Red Jasper.

**372 - Power In Silence.** Spirit is calling you to set aside what is currently happening, so that you can be renewed with Love's presence. The Angels are asking to fill your soul with inspiration and peace, so that you can be guided toward your good, without distraction. 372 is a number of luck, and spiritual support. *I allow the stillness of Spirit to fill me now. All answers lie within the depths of my being, and I take a pause, to listen.*

**373 - The Answers are Within.** This number is a doorway to Spirit. It would be excellent for you to meditate, at this time. The way to find the answers, is in silent harmony with your inner self and guidance. All endings lead to positive new beginnings, and 373 represents an expansive and fruitful future. *I tune in to the inner depths of Self, where I always find clarity.*

**374 - Coming Back to Earth.** The message is for grounding.

Your mind may be on overdrive, or you have too much information coming at you. Maybe you feel a bit hyperactive, or can't shut your mind off at night, when you should be sleeping. You need to ground your energy into the Earth, and bring your mind to the present moment. If you are attempting to make important decisions right now, the answers may be escaping you. Look at things realistically, not emotionally, and find a stillness within you. The right choice will come to you, if you are in a calm place to receive. All things can work in your favor, if you follow your own inner guidance. *I am rooted in the Earth. My mind is clear, and the direction is sure.*

**375 - We've Got Your Back.** This number carries the

promise of good luck, and a strong backing. You have many behind you, cheering you on, or willing to jump in and do what is necessary. What you are desiring, can happen, as people want to work with you, or prove to be blessings for you. This number is a sign that you are under a lucky star at the moment, and things can go your way. Don't get too caught up in your own agendas, and forget to recognize, and thank those around you, that have helped, or got you where you are. *I am blessed with a supportive network of people, and am supplied with everything I need.*

**376 - Loss of Love.** You may have been deeply hurt, recently,

or have been carrying the pain of some kind of loss. You may have a broken heart, or are feeling empty inside. Make sure you are taking time, every day, to be kind to yourself. Stay grounded, and build up your sense of self-worth. Then, no matter what difficulty occurs, you are in a better place to handle it. 376 says that this too, shall pass. Beautiful things are coming your way. Spirit is reminding you to open your heart again, and give love, regardless of what you may get. *It is safe to love. I love myself, and have plenty to give.*

377 - **Towing The Line.** There is work to be done, that

cannot be avoided. You may be experiencing many delays, because karmic circumstances are coming to the forefront. There are situations that need to be released, and difficult experiences that must be resolved, in order for you to move through the difficulties, toward what you desire. In other words, you cannot go from A to C, without first resolving B. *I understand my lessons, and receive assistance in resolving them.* Archangel Jeremial.

**378 - Parallel Lives.** 378 has to do with blocked energies and

frustration. You may have a vision of what you want to do with your life, and have taken action, but difficulties crop up seemingly every step of the way. Your dreams may be subject to reversals, or serious obstacles. 378 says this is karmic in nature. It seems, no matter what you try, you fail, or the time isn't right. This is merely a kickback of previous experiences in past lives, of being held back. Or you held others back, through interference or jealousy. Know that the energy will clear. This is a temporary situation, because it is an overlap of a previous life with this life. A bleed-over. Forgive the setbacks, and know that the time for a clear path is coming. *I forgive myself and others, for that which occurred in any past, present or future life. I understand I do not need to suffer, and that we are all free.* Serpentine.

**379 - A Rise From The Fall.** If you have recently come through a difficult situation, or devastating experience, know that it will be righting itself. Happiness is just a breath away. 379 suggests joy, new beginnings and rebirth. *I have been rewarded for my efforts. I now find happiness.*

**380 - Ends Don't Justify Means.** This is a number of moving up the corporate ladder. It has to do with status-quo, image and ranking higher than the next guy. Either someone is stepping on you, to get a leg up, or you are stepping on others to gain favor and advancement. This is a number that is cold and hard, related to money and gain. It also has to do with squabbling and legal issues, in the areas of inheritances and other people's finances, or estates. In general, there is a focus on ruthless gain and acquiring. Someone is going to lose in the equation. Overcoming 408, means letting go of whatever you are fearing. *I am abundant. This bounty flows to me, and I either accept or resist. It is never taken from me.* Archangel Raziel.

**381 - Driving Into A Cul-de-Sac.** 381 has to do with tensions, causing a stalemate. This is conflicting energies, that keep things from moving forward, in any direction. Two people can't agree, circumstances pop up that put a stop to progress, what you are waiting on does not seem to be showing up, or the decision-maker is not making one. For whatever reason, you are seemingly stuck. Take this time, to observe the situation, and see if another option comes to you, or there is a way out of this impasse. By detaching from your emotional connection to it, you can influence things with new information. *I am free to move forward on my life's journey.* Desert Rose.

**382 - Have A Better Look.** You hold the power, in the current situation you are in. Meaning, how you choose to act, will determine whether this continues, or is lost. It may be time for you to reevaluate the facts, and decide if this is something you really want to be involved in, at all. The way you handle things, sets up what will happen next. Are you thinking only of yourself, or is this all about the other person? There needs to be equal value given to both sides. 382 calls for you to reexamine, and rethink. *I see clearly. I know exactly what is necessary.* Fluorite.

**383 - Writer's Block.** This is a time of mental fogs and fuzziness. Know that the mists will clear. It may be a time, when you are tongue-tied, not knowing what is the right thing to say, have writer's block, or are not seeing clearly on any situation. It is also a message that you may not be able to contact someone, or see them. 383 says to sit and clear your mind, and ask your Angels of Source to cleanse your mind, emotions and whatever else is in your energy field, that does not belong. *My thoughts are clear, and all communication channels are open.* Vanadinite.

**384 - Devil's Playground.** This is a serious warning of dark energies around you. This alludes to addictions (sexual, alcoholism, drug use etc.), entity attachments in your aura, dark cult activity, invasion of your personal space by dark forces, sexual abuse, cheating, or entrapments and the like. Either you are being tempted and influenced, or someone around you is bringing these dark energies into your life. It is time for a serious cleansing, or removing yourself from the vicinity of the other person. If this is in your environment, order it out. Dark energies don't belong or have a right to be there, unless you give permission to them through fear. If it is a work situation, forcing you to be around someone with this energy, then use protection at work, such as crystals, visualizations, sage spray, frankincense oil on your chakras etc. There are many methods. Do not look this person in the eye. Instead, focus on a point of the forehead between their eyes. If you are the one carrying the dark energy, it is time to seek help for a major cleanse. *I am a Child of the One True Creator. Source is. There is nothing else. I am invulnerable.* Titanium Aura Quartz.

**385 - A New Life Coming.** This number talks about endings.

There are areas of your life, or people that are going to have to go, in order for you to continue on your spiritual path, or see progress for your goals. If you are already feeling these endings, know that they are necessary. Try not to resist, for in their removal, is much to fill the empty space. New situations cannot unfold, if one is holding on to people or scenarios whose time is done. 385 has to do with more than one ending, but asks you to look at these, as gifts for the future. You will gain understanding and reward, as you will not be traveling this part of your path, again. *I am open to the future, as I release in the present, what no longer serves.* Oregano Essential Oil.

**386 - Material Increase.** 386 is one of those numbers having

to do with financial and material reward. It is karmic in nature, so this is what you have attracted to yourself, through past life experiences and beliefs. It is especially beneficial, in the acquirement of property, a home, or moving to a beautiful location. Much can happen in a short space of time, and the benefits are likely on their way, or have already found you. Expect good news, soon. *I am bountiful, and enjoy abundance, as my Divine right.*

**387 - Escape to Nowhere.** This number can be connected to abuse, some kind of stimulant, or mind altering substance. If you are around someone with abusive tendencies, or a propensity toward violent behavior, this is a sign to protect yourself. The other side of this number, is being led into temptations of behavior, or habits that drag down the spirit. These lead to a mental depression, as worry, fear and negative thinking prevail. The abuse, and/or violence could be directed at oneself. This is a warning number, to clear yourself of harmful friendships, relationships or anyone that would drag you down in any way. You cannot help yourself, until you are willing to make these changes. A more mundane meaning of 387, is to look at your life realistically. Resist the urge to escape, or bury yourself in illusory pursuits. *I am a powerful being of the light. I take back control of my choices.* Benzoin essential oil.

**388 - Holding Fast.** This number means you have had a lot of challenges to your resolve. It is a sign that you have come out on top, or will very soon. 388 is telling you to keep going, and persevere. Do not give in to dark forces of distraction and fear. You will rise above what has gone before, and be crowned with achievement. This number says it may be darkest before dawn, so remain stalwart. *The past is on its way out, and what lies before me, is a new day.* Tiger Animal Totem.

**389 - The Final Conflict.** - It is crucial to learn your spiritual lessons. You are about to advance, in your evolutionary growth, but must gain the wisdom of the previous cycle. If you do not, you will carry the difficulties with you into the future. They will have to be dealt with again, and at a more difficult level. This may also be a sign that not enough blood is getting to some of your muscles, causing knots, your nasal passages are swelling, or the veins in your head are causing headaches. In extreme cases, you could be having gallbladder or liver troubles. In any case, 389 says to research the spiritual cause of any issue, and clear up the abuses and harmful beliefs, taken on in childhood. It is time for you to be free. *I move into the next cycle of my life, leaving behind old worn-out detrimental patterns that no longer serve me. I am one with my Father.* Dark Brown Zircon

**390 - A Moment's Grace.** Source is blessing you, in your current situation. If you look at things, through the eyes of love, you will understand your good fortune. You are blessed in each moment, and with each step you take. 390 is a number of success, and victory. *I have been given the Keys to the Kingdom. Insight, inspiration and joy fills me now.*

**391 - Fear-Based Sacrifice.** 390 moves you into the next phase of your journey here. It is filled with choices. Having been through many difficulties, you may be at a point where you do not know which way to go. There have been heavy sacrifices, and 390 says that you are still involved in situations that require you to sacrifice. There are two in particular, and it would be wise to remove yourself from these conditions. You may feel you need to sacrifice for the sake of another, or a cause you care about. Perhaps you are sacrificing for monetary reasons. The message is clear. Spirit never requires you to sacrifice. Only the ego does, and the ego is based in fear, alone. If you are sacrificing for your children, examine your own issues of control. Each child has chosen their path and experiences in this life. You cannot change what they must go through, as young children and teens, but rather are here as their responsible guide, until they can care for themselves. This means that you must also live your life, as well. *I am free from obligations that are not mine. Even if they are perceived to be mine, each soul is on its own journey I release myself from prison, and am free.* Barberry Root.

**392 - Your True Inheritance.** This is a message from

Archangel Michael, in alignment with Source, that you are being put on notice. It is time for you to raise your thoughts and heal your wounds. Here in the Earthly illusion, you are a Divine Energy Being. Your true nature comes from Spirit, which is beyond the soul, and is at one with Source. Therefore, the truth of your origin, can be channeled into the illusion construct, and provide healing here. This means that you may not be visible to all beings, or they do not see you the same way. The good news is you may no longer be magnetized to those who would bring you into lower energies. You can avoid and cut ties with what has denied your true nature, and encased you in fear. Miracles are available to you now. *I am a Divine Being of Source. Fear is the stranger here.*

**393 - Universal Expansion.** This is a number of gifts, help

and assistance from others. People are willing to back your creative ideas, or projects. This number especially highlights relationships, as the communication channels are open, and understanding and support is received. This would be an excellent time to heal a relationship, rekindle a current one, repair a separation or come to some kind of agreement. When taking any kind of help from another, this number carries a small warning, to make sure that you are not giving up your dignity, or something valuable, in order to receive this help.

Otherwise, this is a very fortunate number, and promises success. For those seeking enlightenment, this number promises advancement and success. You are on the verge of a highly spiritual experience, that has a profound effect on your life. You can see beyond the veil, and it signals the ending of a final cycle, with a chance to exit reincarnation, death and rebirth. *I accept the Divine healing and support, coming to me now.*

**394 - Losing to Gain.** This number has a lot of antagonistic

energies tied to it, which can bring about loss. It is spelling out danger. It implies that a situation is doomed to fail. It is important to remember that nothing is "doomed" when we view it from Spirit. Another way of saying this, would be, that it is very likely a situation will not turn out in accordance with your expectations. Usually this is related to a misuse of power or control, and therefore the venture is subject to needed change. Know that the foundations are crumbling, and change is almost certain. There will be a reversal of power. On the other side of this destruction, is the renewal of something more simple and real. If this matter relates to health, this number may mean undergoing major decline, but then possible renewal, or if one is declining, then this will come to an end, and health could improve. Whatever has been held onto, is pulled apart. *I release my resistance and fear, and accept that Spirit is bringing what is best for me.* Shungtite.

**395 - Bad Advice.** You have the wisdom, to know the

difference, but your insecurity is making you trust in someone else, instead. Following the advice of anyone or anything other than your Higher Self, is not advised. It may be, that you have already taken this counsel, but know that all will not be lost. This is a karmic situation, and that you will find hope to renew things, on the other side of this. *I trust in what I know. Hope is never lost, and Spirit always comes to my rescue.* Snake Animal Totem.

396 - **Opportunity Knocks.** This number suggests that there

are many opportunities coming your way, or that the chance you were looking for is upon you. If you are being presented with an offering, the advice is to act on it. Go forward. Everything will work out. If this opportunity is not what you were looking for, that is okay, because it will lead you to another one. Others will be receptive to you, and ready to help you along the way. Dispel worry, and know that the Universe is showing you the way. *I am one with Divine Timing. Many doors open to me, now.*

397 - **Breaking Free.** You are expanding to the point, where

this situation no longer fits with your energy. You have moved beyond your current situation, and its constraints, and are therefore no longer in alignment with it. Realize that this is a natural development. Its like you are a helium balloon, that is going to rise, no matter what. Either the situation will go with you, or the string will be pulled from its hands. You are moving upward and beyond, to bigger and better things. Nothing will stay the same. *I rejoice, because I am moving into a space of fulfillment.*

398 - **Stuck in the Wheel**. This number has to do with

powerful lessons from the past. It deals with all manner of previous life karma, and the repeating of that, in this life. Your life, up to this point, has been a continual cycle of these old patterns. This number calls for a release from this prison, but you will have to be willing to face the painful past, and the fears about yourself that go along with it. "Nothing good comes easy", applies here. You can no longer hide your head in the sand, but must face that which has gone before. Your Spirit can no longer continue to go through these cyclic patterns, and it is time for addressing and releasing them. Inner work is necessary. On a more mundane level, the situation you are involved in, has been on a repeating loop, and it is time to look at it for what it truly is. This includes your involvement, and any self-defeating messages you are affirming to yourself. *I know the way out. It is clear to me, what must be done, and I have the strength to do it. I can face fear, knowing there is nothing really to fear. My Spirit cannot be harmed, and my previous actions do not define who I am.* Barite.

**399 - A New Level of Advancement.** This number

correlates with victory, but by taking an odd road. You have taken a path that is not normally chosen, to reach your goals. It has been a long and difficult journey, but you are ascending now, to victory. This is the end of many former cycles in your life, and results of this, are shown to you now. This number means coming to an end of many sufferings, difficulties, relationships and other tests, that have outworn their usefulness on your journey. You are raised to new heights, and accomplishment, and achievement can be yours. Know that each step of the way, was for a purpose, and it was the only way to get where you are now. Things take off from here. *I fly free, into a new way of being. I let the past go.*

**400 - Lifetime Warranty.** 400 is entering a new level of

security, safety and support. You have laid the groundwork for success. Many karmic cycles have ended. A phase of freedom, and the guarantees of good fortune, have arrived. Aspects of the lower nature have been expunged. Rejoice that you have a solid foundation, and will succeed. *I come from a place of strength, and have a rock-solid support system.*

**401 - Lucky Leprechaun.** This is a highly fortunate sign. All things are possible with this number, and what you have desired, will come to pass. Things change or appear, as if by magic. Miracles are the norm. Victory is sure. This is a major "yea" vote for security and moving forward. *Luck is strong with me now. I attract what I need and desire.*

**402 - Tie the Knot.** A harmonious relationship is coming your way. Current relationships are finding balance, and becoming unified. Solidarity is definite, in relationships, so this is a good time to get married, sign agreements, begin a relationship, heal your issues, or make any type of commitment. *I enjoy harmonious and happy relations with all people. My connection to loved ones, is deepened.*

**403 - Larger Than Life.** 403 signifies a time of expansion of psychic abilities, or the uncovering of new ones. Your senses are heightened, and much extrasensory information is coming to you. This would be a good time to communicate with your guides, the elemental realms, or your OverSoul, as these channels are more open to you. This number also increases your spiritual awareness, and desire to learn. 403 also has to do with teaching and sharing what you know. It is the synergy between teacher and student. The mysteries of the Universe are being revealed to you, now. In the everyday life, you are seeing more of the bigger picture, and are acquiring the necessary knowledge. Advancement is sure. *I am a Divine being. I expand into, and connect with all parts of myself.*

**404 - New Vistas.** This is a number of movement, and possibly a physical move in residence. This is a positive change, and enhances your security. Whatever area this is in, things are shifting for the better. This also indicates a gain in financial matters, through speculation and investment. *All shifts and changes, coming to me now, are for my highest good.*

**405 - The Battle Within.** The energy of this number, has a "push-me, pull-you" feel. Your mind works quickly, but interference stalls the completion of your desires. Much gets in the way, of your security. 405 warns against acting on impulse, and says to trust in the wisdom of Spirit for guidance. *I can achieve that which I desire, by trusting in Spirit alone.* Goat Animal Totem.

**406 - One's True Treasure.** You are gifted with a beautiful family, caring friendships, and the achievement of your goals. However you interpret these in relation to your own life, know that you are very blessed. If you have had health issues, they are clearing up, as well as your relationships with others, and any concerns about security or safety. You are given the green light to move forward. *I see how lucky I am, and give thanks.*

**407 - True to Yourself.** This is a number of merging your spirituality with your day-to-day life. Being who you really are, will align with what you are trying to make happen in your life. If you want to connect with others in a positive way, the key is to make sure you express yourself with love. Be genuine, and let this flow through. All the fancy sales techniques in the world, are really leading back to this truth: Be yourself, and communicate with love. Voice coaching may be beneficial for business or marketing/sales success. Notice the inflection in your tone, your facial expressions and your nonverbal mannerisms. Polish yourself. Become a more rounded version of yourself. Overall, this is a fortunate number. *I let my light shine to all I meet.*

**408 - The Means.** Monetary growth and abundance are yours.

Command over the material world, and power and influence play the main role here. Decide what you want, and it will happen. *I have command over my world. All works in my favor, now.*

**409 - New Material.** This number has a lot of potential for

good fortune, but it says you are focusing too much on lack, security fears and what you stand to lose. Your mind needs to be on what you stand to gain. Anything lost, is temporary, and a new life is coming in. You are not going back to the old ways of being, and the situation you are in, is permanently changed. *I open to the new, and release that which has served its purpose.* Fire Opal.

**410 - Miraculous Turnaround.** There are beneficent karmic

experiences coming up just over the next hill. You are about to have an unexpected change of luck, or circumstances. It is up to you, to grab the reins, and go with it. Get ready for a surprise. *I am a child of the abundant Universe. Luck is attracted to me.*

**411 - A Friendly Alliance.** This number involves cooperation between parties. In order for things to proceed, you must work with those, who are involved in the situation with you. It also speaks of cooperating with the Universe, and being open to receive. You may need a helping hand up, or a good friend is on their way to give you support. Accept the help, and don't cause hurt feelings, or step on toes. Working together, and accepting help accomplishes much. This number can apply to artists working with a manager, or anyone who comes in, to solve problems, and get things moving. *I accept help and input from others. I don't have to do everything alone.*

**412 - A Wise Soul.** This number says your intuition is high, and your vision is clear. You know all you need to know. There is great strength behind 412, to overcome adversities and former difficulties. Whatever has been sacrificed, will be renewed. The situation has made you stronger, wiser and more in tune with what you will and won't accept. The message is, you can be unstoppable, if you pay attention, and follow only your own intuition and knowing. *I trust what I get from Spirit. I am divinely guided, and all obstacles are removed.*

**413 - Set in Stone.** 413 says that what you are going through cannot be changed. There are endings happening, clearing the way for something big. Whether this is a positive or negative thing, can be revealed, based on your emotions concerning the issue. If you feel good about the ending, and are excited, or anticipating the future, then 413 is working for you. Your karma is favoring you. If you dread the situation you are in, what is happening, and what is to come, then you are going to experience a lesson. Either way, it has to happen, so prepare, and sit along for the ride. You are moving on to something better, anyway. *I accept that which is necessary on my path. I move through any seeming difficulties, with grace and understanding. My good always awaits me.*

**414 - Losing is Winning.** This number seems to be a battle between two people, wanting the same thing. If you have to fight someone or something to get what you want, force matters, or compete, then it is not what you want. Which means, it is not what you *need.* Or the timing is off. What is yours, will come easily and with very little thought. It comes in a natural way, or as a part of a progression. Two people at odds, are unsatisfied with what they have. If you find yourself in this situation, or some symbolic version of it, the message here is to let go, and move on. *I trust that all things come to me, in their perfect way, at the perfect time.* Rooster Animal Totem.

**415 - Pleasure In Pain.** Anything tempting, comes with a price. There is a reason that you are tempted. This alludes to a belief in lack. To be tempted, means you think you need something, which is not true. Spirit always provides all that is necessary, for you to live your purpose. It is when you block this assistance, and put your own desires or wants first, that you are led astray. Therefore, avoid that which is tempting you. It will only lead to pain, in the end. *I trust in Spirit, and follow to where I am led.* Redwing Blackbird Animal Totem.

**416 - Victory Over Deception.** This number is an uncovering of your true motives in a situation, that may be hidden, even from yourself. Maybe you don't really want to be involved in it. 416 also states that you will be aware of other people's duplicity, and that not much can escape your "eagle eye". If you are not paying attention, however, someone can try to "pull one over on you". However, this number relates to coming out ahead, and on top. You can surmount any obstacle in your way. Just because you love someone, doesn't mean you have to have them in your life. Forgive the petty stuff, and get back to business, living your life. This is overall, a lucky number. *My eyes are open wide, and I let all evil flow behind and away from me.*

**417 - Departure and Return.** This is a tough number,

dealing with lessons and eventual victory over hardship, but only after a long struggle. You are growing spiritually in leaps and bounds, with 417. The difficult areas you are covering, are going to progress your soul growth, and will strengthen your resolve. Your strength of purpose, your steadfastness and dedication to doing what is right, will be remembered. If there is a loss, at this time, such as a beloved pet, know that they will still be with you, in Spirit, sending you love. Another can come to you. Loss will be followed by restoration. *I move with the ebbs and flows of life. All things that end, bring in a new beginning.* Bat Animal Totem.

**418 - Keep On, Keeping On.** Are you a danger to yourself?

Are you having depressed thoughts about a situation, life, or possibly even thinking of ending it all? If so, you need to reassess your situation, and focus on what you do have, and what you can change. Each of us carries our own set of burdens. They all weigh the same, despite the difference in appearances. We each carry a load, whether it is seen by others or not. These types of challenges are what spurs us on, to find answers, do great things, and clear up this karma, so we can finally go home to Source. You are being asked, to examine yourself, your thoughts and your moods. What is causing them? There is always a cause, and you are the solution. *All answers lie within me. I am my own solution, and I take action, to change my circumstances.* Archangel Metatron.

**419 - Full Force Ahead.** 419 is a number of good fortune,

and many blessings, if one does their work. This number achieves. The message is, you reach your goal, when you work through your issues and fears, surrounding it. What needs to be addressed, or looked at, in your current situation? Is there someone, or something you are ignoring or avoiding? Facing fears, concerns or uncomfortable issues now, will open the doors to the happiness that is waiting for you. Say what needs to be said, do what needs to be done, and get it over with. *I face what is in front of me with courage, energy and assistance from the Angels of Source. I surpass all difficulties, and find joy and peace.* Bull Animal Totem.

**420 - Ties That Bind.** This number represents the blessings

of a union. This could be getting married, taking vows of any sort, committing to something or someone, or deciding to follow a health regimen. These promises are ones that you take very seriously, and have importance. Keeping promises to others, and yourself, develops trust. 432 says that what you have committed to, will bear fruit. *I commit fully and wholeheartedly to ________, and am rewarded for my faithfulness.* Ruby.

**421 - Reaching the Peak.** 421 means you have risen above

previous challenges, and are now reaping the rewards of your efforts. You may have something original to offer the world, and you get recognition for this, either on a grand scale, or in your personal life. You are recognized, redeemed and honored in some way. You may or may not want this attention, but 421 says it is well-deserved. It is a good time to put yourself, your creation or your idea out there. Acceptance is most likely, assured. *I am rewarded for a job well-done. I reap the benefits of my efforts.*

**422 - With Eyes Wide Open.** You are trusting the wrong people, or are involved in something that is much more than it appears to be. 422 is a warning to get grounded, and get yourself out of the situation, if possible. When the blindfold is removed, you are most likely going to be confronted with deception, resulting in pain and loss. If you are the victim of this scenario, ask for outside advice, or dig a little deeper into what is going on. Investigate, and then act as appropriate. *My inner self provides me with all I need to know. I understand that difficult experiences are for my own learning and growth. I trust that all is well, and let go of that which is not for me.* Basil Essential Oil, or leaves.

**423 - A Crown of Glory.** There is much to celebrate. 423 promises many benefits, if you flow with the sudden disruptions that can appear on the journey. Something is trying to upset or sabotage your good fortune, but with this number, victory will not evade you. Motivation, combined with common sense and intuition, brings triumph. You will rise above. *I accept that I deserve to be happy, healthy and successful in life.*

**424 - Single-Minded Focus.** Like the number before this one, you are set to succeed. There is nothing stopping you, but your own fears and worries. If you are focused, and stick to the plan, you will come out on top. This means a win. Also an arrival of funding, or money flow. *Abundance flows to me now, and my every need is satisfied.*

**425 - Voicing Truth.** When you speak up for yourself, or state your needs, things happen. Stuff gets done. People show up to help. You may not want their help. If so, you must employ tact, and handle this situation with care. Respect others, but stick to your own judgment. This number says that you are seeing a situation as it is, and that your opinions are correct. Speak out against injustice, and defend the weak. Again, people back you, if you lead the way. Because of the introverted energy associated with 425, you may prefer to be in the background, or work alone. A highly fortunate number. *I have a fine-tuned sense of reality. I trust myself, and respect what I know.*

**426 - Impairments.** This number speaks of handicaps. What is holding you back from what you want? Is it an actual person that is dragging you down, or interfering with a project? Is there some part of yourself, that needs to be developed? This can also speak of actual physical handicaps, such as muscle or bone ailments, or something that you feel prevents you from doing what you want in life. 426 is heavily related to karma, so realize your soul decided to go through this experience. It also says, that if you take the time to meditate on the situation, a solution, or some type of help is at hand. *I am Divine Spirit. I can overcome all obstacles or setbacks.* Blue Sapphire.

**427 - Spiritual Revelations.** This number can mean that answers to your present situation, or life seem to be eluding you. 427 says that these answers are all around you, and within you. Whatever signs or symbols you are seeing in your outer world, are reflecting what is going on in your conscious and unconscious mind. The message here, is to ask your

Angels or Guides to help lead you to the truth you seek. As you turn over your day, to those that can assist you from other levels, you will begin to see your outer world change, as your inner world is healed. Some of this healing may take the form of difficult experiences. This may be the best and fastest route, for you to release what holds you back. Look for your truth. It is coming. *I entrust my day to Spirit. I allow myself to be led.* Archangel Selaphiel.

**428 - Re-naming Yourself**. 428 says that you are like a small kitten, still dependent on your mother, but starting to slowly venture out on your own. It means, that in whatever relationship you are in, project, or goal you have set for yourself, you are still learning and mastering it. It may take a little time for you to put your own unique spin on it, or to get in touch with your true role, in the situation. 428 is a sign, that you are moving into a place of independence and identity. *I come into my own. I am clear about who I am, and my destiny.* Green Aventurine.

**429 - Superficial Beauty.** This numbers speaks of things that aren't real. It may mean, that you are thinking of enhancing your looks or physical appearance, in some way. It also relates to those around you, who may be judging others, based on appearance, alone. 429 invites you to look deeper, at what a person is saying and doing, before deciding to bring them into your inner circle, or be intimate with them. This number suggests that you look in the mirror, and appreciate what you see. Tell your body thank you, for all it does for you. If you are the one judging others on looks, again look deeper, into who the person really is. It may be time to unload your judgments, or unload people. *I am perfect, as I am. I am so much more than a body. I am Divine Spirit.* Silver.

**430 - Sunrise.** You may have just come from a "dark night of the soul". We can have several of these, on our life journey. Maybe it was less drastic, but still difficult. 430 says it is time for a respite. To let go, and be reborn, into a new phase of life. You have the insight, now, and no longer need to stay in that space. The problems may go with you, but you have the wisdom, to do things differently this time. In general, 430 is telling you to trust your inner self, and deny the ego. All is possible now. *I have come through the dark, into the light. All is revealed to me, now.*

**431 - Family Circle.** This number can be very fortunate, if you do not isolate yourself. 431 says the temptation is strong, but you must get out, mingle, network and interact, if you are to achieve your desires. Your connections with other people, are the key to your success. You must also take into consideration, their opinions. You need input, at this time, and going it alone, or relying on your own judgments, could prove contrary to your objectives. *I welcome others into my personal space, and my life. It is ok to need and be needed.*

**432 - Energy Drains and Attachments.** This number talks about energy drains, and includes as the source: other people, depression from childhood abuse, substance use (legal or illegal), negative thinking, watching violent and drug-related movies of dark content, and anything else that brings you down into lower energies. A full cleansing of mind, emotions and body is in order. You have engaged in activity, or been around others who have caused damage to you, or taken on some of their negative or dark energies. If you are utilizing substances that alter your mind, in any way, the advice here is to stop use, and see a shaman for removal of that which may be in your energy field. A house cleansing is in order, as well. Family matters, that originated long ago, include abuse, defining love through abuse, and other wounds that have followed us into our present lives as teens or adults. Set boundaries around yourself, and your home, and take time to heal. *I am a Divine Child of the One True Creator. I am of the light. There is only my creation.* Manganite.

**433 - Second Chances.** This is a number of gifts, rebirth and

second chances. You have been given an opportunity to redeem yourself in a situation, or you are considering giving someone this opportunity. This number says to make sure you really mean it this time, if you are the one being given the new start. If you have been having a bad time, know that everything is looking up. If you have been denied something, it should be arriving on your doorstep. *I open myself to a new energy, and the gifts that are finding me now.*

**434 - Stubborn Mules.** This number speaks of a stubborn

situation, where lines are drawn, and communication has been at a standstill. Two people are hostile, or cannot agree. Or, at best, are being disagreeable. 434 is asking you to look at the experience with new eyes...the eyes of Spirit. See the other as a part of true Spirit, rather than the personality they are acting as. Give a little, to get a little. Compromise. See both sides. Watch what you say. This situation needs healing, and neither party is right. It is a neutral stalemate. 434 says that healthy communication is necessary now. *I silence the ego, and accept my friend/partner/employee/boss etc. as part of the overall design and plan. I communicate with love, because that is all there is.* Blue Topaz

**435 - Rose-Colored Glasses.** Romantic fantasies and illusions are tied to the number 435. If you are involved romantically with someone, give the relationship time to develop, so that you will see their true character, motivation and long term intentions. If you are without a partner, pining for one, is a sign that you are out of balance, and trying to fill a void. Realize that this void can never be permanently filled by a partner, and that you may be better off by yourself, at this time. Romantic partnerships are difficult, over long periods of time. Better to look for your best friend. Either way, you will be lulled into romanticizing some situation or person, and are not seeing clearly. It is best to wait, and ask for clarity from Spirit, instead. *I am Divine Love. Only this recognition, can truly satisfy me.* Amegreen.

**436 - Lose to Win.** This number is a message, that gain will come, but through loss. This is especially true, in family matters, estates and issues with the home, but can apply to any area. Either you have to sell your home and move, or you are required to let something go, in order for the situation to improve. The announcement of good news, will follow, or you will be in a better place on the other side. *Change is necessary, as I welcome in a new phase of my life.* Archangel Jophiel.

**437 - End of the Rainbow.** This number has to do with stories, fairy tales, and the telling of stories. Perhaps you are a writer, or want to try your hand at it. 437 says this is a good time, for creative flow (you may want to read Julia Cannon's

"The Artist's Way"). Also, fairy tale endings are possible. Much luck and abundance is available for you at this time. It may be due to your creative efforts, or something trying to manifest. Have confidence and faith, that you will be rewarded, no matter how seemingly impossible. *I open my creative abilities and imagination. All is possible for me, now.*

**438 - Unconscious Memories.** This number suggests karma, and a need to understand why certain things are happening. 438, says it may be a good time for a QHHT session, hypnotherapy, past life regression, channeling, meditation or some other healing method. These can help uncover where the current difficult energies are coming from, and give you insight into nullifying their effects. Just because we signed up to experience unlucky karma, does not always mean we have to go through it. This number says, in this case, you have a choice. *I am willing to free myself, by facing the past, and uncovering that which lies in my deep unconscious.* Scolecite.

**439 - Respect Yourself.** This number has to do with things being taken away from you. In a material sense, this may be your time, your privacy or actual physical possessions. This is coming from a lack of respect, and becomes a loss for you in some way. People aren't respecting your right to live your life, your personal property, or your body. This could be related to an actual form of physical abuse, or attack, and if so, the perpetrator should be reported. Take measures to protect yourself. 439 is saying to put up your fences. Keep you and your valuables protected from exploitation by others. In a spiritual sense, 439 says that you need to treat yourself with honor and respect. *I love and respect myself. I only accept the same, from others, and I forgive those who are incapable of giving this in return.* Melanite.

**440 - Boundary Lines.** This number has to do with outside stresses, and worries. It deals with control issues. Whether you are the controller, or the one being controlled, 340 is alerting you to pay attention. You need to know when tell another to back off. By letting others interfere, you get drawn into the dramas and unnecessary distractions. 340 asked you to look at the situation you are in, and reassess your role in it. *I allow others their space and focus on my own responsibilities.* Dalmation Jasper.

**441 - Me, Myself and Me.** This number deals with issues of narcissism. This may apply to you, or someone around you. It is the "all about me" attitude, and "my way, or no way". If it is someone else, who has made your needs take a backseat to theirs, know that you were involved in an unhealthy relationship, or association. With this type of energy, the narcissistic person, may try to isolate others, and prevent anything that is not focused on them. This is an abusive relationship. It can be difficult to get away from a narcissist because they tend to tear down your self-worth and self-esteem. If this is someone around you in business, at church, or social events, the advice is to bless them and spend as little time in their presence, as possible. *I attract healthy relationships. I honor myself and others.* Peacock Animal Totem.

**442 - The Light Returns.** The Angels are around you, but it is up to you call upon their assistance. You may sense their presence, or at the very least, know that you are not alone. It is almost like a feeling or mood in the air, that your luck is about to change. Even though you have assistance, the positive changes that are about to occur, are largely up to you. What you choose to do with the situation, will be what manifests for you. In some cases, you may be needing alone time. *I have everything I need. I am always surrounded, by the loving presence of my Angels.*

**443 - The Guilty and the Innocent.** This number has

messages about placing blame. You, or someone else, may need to plead innocence, or seek legal help. Sometimes this is on a small scale, such as others pointing fingers at work, or placing blame on the scapegoat. If you are being targeted in this scenario, know that there is help available. Speak the truth, and let the rest work itself out. If you are guilty, sticking to the truth may be difficult. Use wisdom, and seek professional counsel, or spiritual advice. *I forgive myself, and others. I learn to trust again.* Rhodolite.

**444 - Home Away From Home.** This number signals the

converging of many, from different places. Beings are coming to this planet, from different parts of the galaxy, in order to assist in the growth of humanity. You may be a nomad, calling many places home. You are most likely from another dimension, place of energy, or planet. Earth has become home to many off-world beings, in order for the survival of the human race. They have joined in the struggle, to bring back the light. These outsiders are a gift to Mother Earth. They ground their energy with hers, to hold the planet stable at this time. Whether you feel as if you are one of these beings, or not, 444 is a message that whatever situation you find yourself in, many of your needs may be denied, for the greater cause. It does not mean that you do not have support or assistance, but rather personal agendas should take second place, to what needs to be done here. Make sure your home and affairs are in order, and take care of loved ones. *I am at home, in the Universe.*

*I am one with all of my brothers.*

**445 - Ascending Energies.** This number is connected to the previous one, in that this is the transition period, where there may be much upheaval and change. It is the movement out of the old, so that the new and enlightened can come in. Many souls may be choosing to leave at this time, but know that these were contracts made long ago, before incarnation. All who are supposed to be here, are in position. The Earth, her people and all life beings, are moving into a new phase of being. 445, in a general sense, suggests that you are being too stagnant and controlling in certain situations. You must flow and move with the tide, allowing new energies to penetrate and enter. You are being lifted up, so allow this to happen. *I join with my brothers, and ride the wave into the future. I am at one, with all.* Malachite.

**446 - Charismatic Leader.** This number means you have the power of command. You have the ability to control the mob, or calm the storm. You have a lot of public appeal, and people like what you say, and how you say it. They want to follow your lead. You have the ability to turn situations to your favor. If you are in sales, this is a huge benefit. Use your influence wisely, and for the greater good. *I allow spirit to speak through me, and direct my thoughts and actions.*

**447 - Fair Weather Friends.** The number 447, speaks of a focus on materialism and possessions. It can also relate to home life, and whether that reflects relationships based on money and gain, or love. What is valued here? This relates to those around you, such as friends, spouses, lovers or family members. What seems to be a pleasurable connection, may be based on shallow desires. When others only want you, for something that you can provide, or as a source of fun and enjoyment, then you are devalued. You would be better off alone, then in this transparent relationship. This number could also relate to being left out in the cold, or kicked out of somewhere, that you thought of as home. This includes work situations or romantic relationships, where you felt part of the team. 447 asks you to re-evaluate the situation, and claim your true worth. *I am a Child of Creation. I focus my mind and heart on what is important.* Dog Animal Totem.

**448 - Pending Destruction.** This number has to do with

extreme abuses of power. If the situation continues as is, there will be consequences, as a result. This is a highly karmic situation, that has been replaying over and over, throughout multiple lifetimes. You are involved in a power struggle, and the end result, is the destruction of the situation. One party is suffering, while the other is dominating. This is an imbalanced relationship. 448 also relates to experiences, that hold you in their control. Know that anything we hold onto, too tightly, will be forced from our grasp. The wisdom, here, is to leave the scenario that controls you, or to release your control on the scenario. *I trust my life to Spirit. I am led on the wisest path, for the highest good of all.* Skunk Animal Totem.

**449 - Phoenix Rising.** This number is related to the one

before it, and is the eventual destruction, spoken of in 448. All has come to a head, and must be resolved. This number is a message, that you are moving through the worst, and will come out on the other side. This is the rebuilding from the ashes. There will be endings, or they have recently occurred. This rebuilding process, may take some time, but know that what has been torn down, will rise again in a new form. *I forgive myself and all involved, who are connected to me, through difficult karmic circumstances.* Eagle Animal Totem.

**450 - Ready for Launch.** Things are moving very quickly into manifestation. Whatever you have been wanting, is on its way. The energies have sped up, and sunny skies are ahead. 450 says to be prepared for this windfall of gains, as their appearance may require quick decisions, and a solid platform, from which to launch. Things take off with 450. If you are rushing to catch up, because you have wasted the opportunity to prepare, then this good fortune could pass you by. *I make sure I have planned accordingly, for what I hope to accomplish. I organize and prepare what needs to be done, now.* Gold Star Muscovite.

**451 - Reaching the Pinnacle.** 451 can shoot you straight to the top of whatever mountain you were climbing. The warning is to watch for those behind you, trying to hold you down, or knock you out of the way. This is a number of high aspirations, and determination. You get what you want, because you have put in the effort, and the end is in sight. No matter how minor, or grandiose your goals, accomplishment is yours. Whether you stay "on top", is up to you. *I have overcome adversity, and celebrate the arrival of my desires.*

**452 - From The Ground Up.** See 352, although a more conservative approach is advised. You have a stable foundation on which to build, so get busy, and create your dreams. *All is well in my world. I have all I need to succeed.*

**453 - There is No Lack.** This is a "poor me" number, of longing, and of feeling a lack of worth. This lack translates into literal terms, in your outer world. You may be experiencing scarcity, or "not enough". You might have to scrounge for every penny, live paycheck to paycheck, or cannot buy what you want. In other ways, you feel left out, and a victim to life. This could be a feeling of being tied to a partner, or marriage you cannot escape, or someone holding something over you, which keeps you trapped. The energy of this number, is there is no way out. Because you are so used to feeling this way, it has become a habit, and part of your personal energy. Like any other bad habit, you must break out of this holding pattern of victim-hood, by changing your thoughts about yourself, and life. The Universe is abundance. *I am so much greater than the personality I incarnated as, and can experience that limitlessness now.*

**454 - From the Bottom Up.** This number is a warning, to invest conservatively. If you are thinking about taking a risk, of any sort, the advice here, is to make sure you can afford to lose, if that happens. How strong is your ability to handle setbacks? Do you have back-ups and a strong foundation? Caution, prudence and preparation is recommended. *I take care of my responsibilities, and act with common sense, and foresight.* Guardian Angel Haamiah.

**455 - Golden Touch.** 455 is a number that says the goose has laid the golden egg. You cannot do anything other than win. Whatever you bet on, engage in, speculate about or choose is a winner. Trust your instincts, and pick what you are drawn to, or go with what you are already contemplating. Do not listen to the advice of anyone else, and do not wait. Act now, and the rewards follow. *I cannot fail. I am in Divine Timing; in the right place, at the right time.*

**456 - All That Glitters.** This number has to do with luxury, the aristocracy, royalty and appearances. It has a completely materialistic focus, and can mean being caught up in playing a role, and displaying an image of wealth. This can be a warning of the temptation to go into debt, in order to keep up with someone else, or have what they have. It is a number of extravagance and excess, and you need to pay attention to whether you can afford to spend. The advice is to get comfortable being in your own skin, and being who you really are. Being jealous of, or trying to mimic someone else, is always a recipe for unhappiness and failure. 456 reminds you to face yourself, and find a higher meaning in life. If you are the one that others wish to emulate, you can have feelings of loneliness, as those around you would easily wish to take from you, or only value what you can provide. *I value my true self, and my purpose in being here. The world is transitory, therefore, it has no real or lasting happiness to offer me.* Llama Animal Totem.

**457 - New Exposures.** 457 gives the urge to travel and see new scenery. This number says that you need a break from the usual routine. Immersing yourself into a different culture, will do wonders to shift your mind out of the doldrums. You need a spark of inspiration, and something to stimulate your mind in a different way. If you don't have the funds for long distance travel, then find a restaurant serving foreign fare you've never tried, or visit an ethnic shop or event. Read up on a country you've always wanted to visit, or research the history of a civilization. Be around someone, or something different. *I open up my horizons, and seek the new. Interesting experiences find me now.*

**458 - Wise Use of Authority.** This number carries a lot of power. You have influence, and the ability to sway others to your opinions. Or, you believe someone else is the authority on a matter, and give your power away to them. Either way, 458 talks of intense impact, and the stirring of emotions in others. This would be a good time to ask for a raise, if you deserve one, or make a play for anything that you have on your radar. Use your power wisely, and take responsibility for your influence. If you are idolizing someone else, who seeks to require your deference, than the advice of 458, is to realize your own value. *I acknowledge my own power, which comes from Spirit. I am capable in my own right.*

**459 - Desperate Measures.** This number represents hard pushes, and doing whatever it takes to get what one wants. The image for this number, is someone holding on with their claws, and not letting go, even if blood has to be shed. The underlying motivations of this image are fear, and desperation. This can represent smooth talkers, who, if called out, become hostile. If you are around someone like this, or in this energy, the message is to listen carefully, and if possible, remove yourself from their space. You may be forced to go along with this person, by agreement, or by force. If you are this person, understand why you think you need this particular agenda, and what is it that you fear, if you don't get it. You do not need to fight for what you want, even though you may believe this. There is room for everyone. *I am a being of Divine Love. As such, I am in harmony with the Universe, and I get back what I give.* Sweet Woodruff Herb.

**460 - One Big Family.** This is a very fortunate number, and suggests family reunions, get-togethers, friendships and fun. If you are looking for a new relationship, 460 is telling you that your best friend is on their way to you, now. Opportunities are coming in, including job offers, partnership options and having children. 460 has to do with all your relationships, and connections. It is a good time to buy, sell or create art, and decorate. Throw a party. Buy something really nice for yourself, your home or a loved one. Celebrate what you have, and who is in your life. *I rejoice in the knowledge that I am part of a larger whole. Everyone is a gift to me, and I treat them with gratitude and respect.*

**461 - Sounds of Silence.** The message of this number is a need for silence. Being in a quiet space, as well as keeping silent. It would do you good, to try to go for a period of time, without speaking. Silent meditation, on a regular basis is a suggestion. It is not time to say how you feel about someone, or what you think about their actions. It is not time to speak up, about anything right now. It is a time, however, to get back in touch with your ability to see beauty, to appreciate life, and connect with your inner being. Freeing your mind from the problems, worries and stresses of life, is a must. Develop the ability to be silent...all it takes is a little practice. Observe in silence...this means also silencing your thoughts. View the world from this space for awhile, and on the other side of this period, you will see why it was necessary. *I am silence. I commune with my True Self. I am.*

**462 - Denied Love.** This number has ties back to a childhood, where you were psychologically or physically abused, or put in a subservient position. It can also relate to situations as an adult. It speaks of a dominant party, or parent, that you seek forgiveness from, because you were found lacking. You seek love and acceptance. Regardless of what you think your crime was as a child, or what you were made to believe, you were not responsible for your actions. You were deprived of the love, support and guidance that was the job of the parent, or parenting system...the adults, teachers etc. If these systems failed you, then it is time to forgive yourself. You have no one to seek forgiveness from, and were at the mercy of someone incapable of love. If these patterns are replaying as an adult, then again, forgive yourself. This is all about the lack of love, calling out for love, denying love and feeling undeserving of something you inherently already are. In financial areas, however, this number is a sign of abundance. *I am a Child of the Divine. I am love.* Smithsonite.

**463 - Karma Chameleon.** Things can change overnight. Fate is ushering in a new phase, and this could prove uncomfortable for you. Whatever happens, know that this is temporary, and you will recover. *Spirit uplifts and supports me through any and all challenges, and makes my path straight, and my burdens light.* Orca Animal Totem.

**464 - Six Degrees Of Connection.** 464 represents the building of a solid relationship, as well as karmic connections that are lucky. You cannot fail. Go forward with any plans, or initiatives. *I am joined by the beauty of kindred souls. I am blessed with many friends, and those who wish the best for me.*

**465 - Returns on Ill Wishing.** 465 is related to the deliberate use of dark forces. Whether this is in a literal sense, such as using black magic, being jealous, or wishing ill on someone, the result is the same. This will rebound on you. You cannot get around the law of the Universe, that what you put out, comes back, multiplied. If you are harboring ill thoughts, know that even this type of thinking is having an effect. Anything you speak or think into existence, has a result. The solution is to practice a higher form of forgiveness, such as Radical Forgiveness, or asking yourself if this will be of any importance in 500 -1000 years. Or 10,000 years. Watch a video on you, compared to the size of the Earth, the Sun, the Solar System, the galaxy etc., to regain your perspective. If someone is sending you these ill thoughts, learn to protect yourself, and remove that which doesn't belong in your energy field. *I am Divine Love. That is all that matters. It is all there is.* Dill Herb.

466 - **Much Ado To Undo.** This number carries fear, and a resistance to letting go. Even though solutions to problems may be showing themselves, you continue to remain stuck in, or recreate them. Being up at night worrying, and sleeping in, leads to exhaustion. By anticipating the worst, and entertaining negative thinking, you are making things worse, with pessimism and fear. The advice here, is to cultivate positive thoughts, bless those around you, and give thanks that Spirit is taking over for you, and making things right. *I do not block my good from coming to me. I ask for good, and see only good.* Vetivert Essential Oil.

467 - **Superhero.** You have overcome great odds. You are in the process of conquering the lower nature, and getting in touch with your true Self. It may have been difficult for you to give up the control that the ego desires, but you have learned, or are in the process of learning detachment and trust. Having

faith in Spirit, takes courage. When the ego dies, there is only love left. This may be a lifetime process. In a more mundane sense, this number speaks of surmounting difficulties, learning your lessons, and doing what is right. *I allow my true love nature to come forth, and guide the way.* Vesuvianite.

**468 - Meteor Impact.** This number has explosive tendencies, and tempers that could ignite out of nowhere. Because of its volatile energies, one must be prepared to come up against enemies and those who would thwart your plans. Be careful what you put out into the world, and be prepared for disasters, whether man-made or natural. Tend to your health, and cultivate a healthy lifestyle. Prevention and awareness is key. *I diffuse situations that I know could be problematic. I act with love and integrity, toward myself and others.* Vervain Herb/flowers.

**469 - Responsible Party.** This number has to do with family issues, and yourself. Were you adopted? Did you have an absent parent, or divorced parents? Are you a single parent? This is a number of doing it alone, and lacking family support in some way. Issues from the past, such as abandonment, having to take on adult responsibility too early and the like, have carried into the present. The good news is, that 469 says this energy can be released. Being your own child and parent, fosters a love of self, and in turn, overcomes feelings of emptiness and betrayal. In a general sense, this number can also relate to taking on other people's responsibilities, or being left to fend for yourself, in any situation. *I nurture myself, and take care of my responsibilities.* Lion Animal Totem.

**470 - A Foreigner in a Foreign Land.** Are you trying to learn another language, or applying for citizenship? This number has to do with fitting into alien territories. Maybe you need certain certifications or know how, in order to be accepted. 470 is saying to adhere to the task of acquiring that which you need, so that all goes smoothly. It also relates to those who have had alien UFO encounters, or memories of being abducted. If this is the case, you may need to assert certain boundaries, and intentionally negate any contracts or agreements that were made, with you, or without you, anywhere and in any time period. Whether made in past lives, in between lives, on other planets or unconsciously, you are no longer honoring these pacts. They are against your free will, and rights. *I am at home, in the Universe. All is one.* Calendula Essential Oil.

**471 - Body's Defenses.** This is a warning number, to watch

your health, and keep your immunity up. This is about enhancing the immune system of the body, as well as protection from negative people and thought patterns. It can also relate to someone with hypochondriac tendencies, or you are worrying a lot. It may be a time for a check up, and to amp up your nutritional intake of whole foods. Keep your thoughts happy, watch a funny movie, or lighten the mood. This will brighten your energy, and improve your health. If you are experiencing allergies, this is a sign that you are rejecting, on some level, what or who is around you. If negative environments are bringing you down, get a change of scenery. *I protect myself, by bringing my mind back to its natural state, of love. I am healthy, happy and whole.* Quantum Quattro Silica.

**472 - Divine Revelation.** This is a number of reward, and

states that you are in a space of Divine inspiration and connection. Communication from your guides is clear, and you have nothing to fear. If you have a question, ask now, and you will receive a clear answer. It would also be a good time to use this book, and ask your guides for another specific number that relates to your situation. In a worldly sense, you are feeling inspired to create and take charge of your life. You are in the flow, and sense that things are moving forward toward a more joyful state. Love energies are reaching you. All is working out as planned. *I am at one, and connected with Divine Spirit. All is well.*

473 - **Ancient Present.** This number is related to studying the past, and the mysteries of the ancients. This includes old manuscripts, the Akashic Records, past lives and ancient teachings. You may be motivated, to delve into this information, to assist you at this time in your life. This number can also symbolize learning from past mistakes, so that we don't make them again. The message is to have patience, and take time to study what is really going on, and what has gone before. *The past, present and future are all one. I am aware of how they tie together, and reap the rewards of old lessons.*

474 - **Wrong Road.** This number deals with being led down the wrong path, or things that seem attractive, but are actually not good for you. It can indicate a loss of control, if one gives in to these enticements. When you are exploring, it is easy to lose track of what is right, in favor of what feels or looks good. Take time to step back, before acting or making decisions. *I see clearly, what is real, and what is emptiness.* Komodo Dragon Animal Totem.

**475 - Expert Counsel.** This number means that you have authority to teach, and must use it wisely. This could mean being a literal teacher, especially in areas of spirituality, such as a minister or being involved in your church. 475 can mean teaching New Age principles, or doing lifestyle coaching or anything where you are uplifting the other person. This could also relate to everyday life, and that you are teaching others, by what you say and do. It could mean being an example for your children, or being the party in the relationship who is helping the other person. If work-related, it could mean training others on the job, or simply teaching your customers about what you are selling. It also means that you do not have anything to learn, in your present situation, and have mastered something. *I trust what I know, and help others along the way.*

**476 - The Light of Truth.** If you are experiencing this number, it means that people's opinions of you are changing, for the better. If you were being accused of something, or were cast in a poor light, know that the truth of your intentions and motivations are becoming known. For those who continue to blame, or find fault, the time has come to let them go. Know that the people that should be leaving your life, are going to go now. If you are losing someone, and this is upsetting for you, know that they chose this time, karmically, to leave. *I am truth. I forgive myself, and others, in _____ situation.*

**477 - Nothing Lost.** This number means that you are undergoing spiritual changes and tests. What Spirit is trying to teach you, is that there is no need to suffer. There are many parts of you, of your thoughts and your unconscious mind, that believes you must suffer. Some of these beliefs, you don't even realize you have. Contrary to what the ego tells you, Spirit does not want you to sacrifice anything, but simply to become who you really are, and that is love. This number also relates to the time of autumn, when things clear, the tests are over and the pace picks up. *My true being is love. There is nothing else.* Roman Chamomile Essential Oil.

**478 - The Undeserving Myth.** This number speaks of a life spent struggling. You may have had many goals, but did not believe in yourself, or thought you were undeserving in some way. Know that the door is open, for you to accomplish all that is necessary. You have learned confidence, from your many trials, and learned to stand on your own, instead of letting someone else tell you what you could, or could not do. 478 says it's an excellent time to achieve goals, and to become the person that you always were. *I have accomplished much. I am capable, strong and filled with purpose. Vivianite.*

**479 - Disowning the Past.** This number has to do with all the things that hold you back, and all the ways you hold yourself back. The message is similar to the previous number, 478, in that you have old wounds from a difficult past, that continue to haunt you. These hurtful experiences, have shaped you into the person you are now. The only way to let go of the feelings of lack of self-worth or esteem, that were formed long ago, is to use spiritual forgiveness. Reaffirming and finding your connection to Spirit, your Guides and your reason for being here, are what will give your life new purpose, and release the hold that the past has on you. *I am not, who I was told that I am. My true nature is love. I am a Sovereign Being,* Rhodonite.

**480 - Standing Firm.** This number can mean you are coming up on an exit point, which means there is an opportunity for you to leave this plane of existence, if you so choose. We do have choices in this, regardless of what society or religion may tell us. Some of us are just simply unaware they exist. Exit points, are a backup system, that the soul chose, in case life got too difficult to handle. It is my opinion, that one should *not* take these exit points, unless you are being told otherwise by your Guidance. There is much to be done here, and your soul came in with its own mission. In a more general sense, you may experience some type of ending, that leaves you in a limbo-like state. Realize where you have been, and if you want to continue in the same loop. It may be time for a new direction, a new way of doing things and a new perception of life. Take time to meditate on this, and break destructive cycles. *I am at one, with my soul's higher purpose.* Owl Animal Totem.

**481 - Running to Nowhere.** This number says you may be moving to a new physical location, or moving into a different phase of your life. This movement is related to karma, and may not necessarily be what is best for you, at this time. What is the reason for the move? If any of your decisions are fear-based, then you are going in the wrong direction. If this is the case, plans may fall through, or permanent endings could happen. If the movement is made out of wisdom, and counsel from your Guidance, then move forward with strength, knowing that you are beginning a positive new upswing of experience. *I make changes with ease. There is no force, hurry or fear, in my decision-making.* Guardian Angel Elemiah.

**482 - Now My Problem.** 482 is saying that others around you, or close to you, are having an effect on your health and well-being. It may be in your best interest, to limit your contact with these people. Their responsibilities are not your own. Taking on the energies and dramas of others, when you are already run down, or have enough on your own plate, is never wise. You are manifesting this exhaustion, in your health, your emotional state and in your life, as the pace has picked up dramatically. Note that these relationships have past-life connections, and state your intention to Spirit, to end your role in them. *I take care of what is mine. I allow others to live their own life.* Hyssop Essential Oil.

**483 - I Am Who I Am.** With 483, you have strong ambitions, but reaching your desires, could require unsavory tactics. What you're being asked to do, or who you need to become, to accomplish your goals, may be against your ethics, or better judgment. This number is asking you, to analyze carefully the direction that you're headed. Realize that once you start down this path, it will be that much more difficult to exit. Tread carefully, and look intently, at those you are doing business with, or are involved with, and pay attention to what your gut is telling you. *I live my higher purpose. My will is in alignment with Spirit.* Crow Animal Totem.

**484 - The Maze.** You are being kept, in a rigid box. You may be stuck in a situation, that is denying your power, and your ability to leave. It is a mix of power plays, and unhealthy control. The person you are tied to, is someone you have spent many past lives with, playing this type of scenario, over and over. It speaks of sudden, and dramatic shifts, and bolts of lightning that come out of nowhere. Nothing is predictable with the situation. It is for you to find the way out, as much damage is being done, or you will be forced out, with much fallout. Leave now. Find a way to accomplish this, and free yourself. If it is beliefs that are imprisoning you, now is the time to make the extra effort to overcome their hold on your mind and life. *I am a free Spirit. I make the choice to be who I am, now, and assistance comes to me, when needed.* Deva Quartz, Green Phantom.

**485- The Good, The Bad and The Karmic.** This number has to do with deep soul contracts. This usually has to do with other people, although it is also contracts of certain types of experiences, that you signed up to go through. It is usually a sign of soulmate relationships, and these are either one extreme or the other. The relationship, whether it's a friendship, a spouse, a child, or someone you work with, will be really good, or really difficult. Sometimes you may think it's both, but if this is the case, it is usually the latter. These are experiences, that you signed up to go through, and 485 says that these relationships can be financially beneficial, even the difficult ones. Usually there is a lot of emotional heartache and loss connected to difficult soulmates. Understand that even though your soul contracted to go through this experience, you always have a choice. You can stay or go, and alleviate some of the difficulties, through learning your lessons. *I attract healthy and happy relationships*. Blue Chalcedony.

**486 - Explosive Tempers.** The advice, with this number, is to step carefully into any scenario, in which you are involved. The situation could be volatile, and the best course of action, could be no action. There are risks, that could be dangerous, and things that aren't clear. Deception, violence or disaster, are the more extreme outplays of 486. Combinations of people, can prove unfavorable. Whatever you are trying to accomplish, or wherever you have found yourself, you may want to wait this one out, or bow out gracefully. There are health concerns here, as well as personal safety. It may be time to get counseling, and heal what the issue is. *I am centered, and satisfied with where I am. I do not feel a need to push or force, to get what I want.* Amaranth Leaves/Flowers.

**487 - The Climb to The Top.** This number speaks of having

high ambitions, and meeting with conflict. The situation you are in, has potential, but it is an uphill climb. Know that you will reach your goals, but must endure testing or interference. This could be in the form of competition, rivals or general tests of your measure. If you want it badly enough, you will have it. Just make sure it doesn't conflict with your spiritual desires or true nature. *I can accomplish anything I set my mind to achieving.* Grasshopper Animal Totem.

**488 - Psychic Vampires.** This number has very oppressive

energy. You are being drained by negative energies, that can follow you, from lifetime to lifetime. They wish to drag down the Spirit, and subdue the will of the targeted party. Dark forces do not want you to succeed, especially in spiritual progress, and may be working against you. You may be facing one of the toughest tests yet, and should search out healing work, and decide that you will extricate yourself from those draining you. Put up protection. Ask your Soul for guidance, so that you will have the strength to do what needs to be done. *I am shown the way, no matter how difficult the path.* White Copal Resin.

**489 - Dangerous Waters.** This number is directly related to 486. It is a very explosive situation, or has the potential to get out of hand. Proceed with caution. Its like handling dynamite, whether you know that is what you are holding, or not. 489 says that you will eventually be removed from this energy, if you handle things correctly. *I am safe in Spirit, and know what is the correct action to take, in all situations.* Nettle Herb.

**490 - Tremors Below The Surface.** This number has the same meaning as the one before it, as it has the potential to be unsettled. The energy here, is not as precarious, as long as you do not give in to your lower nature, and low vibration emotions. Especially anger. All can be overcome, with higher Divine Love. *I acknowledge my true being, which is love, and only act with love.* Tasmanian Devil Animal Totem.

**491 - Wise Investment.** It is important for you to meditate, stay centered, and keep your emotional state balanced. Do not give in to lower base emotions, and allow them to take over. This can be a lucky time for money ventures or investing, as long as you take measured action, and a balanced position. Check the facts, and don't involve yourself with anyone who is giving you reason to doubt them. *I move forward, with wisdom and a well-devised plan.* Elephant Animal Totem.

**492 - What The Eyes Don't See.** This is a warning number, of keeping your eyes open. There are those around you, who would steer you wrong, just for the sake of doing so. This number promises assistance from others, but be aware of their scruples and ethics. Your intuition is strong, so learn to define between that, and emotional reaction. If something seems good, but your gut is telling you something doesn't feel right, it probably isn't. There can be much enjoyment at parties, celebrating and the like, but possible run-ins with people from the past, or family members, who want to start drama, or trouble. Be wary with this number, but go forward with what you are trying to accomplish. *My instincts are crystal clear. I know what is good for me, and what is not.* Magpie Animal Totem.

**493 - Save For A Rainy Day.** This number is speaking of a

failure to plan ahead, for difficulties, or kinks in your plans. What you are striving to achieve may not work out, because you have not prepared for possible difficulties. You need back up, savings, and a contingency plan. Things may be coming to a standstill, or an ending. Know if this happens, you will need to regroup, before going on from here. What is supposed to happen, will happen, and it will be for the best, regardless of what you may think, at the time. *I am ready to succeed. All is happening for a reason.* Green Calcite.

**494 - The Gateway Home.** This number is a sign of a final

test you are passing through, in relation to letting go of the fear of not having enough. Making sure you are taken care of, but don't hold on and horde. As you release the hold materialism has on you, you experience the wonders and joy of this number. You have true power, because you are not controlled by want and seeming need. True freedom lies in being able to release your fear, of even death. *Nothing can hold me down. I am true Spirit.* Red Agnitite.

**495 - Make Believe You Believe.** This number points to emotional blocks in your meridian system, and the flow of energy in your body. There may be blockages in your circulatory system, your lymph, or your air flow. Acupuncture would be helpful in restoring your health, as well as dietary changes. Seeing someone versed in Chinese medicine and the acupuncture points, can help get your system functioning again, and as a mirror effect, remove obstacles on your path. If you want something to happen, you have to believe it is possible. You create the obstacles. Success is your birthright, and only you, can screw it up. *I let my energy and mind flow in harmony with the Universe. I am led to where I need to be, and all is well.* Anandalite.

**496 - Gifts From The Universe.** Things come easily, with this number. If you want something, just ask. There will be someone to give it to you, or the Universe will bring it. Trust is the key, here. If you are demanding, or manipulating to get what you want, this will backfire. You will always pay a price, when things aren't done for the higher good of all. A sunny path is in front of you, and a new birth. This can be literal, such as a baby, the beginning of a project or business, an artistic creation or a rebirth of you and your belief system. All is new, and the answer is "yes". *I join with the higher good, and my blessings flow.*

**497 - Shedding Your Skin.** This number has to do with situations that don't live up to your expectations. What you are wanting may not be what you are getting. People may appear one way, when they are really another. This number also has to do with unrealistic expectations, or putting too much pressure on someone, to be a certain way. 497 is a message, that you are choosing to be someone that you are not, as a way of hiding from, or not accepting yourself. This usually comes from childhood identities, and the ways that we were taught to perceive ourselves. This is not always accurate, to what is actually true. 497 is asking you to look deeply within yourself, without fear, and see who you really are. Be more authentic, and know that it is safe to be you. *I love and accept my true self. I do not have to please anyone, or meet their expectations. I am who I am.* Mockingbird Animal Totem.

**498 - Meeting Challenges.** 498 is a sign that you will get

where you're going, but you will have to make it through the obstacle course first. There are hills you have to climb. The message with this number is, if you stick to the path, you will eventually accomplish your goals. There may be parts of yourself that have to develop first, in order to become that, for which you are striving. *I have strength of purpose. I am willing to do what is required, to reach my goals.* Fox Animal Totem.

**499 - Stay Present.** This number can mean that you are not

paying attention. You are too focused on going where you are going, and not noticing the scenery or who/what is around you. Not being aware, can lead to difficulties, or lead you into situations that were not what you thought they were. Being in a rush to get where you're going, can make you trust people that are not trustworthy, or sign documents that shouldn't have been signed. This number is urging you to slow down and take notice, before plunging ahead. This is also a number of completions, and the end of old cycles. *I am fully present in the moment. I am aware, and take notice.* Mouse Animal Totem.

**500 - 5$^{th}$ Dimension.** This is a powerful number, of change and miraculous occurrences. This is "life in the fast lane", the movers and shakers, and those who are making things happen in the world. You are able to manifest, a lot quicker. There is a lot of movement and activity. 500 says that you will almost surely succeed. 500 is also symbolic of a new race of mankind. A fifth dimensional reality, and a shifting of the spheres. *My thoughts become things. I manifest quickly and easily. I maintain my energy at a high vibration.*

**501 - Choices in Value.** Do you love yourself, or do you seek

this love in possessions? Be your true self. Act as that self would act. Be an incarnation of love, and all the so-called pleasures of the world will be but pennies in comparison to the riches of the Spirit Self. *I am love. I am one with all things.*

**502 - We Are Family.** This is a number of magical

partnerships. You are with, or about to meet, someone you can join with fully, on a soul level. This is a pairing of kindred spirits, soulmates, Twin Flames and other powerful relationships. It is a joining together of like minds for a higher purpose. You have much in common, on many levels, or are complimentary opposites of each other. Either way, this coming together has brought much love to the planet, and much satisfaction and support to your life. Whether this meeting is for long or short term, depends on the higher purpose. Know that when you meet this person, you are fulfilling a large part of your spiritual destiny, here. 502 is also a merging of your opposite selves, such as masculine/feminine tendencies etc. *I am merged fully with the Divine. I have all that I need, and am blessed with my soul family.*

**503 - Winning Ticket.** 503 brings the message of money and abundance in all forms. It is a worldly number of increase, gain and riches in all undertakings. This would be an excellent time to take a chance in the area of speculations and investments. Whatever you are investing in, whether it be a relationship, funds, a business idea or a creative project, 503 says you are set to win. *I am in the direct flow of abundance. Prosperity is mine.*

**504- No Place Like Home.** Another level of karma is being experienced with 504. It is a number of home life, and feelings of security. Do you have a home that feels like home? Are you comfortable in your own house? 504 can also relate to arguments in the household, or tensions. On the other hand, it relates to issues with monetary security, with the home life as the focus. 504 is a need for grounding, worrying about issues with mortgages/rent payments, missing old childhood homes, and needing to feel at home in the world. Know that what you are searching for, is your real connection with Divine Spirit. *I am at home in Spirit. I am one with all, and I ask to experience this now.* Comfrey Root.

**505 - Evolutionary Choices.** On a spiritual level, this number, means that you're being a given a choice. Stay at a lower vibration, or advance on to a higher plane spiritually, and move yourself forward on the path of evolution. Abilities, that are considered “not normal”, or unfamiliar are developing. This number also deals with thoughts of brotherhood, and higher-minded thinking. You are thinking more of the overall good, rather than self. There are elevated thoughts, and higher knowledge, channeling through to you. Your Guides are with you, and asking you the question,

"Which is it going to be? Staying as you are, or progressing at this time of evolutionary leaps and growth?" *I walk the path of Light, and trust that I am being led to where I need to be.*

**506 - A Helpful Companion.** This number says that small tasks and everyday work, may be the focus, at the moment. Finishing things, and tending to what needs to be done, is important right now. You are very busy. Do you need a personal assistant, a nanny, an organizer, or help to take the load off? Don't resist delegating to someone else. Not everything has to be perfect, and neither do you. You will be of more use to yourself and others, if you get help carrying the overload. You will be able to communicate with kindness, from a more centered, less harried space, and you may find, that your life becomes infinitely more fulfilling, with time for much-needed fun. *I find calm, in sharing the load. It is okay for me to let go, and accept help.*

**507 - Peaceful Space.** This is a number of spiritual challenge, where certain things may have to be given up, in order for you to have the peace and serenity you seek right now. 507 says to let go of what is unimportant, does not serve you, or requires you to be something that you are not. What seems a sacrifice, or hard to leg to of, will actually bring relief. You can then have much needed private space to think correctly, and perceive your future. Peace of mind is the most valuable commodity there is, other than time. You get both. *I choose to do what is needed, to enable me to find my center, and be healthy and in harmony with life.*

**508 - Guided Support.** This number is a sign, that those on the Other Side are trying to contact you, your mediumship skills are very strong, or they are developing. You are strongly guided, at this time, by your Spirit Guides, Angels, ancestors, loved ones who have crossed over and those that are from your world of origin. Listen to, and pay attention to the signs and symbols being given to you. Ask for information that you need, in order to help you on your journey. *I trust my guidance, as I am surrounded by Guides and Angels of the highest caliber.*

**509 - At Your Request.** This is a number of strong will, and magnetizing what you want. You have an extremely strong presence, and what you focus on, is coming to pass. Your desires are being met. You have strength, and leadership ability. You are a visionary, and set the tone for others. What you say, goes, and your wish is the Universe's command. Call forth that which you need. You will have it. *I am thankful that I am provided for; I call forth ______.*

**510 - Nose To The Grindstone.** 510 says, if you do the hard work that is necessary, you will achieve success, make a name for yourself, or whatever is your goal. Hard work can mean actual work, as well as working on your fears that block you from achieving. What needs to be done, in order for you to get where you want, or have what you desire? You have a lot of positive energy backing you, at this time, so if you get busy, you see results. Remember the journey is as important, as the finish line. *I am willing to do, and face what is necessary, to reach my goals.*

**511 - New Being.** This number means the choice has already been made, between the light and the dark. 511 has to do with the shifting into fifth dimensional reality, and choosing the path of light. The ascension process has begun with you.

Know that lifetimes of spiritual progress, will be made in this lifetime. 511 also means networking with spiritual friends, or groups. Connecting with like-minded individuals, will be beneficial for growth at this time. Camaraderie and the sharing of viewpoints will be helpful for you, such as a meditation, or discussion group. *I am becoming light. That is all there is.*

**512 - Forward Vision.** This number says you have the ability

to see backward into the past, and forward into the future. If you are not using your psychic abilities, 512 is asking you to spend time developing the one which is your strong area. This number says you are a seer, which would suggest the ability to see visions. 512 is also sensing or knowing certain things, with no explanation of where the information came from. If you are needing information, 512 says, the answer is within you. *I see clearly, all that I need to see.*

**513 - Forecast For Change.** This number is saying that good

news is coming, and things are about to change. Look for trips being planned, or adventure coming to the forefront...long distance travel for business, pleasure, or opening your mind to new philosophies. If you were waiting on an answer to a problem, know that resolution is coming, and it will be positive in the long run. *All change happens for the better. All is righting itself, in _______ situation.*

**514 - Present Company.** If you live alone, it may be time for

you to find a companion, or some company. Sharing is called for, here. If you are with someone and feel alone, then spend more time together. The message is the same for any relationship...share time and love. *I open myself to others, trusting that Spirit brings to me, what I need. I let love flow through me, now.*

**515 - Magical Energies.** This is a number of high magic, and represents energies being pulled through, from intentions sent out. It is a warning to be careful, what you are engaging in. A single-pointed focus, brings results. Be sure that your focus is for the good of all. If someone is practicing magic against you, protect yourself, and send them blessings. Spell work uses dark entities to deliver the desired result, and this is harmful energy you do not want in your life. *I take care, with my words and thoughts, as they manifest into reality.*

**516 - Loosening Your Grip.** The need for control, and trying to get things perfect, is resulting in endings and pain. Take all others into consideration, before insisting on having your way. If you can go with the flow, and not insist on your own way, then life can lead you to more pleasant experiences. You will have more enjoyment, and happier outcomes. You can be shown a new way of looking at things. *I let life be, as it is. There is no perfect, as all is changeable and in continual motion.*

**517 - Coming Full Circle.** This number relates to soul growth, and your mission here. You have accomplished a level of mastery. It hasn't been easy. You have come through a difficult time period, recently, but are not returning. The past situation has ended, and you are moving into a new phase. On a soul level, you have achieved much. Be kind to yourself, and know that you have support from the Archangels, and all of those, in alignment with true Source. *I fulfill my purpose, because I have come through the storm. I find strength to carry on.* Pink Tourmaline - Elbaite.

**518 - Completed Tasks.** This is a very fortunate number, and means rewards are coming for a job well-done. This number is saying, when you knock, it will be opened. You have good karma coming to you, for your progress in past lives, and in this life. There is not much that is preventing you from succeeding, with 518 at your back. *I accept my rewards from the Universe. I am deserving of all good.*

**519 - Candle in The Dark.** You have a lot of light energy, and therefore may be surrounded by psychic vampires. These are in the form of people (boss, coworker, codependent friends or lovers, etc.), as well as energy entities. Just as the moth seeks the flame, so is the dark drawn to the light. Darkness seeks to extinguish your light, so that it can feed off your negative emotions. But darkness cannot smother light. Light shines through the dark, and makes it disappear. *I am the light. I cannot be anything, but light.*

**520 - Family Picture.** This number alludes to problems in early family life. 520 asks you to focus on where you are at, now, and the bigger picture. On higher levels, we are all connected together as a family, whether we are biological or not, and can choose who we want to be, as adults. Make your life new. Connect with the One Spirit, and feel the sense of unity. Know that you can come out of the past, and be born anew. *I release old pains, as no longer being in alignment with my true Spirit. I am one with all, and I join in that energy, now.*

**521 - Holds Barred.** 521 is a number of acquisition, with a possible delay. This number can bring in great riches or wealth, great ideas and gains. It is a power house. Rewards come with a karmic price. It is up to you, whether it is worth it. Your willpower can carry you through. *I allow Spirit to direct my path, for the highest good of all.*

**522 - Differing Views.** 522 says very different energies are trying to work together. There may be frictions or issues that come up but as long as you are realistic about the situation, everything should turn out fine. 522 says do not walk blindly into anything, assuming that everyone has your same intentions. Keep your eyes open for deceit, and act with wisdom. *I acknowledge all viewpoints, but stay true to the vision, or goal.*

**523 - Universal Guarantee.** This is a number of good fortune, and ease of accomplishment. Everything is lined up for you to succeed. You cannot fail, and should continue forward with any undertaking. *I am successful. Everything and everyone blesses me, and I bless them in return.*

**524 - Says or Does.** This number has to do with partnerships. Pay attention to someone's actions, rather than their words. And watch that you don't say too much, too early. Keep some things to yourself, and this should prove to be a positive relationship. This number is fortunate, in a general sense, but carries the same warnings. *I approach relationships with caution, and let them develop in their own timing.*

**525 - Prophesied Arrival.** This number is related to the one before it, and states that analysis is needed in relationships. In an added sense, 525 predicts new relationships coming in. Have you sensed someone important about to enter your life, or have you had a reading where this meeting was predicted?

Maybe your guides have been telling you a partner or someone significant is coming. This is the waiting, or in between stage before this occurs. *I open myself to beneficial relationships.*

**526 - Stick Around.** This number says your situation has harmony, but there are things brewing beneath the surface. You may think someone involved, is here for the long term, but this may not be the case. Or aspects of the situation are not solid. Know that whatever you are involved in, has potential, so don't give up. *I accept that things may not be as they appear, and if change happens, it is always for the best.* Monkey Animal Totem.

**527 - Magic Wand.** This is a very lucky number, and means that anything you undertake, has a magical quality to it, and is set to win. Especially if you are the one in charge, or who put things in motion. Whatever area of life this applies to, the message is to go for it. *I can and will succeed. Everything works in my favor.*

**528 - Do Over.** A lot of people and situations, that you are encountering, are related to past lives, and some of these memories and lessons, may be coming through, at this time. You have been held back from a lot of things, or from getting what you want. There's been a lot of drudgery and continual work, with no signs of progress. Know that this is connected to these past and future energies, and it is time for you to start uncovering the layers of fear that lie within your unconscious mind. This will release you from this endless cycle of repeat. *I bring my consciousness fully into the present moment. I do not allow fear to rule my decisions, or my thoughts.* Howlite.

**529 - Friendly Foes.** This number has to do with betrayals, from those you consider to be friends or loved ones. You have certain people around you, that would backstab, or do what was necessary to save their own skin. 529 says these are people that you trust, and their deception is unexpected. Realize that people act in this way, because of fear. Forgive them, and let it go. Understand that some of these relationships may be coming to an end. Better friends, associates or partners are on their way. *I attract loving relationships, based on trust and genuine caring.*

**530 - The Guiding Light.** 530 says that you are the master of your fate. You have come through many lessons, hardships and karmic circumstances. You have learned much, and cleared layers of fear. Now it is for you to choose your destiny, and know that you can determine your course. The way is no longer set, and the script is open for you to decide. Therefore, choose wisely. *I have made much progress in self-mastery. It is up to me to choose, and I align my will with Spirit.*

**531 - Hiding From The Past.** This number has to do with resistance. You are avoiding something, because it is easier to hide, then resolve it. This may be a particular situation, or just issues within yourself. The war is within, and it is up to you to end it. No one can do it for you. You are no longer your past, and must let go of this, as you are becoming more of your true self. *I choose happiness, therefore I trust in doing that, which I fear to do.* Guardian Angel Barakiel.

**532 Goodwill Rewarded.** This number is speaking of the depths of wisdom. You possess this, as well as a good amount of luck. What you put out into the world, with your thoughts, will instantly manifest. *I align myself with good fortune. I wish the best for everyone.*

**533 - Penny In The Fountain.** There is not much that holds back the success of this number. It is extremely lucky, and wishes find fertile ground. *All my dreams are fulfilled. All is available to me.*

**534 - U-Turns.** This is a number of insight and illumination. Situations that were headed one way, may be reversed, and what you thought to be true, may turn out to be the opposite. Be prepared for switch-arounds, as what you thought was sure, may be unraveling. This is happening, so that you learn a new way of seeing. 534 is a sign that you need to be focusing on spiritual matters, and your inner guidance for direction. *I have Divine Clarity. My way is sure.*

**535 - Executive Influence.** This is a powerful number of advancement and recognition. If this is related to business or work, it signifies influence over others and that your opinion has sway. Your word is law. Beware of those around you, who try to block your progress, or are jealous of your accomplishments. Try to work alone, if at all possible. If related to personal relationships...love could be hard won. *I use my power wisely, and with caution.*

**536 - Perfect Aim.** A highly fortunate number in career and your personal life. Things become easier. It may get so busy, that you may be inclined to neglect your health, or take precautions. Enjoy the abundance that flows your way now. *I* *am in the Divine flow, now. All that I aim for, comes to me in a perfect way.*

537 - **Sign Post.** This number is a crossroads, with choices to be made. There is no wrong decision; only your personal preference. Whatever you decide, or if you have already made a decision, know that you will have help and assistance for whatever you need. *The choice is clear. I know exactly what I want.*

538 - **Equal Measures.** This number says that you need clarity, on whatever you are considering. Some of what you are envisioning or wanting, you are not ready for, and the advice is to reevaluate. Are you truly up to the task, or is it in alignment with your goals? If you take action before you are ready, the result may not turn out as you had hoped. Start smaller and take one step and one piece at a time. *I move and act with patience and forbearance. I take the next logical step.* Analcime.

539 - **Importance of The Journey.** 539 says you are jumping ahead, and skipping an important step in between. It is related to the number before it, 538, and asks for patience and concentrated effort. In the end, you will succeed, but the means is what is important. *I succeed through careful thought, planning and action.* Guardian Angel Asmodel.

540 - **Separate Lives.** This number is a sign of loneliness and isolation. You may be living like a hermit, or avoiding people. Perhaps you need this time away, to regain your energy and recharge. If you are separating yourself, due to anger, this is not healthy or beneficial for you. Maybe the separation is only

at the mind level, or maybe you are ignoring someone. The advice is to face the situation, and find resolution. Hiding will change nothing. *I bravely face that which may seem uncomfortable, so that I might find comfort again.* Platypus Animal Totem.

**541 - Surprise Party.** This is a sign of success in all

undertakings. Something really good may show up out of the blue. Be on the lookout for surprises. The answer is a resounding "yes"! *I am in the Divine flow of blessings and miracles.*

**542 - Lucky Star.** 542 is very lucky! It can overcome any

seeming difficulty. This number is connected to the one before it, and promises blessings. *Divine prosperity finds me, now.*

**543 - Watch Your Back.** This number is a warning about the

path that you are treading. You may want to think carefully if you continue. Be wary of friends, coworkers or associates at this time, as there may be a bad apple in the mix. Other people may be willing to let you take the blame for something, or aren't taking you into consideration, with decision-making. *I choose my path wisely, and allow Spirit to lead.* Cat Animal Totem.

**544 - Home and Hearth.** This number is a sign of unexpected

changes, that create success, in a worldly sense. It may also signal a time, when you are having emotional ups and downs. Otherwise it portends material security, especially within the home. *I am at one with my good. I always have all I need.*

**545 - Creating Love.** This number is connected to creative energy and all the forms it takes. This includes children, ideas, enjoyment, hobbies and romantic love. Anything brought forth, at this time, is extremely beneficial. Let the creative force flow through you. Your creations have far-reaching effects. *I am one with the energy of creation. I allow myself time, to explore this area of my life.*

**546 - Price Tag.** This number is tied to exploitation, or using others for gain. You could be tempted to take an offer, because it is a stepping stone to where you need to go. Be sure of what you are getting yourself into, and that no one else is getting hurt in the process. Although temptation can be strong, remember that you always get back what you give, or in other words, there is always a price. *I have all I need. Spirit provides that which is necessary for my life.* Hawk Animal Totem.

**547 - Power of The Word.** This is a highly lucky number, if one is careful with their words, and doesn't walk on other people's feelings. It relates to quick and sudden changes and emotional interactions. *I honor and respect others. I speak with kindness and love.*

**548 - Hidden Intel.** The goals you have in mind, are achievable, if you are willing to do what is necessary to make them a reality. This number has a lot of support behind it, and in-depth information that can help you in your quest. You know the way, so get started. *I can reach my goals. I support myself and have confidence in my ability to succeed.*

**549 - Slave and Master.** This number warns of confrontations, and feelings of superiority. You may have someone around you, who thinks they have all the answers (or the situation is reversed). You may be put in a subservient role, but it is not where you belong. Bless those who would treat you as such, but allow these scenarios to end. You need to be uplifted. *I am at peace with myself, and with all.* Wood Thrush Animal Totem.

**550 - Leprechaun's Gold.** This number has to do with fast movement and change. It is high success and victory. Luck abounds. *I am in the flow of luck.*

**551 - Enough For All.** A number of luck, combined with caution. Other people want what you have. This number says to watch your back, as other people may be saying things that are not in your favor. Curb the urge to retaliate, bless your enemies, and give thanks for what you have, in order to shift this energy. *I am grateful for my many blessings, and wish the same for others.*

**552 - High Positions.** This is a good number for intuition and guidance, but warns in the areas of advancement and promotion, relating to material goals. Even though you may succeed, you are in dangerous waters. Take care to acknowledge your surroundings at all times. I am protected by Spirit. *I am always in the right place, in the right timing.* Opal.

**553 - Abundance Earned.** This is a number of luck, coming from past life reward karma. It has monetary gains connected to it, but implies general luck in all situations. Ask for what you want. *I am in the flow of luck and abundance.*

554 - **Homework.** To accomplish what you want to do, more schooling or education is necessary. You don't have all the tools or knowledge needed, as of yet, to succeed. Realize that this is a step by step process, and you are in the beginning preparation stage. *I apply myself to the task at hand, knowing that in the end, I will achieve my dreams.* Red Amethyst.

555 - **The Sky's The Limit.** This is a high vibration number, of extreme talents in art and music, mastery of language, eloquence of speech, and luck with business and investing. Your mind moves quickly. Assistance comes when needed, for any accomplishment. The world is your oyster. *I give thanks for my good fortune.*

556 - **Warning Whispers.** This number asks you to pay attention. There are things being said, that you need to listen to, and heed. This may be from someone around you, or from Spirit. Whatever message you are being given, follow its advice, and take it seriously. It could relate to a change you need to make, or a warning. Otherwise this number ensures luck. *I listen with open eyes, ears and heart. I am always told what I need to know.* Yellow Scapolite.

557 - **The Lure to Lull.** 557 is telling you to slow down, and take a better look at things. It encourages you to get in touch with your spiritual self. It is a wake-up call, to jar you out of the lure of materialism, and acknowledge your true purpose in being here. You have come, as an agent of love and peace, and Spirit is asking you to carry out your mission. Have you been too bogged down in everyday life, goals or material desires? It is time to find some balance, and see that there more important things going on, in the overall bigger picture, than

what this transitory life could offer. *I align myself with my true nature, which is Spirit. I rediscover and remember my true purpose in being here.* Manatee Animal Totem.

**558 - Weeding The Garden.** This number asks you to release all that is not serving you. It will be released anyway, but you cooperating makes it easier. Get rid of unnecessary items, and deadwood. Get back to basics. Realize that some needs to stay. Just as some weeds are beneficial, if one looks carefully, so prune only that which no longer serves a purpose. This relates to your material life, as well as unnecessary emotions and thought patterns. *I shed the old, so that I can thrive, and the new can be born.* Spruce Essential Oil.

**559 - Angel Trumpets.** There is nothing stopping you from reaching your goals. This is a happy time. You are given what it is, you desire. *I enjoy my happy life, and give thanks.*

**560 - A Bridge Of Words.** This number comes with a desire to be useful, or of service. It may require you to speak out, and defend others, or say what needs to be said, when you would normally hold back. You are a champion for other people, and your role, right now, is important. You have a way of expressing yourself, that will be accepted, and get done, what needs done. *I am the vehicle for truth. I am essential to the overall plan.*

**561 - Entwined Worlds.** This is a number that talks about the "in-between". It is the times that fairies and nature spirits are most active, and most likely to be encountered, in magical places that live outside of this dimension, and its rules. These times can be dusk, sunrise, and other instances when the energies are not definite, or are shifting. If you are in a high meditative or trance-like state, these beings are more visible. When our dimensions overlap, they are accessible. It is also a time, when your Guides can deliver relevant information, guidance and prophesy. Heightened awareness and senses come with 561. Look for the invisible, and the "impossible". *I am in tune with all life, in all dimensions of time.*

**562 - Circular Passages.** This number has to do with things

that go in circles, and oracles. Anything that predicts the future, or is connected to time-lines from the past to the future is 562 material. It is related to oracle cards, tarot, crop circles, runes, the I Ching, and anything else that contains messages of old, for the present and future. Things go in cycles, and this number clocks our revolutions around the Wheel. What was old, is new, and what has gone before, will come around again. This can be applied to your current situation. Much success comes from being able to see the whole spiral, and make a wise choice. *I have clear vision. I see the past, and its relationship to my future.*

**563 - Advantageous Associations.** This number speaks of

privileges, and having inside information. You are connected to the right people, and have many opportunities open to you. This is a number of divine success, and succeeding through word-of-mouth promotion. *I am divinely connected to all who can help me. Everything always works out for the best.*

**564 - The Veil Of Pretense.** This number says you may be

blinded by someone's appearance, or unaware of your own motivations/intentions. It asks you to look carefully beneath the surface. What are the inner values, of the people you are dealing with, and what are your own? These are important questions, as they will determine what happens. If trust is placed in the superficial, or the uncaring, the results may not benefit you. Do what is right and ethical, and think of the whole, not just the ego-self. *My true nature is Love. I only attract those, with honorable intent.* Green Apophyllite.

565 - **Righteous Reward.** This number can go one, of two

ways. It is connected to 564. If your intentions are in the right place, and you are aligning yourself with ethical people, then the material, emotional and spiritual rewards of this number are many. If you have chosen the left-hand path, from 564, then your situation is set to fail. Betrayals and power struggles destroy what was built. *I choose wisely, and hand over decision-making to Spirit.*

566 - **Top Honors.** You are the whole package, and with this

number comes advancement. You have the wisdom, work ethic and know-how to be considered for high level positions or esteem. You are recognized, and compensated, for being you. *I am whole and complete. I have everything I need, to succeed.*

567 - **Prospering Through Planning.** This number

symbolizes an unorganized mind. You need a plan, for things to work in your favor. If you are at the beginning of an ending, you must plan your exit, as well as what comes on the other side of it. Worrying and obsessing will not help the situation, and is unnecessary. You have the strength to see this through, and come out ahead. Focus on this, in order to bypass the unpleasant. In this way, is a happy ending found. *I am calm, and poised for success. I am organized, and make a plan to triumph.* Horehound Leaf Herb.

**568 - Labors Of Love.** This is a number of success in the careers of writing, journalism, speaking, life coaching or anything where you are interacting with others, through communication. It is a career focused number, with the message, that you can do what you love. This number says to explore, and find out what that is. If you are already doing what you love, 568 is a number of success and advancement. Overall, this number is lucky for any area of your life. *I enjoy the fruits of my labors, as my work is love, and love is my work.*

**569 - Extrasensory Energies.** This is a number of psychic energies, and their influence on you. It is a sign of enhanced psychic abilities, but also a lot of paranormal activity around you. If you are in fear, these energies can be disruptive and possibly harmful. Make sure to protect yourself, and eliminate fear, or any vengeful thoughts, anger or sadness. These emotional energies, will lead you down the wrong path. Otherwise this is a positive number, of assistance from others. Just be careful of your motives. *I am of the light. I attract only the good.*

**570 - Crystal Ball.** This number is connected to the one before it, as it deals with psychic abilities, information and revelations. Your ability to see the future, is increased, at this time. If you are having predictive dreams, or information coming to you about the future, pay close attention. It may be good for you to sit quietly, and receive information, in areas that are of concern. 570 says, that the predictions will come to pass. *I am given all that I need to know, so that I may act with wisdom.*

**571 - Soul Contracts.** 571 says that you are either in a relationship with a soulmate, or about to meet one. It warns that you are not seeing the person, or the situation from a clear and logical mindset. What may seem to be a joyful reunion of souls, is actually hard lessons to be learned. If you learn these lessons, and go through the experience, it will either end in its own natural way, or the situation will improve, as if reborn. If the relationship ends, this is a signal that there is a better partner for you, coming in. The soulmate can be any type of relationship to you, not just a lover. Know that some of the difficulties involved with this person, are not really lessons, and therefore unnecessary for you to endure. *I am love. I attract divine loving relationships.* Swan Animal Totem.

**572 - Taking A Trip.** 572 may be giving you the opportunity to travel, especially if that involves traveling for educational purposes. It involves fast movement, higher learning quick changes and growth. It would be an excellent time for you to take a trip, to a mystical site, such as Stonehenge and other stone circles, Machu Picchu, Sedona, Newgrange, healing wells, etc. If you are unable to travel, reading about and looking at images of these places, can help shift your energy. In general, this is a lucky number. *I raise my vibration, by learning ancient mysteries. I am always in the right place.*

**573 - Manifest Your Desires.** This number has to do with manifesting your intentions. It is a very fortunate number, that brings your desires to you. 573 says to visualize what you want, communicate that to others and see results. *I know exactly what I want. All that comes to me, is for my highest good.*

**574 - Overcoming All Hurdles.** This is a number of goodwill and good luck, in overcoming any obstacle or difficulty. It is a winning formula, and brings that which you desire. These gifts from heaven, will come in a natural way, as they are karmic rewards. *I am confident that all works in my favor, for the good of all.*

**575 - Suspension Of Time.** This number says that you are in

a waiting period. It is a time for you to contemplate, understand and receive guidance, before moving forward. The temptation is escapism, fantasizing, frustration, nervous anticipation, boredom or despair. Use this time for what it was meant for, and the rewards of clarity and joy will be yours. If your life is at a pause, it is for a reason. *I see clearly, the path that I must follow. I am led to my good.* Snail Animal Totem.

**576 - Powerful Responsibility.** This number says to use

your power wisely. With 576, the Universe is reaching out its hand, and giving you what you want. Unless you are a fairly evolved soul, the danger here, is that your power over others will have a destructive influence. You must be coming from a place of concern, not losing sight of the other people that are affected by your decisions. Denying ego desires, and relying on your inner self, for the direction of your thoughts and choices is necessary. *I use my power wisely, and Spirit works through me, for the highest good of all.* Sardonyx.

**577 - Spiritual Mastery.** This is a number of high spiritual

advancement, direct communion with Spirit Guides and teachers, as well as the possible apparition of Ascended Masters. It is a number of high honors, and spiritual evolution. Your skills for channeling, psychic interpretation and healing are at very high levels. This is a number of worldly and spiritual abundance. *I am dedicated to my path. I am supported in my purpose.*

**578 - The Oppressor.** This number shows a lack of

acceptance, and goals not lining up as desired. With 578, you may be having feelings of not being good enough, having to act a certain way, or play a certain role, in order to be accepted by another. It has oppressive energies, of not getting what you want. Your desires, or desiring another person, seem to dominate, or have control over you. The advice here, is to release and let go of anything that challenges your self-esteem, value or integrity. *I am one with Divine Spirit. I'm a child of Source, and worthy of all good things.* Woodpecker Animal Totem.

**579 - Duplicitous Double-Dealings.** This number has to do

with psychic boundaries or space. It is connected to invading other people's thoughts or psychic energy, as well as manipulation for control. This can be likened to someone reading your psychic energy, in order to gain information, or fool you. Psychic charlatans, scammy businesses, or propositions are included here. *I maintain my boundaries and personal space. I interact, only with those who have my best interests at heart.* Porcupine Animal Totem.

**580 - Position Of Leadership.** 580 is a number of success.

Because it is a number of worldly and material success, it is sometimes used by those who are devoted to dark side worship. However, for the light worker, or for the mystic, this number connects you with those in high places of power and influence, and you generate their support. It also relates to being moved up into these places of power, which allow financial prosperity and the realization of your dreams. 580 says that you have tremendous influence. *I use my gifts for the benefit of the higher good.*

**581 - Eye Of The Tiger.** This is a number of achievement,

while enduring frustration and setbacks. It may feel as if you are fighting against constant obstacles, or against yourself. There is a lot of energy, however, behind this number which suggests accomplishment, regardless of the difficulties. You will fight through, and succeed, because it is your destiny to succeed. The obstacles are lessons and strengths that need to be learned, in order for you to reach your goals. *I am determination. I am willing to fight through that which is necessary, in order to achieve my end goal.* Yellow Opal.

**582 - Humble Leader.** This number is a warning, and is

connected to 580 and 581. When we are put in positions of power, whether that be in a relationship, or a career, our weaknesses can become problems, and interfere with our ability to lead. Power for the sake of power, desire to dominate, manipulation and treating others as inferior or without value, can be the trap into which we are drawn. 582 says to resist the habit of giving into your own insecurities, which will make these negative traits come out, in your leadership position. For no one is a true leader, without also being a follower. The student is also the teacher. For long-term happiness, you must understand that any type of leadership or superiority position, is a gift that can be taken away, at any time. Treat others with respect, and you will be respected. *My role as leader, is not about me. I serve Spirit, and the higher good.* Iolite.

**583 - Small Steps To Success.** This number suggests being in a situation, where you are just maintaining, or existing. It seems as if your dreams are forever crushed, by the need to maintain a daily existence, or responsibilities to others in your daily life. Sometimes it can feel as if you're just going through the motions, but this number says what is needed here, is a more realistic view. If you will work within the confines of your situation, instead of trying to escape, you will begin to see your dreams build on a daily basis, with daily effort. Decide what your life will be like, and begin to take the small steps, that you are able to take, to reach this goal. Determine whether time, finances, responsibilities etc. are the obstacle, and find small ways to get something accomplished. *I do not have to give up my dreams, I simply need to keep my feet rooted in reality, and create from where I am.* Spiderman Jasper (black and orange).

**584 - Building The Dream.** This number is connected to 583, and suggests certain areas that one may need to sacrifice, and order to make daily steps toward your goals. Discipline and determination, are needed here. 584 is a fortunate number. It is a guarantee of success, not through sacrifice, but through giving up the unnecessary, and that which blocks progress. *I can reach all of my goals and dreams. I am successful.*

**585 - Tug Of War.** Opposite ends of the spectrum meet here, and try to influence the outcome. Your drive may be motivated by emotional responses, and not by clarity. The changes that happen here, happen quickly, and may not be for the best. Try to sit back, and calmly analyze a situation rationally, or get input from someone objective. Once you have centered yourself, you will see what action, if any, is wise for you to take. Otherwise, you are swinging between extremes, and will make a mistake. Find the middle ground. An energy balancing may be needed. *I always act from a calm and centered space. This is where all answers are found.* Baltic Amber.

**586 - Crowning Achievement.** There is not much stopping

you, with this number. All systems are go, and whatever you wish to accomplish, has the blessing of the Angels. Serendipity abounds. *I am luck. I am good fortune. I celebrate my success.*

**587 - Predestined Pain.** This number carries heavy energies,

of oppression, depression, and a materialistic negative outlook. You may have gone through many difficulties in childhood and in life, which has brought you to this present state of negativity. The message from this number, is to realize, that your current situation is a result of previous karma. Understand that you as a soul, decided to come into this life, to pay for past mistakes. Therefore, forgive those you are involved with, forgive yourself, and decide to change your path and break the cycle. It is not necessary for you to undergo these experiences, and once you wake up to the truth of where it has come from, you can begin again. *I am renewed in Spirit. I have not left my source, for Spirit is always with me.* Tangerine Quartz.

**588 - Eventual Victory.** Any number containing 88, is

connected to dark side energy. However, since I don't want to add to their influence, I always encourage everyone to use the higher side of numbers. This is a number of important karmic choices. If one makes the wrong choice, and aligns himself with greed and other dark force energies, one will eventually fail. This is a number of overcoming the lower self, and learning that this is not your true identity. 588 says that you will be victorious, after the karmic struggle is over. This struggle is with yourself. Know that you are a Divine being of light. *I choose the higher path of forgiveness, and light.* Chrysoberyl.

**589 - Cold Hard Look.** This is a hard number, of extreme

difficulties. There is much conflict, possible violence and challenges with this number. You must get out of your emotional self, and use logic, reason, and see reality as it is. Your intentions may be pure, but the situation or the people that you are involved with, are not. Look with new eyes, and see your value. You are deserving of love, happiness, respect and peace. *I am a child of the light. I understand, and see clearly.* Bowenite

**590 - Crowning Achievement.** Knowledge and wisdom

have brought you far. This number is connected to using your gifts, to attain your goals. This is a highly fortunate number, and should be regarded as certain success. *I use my gifts, with wisdom and enjoy the benefits.*

**591 - The World Is My Playground.** This number has to do

with beauty, personality, charm and getting your way. You are magnetic to your good. It is a number of powerful success, favors from others, and reaching your destination. You have been given the keys to the kingdom. Use them wisely. 591 suggests the ability to procure beautiful surroundings, a likable personality, talents and assistance. *I am gifted, and share my good fortune with others, as there is enough to go around.*

**592 - Student And Teacher.** This number has to do with learning new skills or pursuing new interests. You may be led to explore astrology, numerology, or other metaphysical practices. Study and personal growth are highlighted. Returning to school as a student in any capacity, or a teaching role is indicated, with this number. New subjects for learning, change your perception on life, and replace old ways of believing and seeing the world. Explore your passions. *I am ready to learn. My mind is always stimulated by taking in new information.*

**593 - Waiting Your Turn.** This number talks about a struggle between getting what you want, versus giving up your needs for other people, or responsibilities. Know that your efforts are not in vain, and you are doing what is necessary, at this time. Things will eventually shift, and you'll be able to move into a more satisfying phase. *I take care of what is in front of me, trusting that Spirit knows best.* Frog Animal Totem.

**594 - Face The Music.** 594 is hidden frustrations that lead to outbursts of anger, and loss of control. The draw to escape through self medicating, or masking emotions with medication is strong here. Know that this cycle can end, if you don't ignore the issues, and work through what is causing the upset. *My happiness is not an escape. I am strong, and have faith that wholeness is restored.* Black Spinel.

**595 - Sunny Side.** This is an excellent number of good health and good fortune. Put plans into action, and celebrate the good news coming your way. *I am in the flow of the Divine. All good awaits me.*

596 - **Knowing The Way.** Your intuition and sense of

emotional currents is high. Your life has taken, or is about to take a turn for the better. Much help and assistance is coming. You should be able to accomplish your aims. You are being led, and sense the right way to go. *I am in tune with all of life. Everyone benefits me, and I benefit all, in return.*

597 - **Out Of The Rain.** You may be going through

difficulties, but 597 says that you will break through and reach your goals. If your focus is on the higher good, and you follow the advice being given to you from your inner guidance, you will eventually break through and be victorious. *I am fully aware of my inner self, and hear it's voice clearly.* Guardian Angel Emmanuel.

598 - **Faithful Follower.** This is a number of trusting, or

putting faith somewhere it doesn't belong. If your answers, or happiness is in something outside of yourself, you will experience difficulties and disappointment. This number can mean giving time, or money to a cause, or to something that is not what it seems. Put your faith in your inner knowing alone, and not in the world, and you will find peace. *I trust Spirit to lead the way. My true happiness lies within.* Chamomile herb.

599 - **Lucky Days.** This is a fantastic number of walking into

the sunset. It is the final phase of trials ending, and life working in your favor. It is reward for lessons learned. A highly favorable number, for any venture. *I am grateful for my good fortune.*

**600 - Beauty Of Love.** This is a very high energy number,

that is fortunate in the areas of love relationships, service-oriented business, the arts and good health. It is a number of direct angelic contact, via visions, voice or inspiration. It is the joining of others, to bring the beauty of love to all. *I am blessed daily, in many ways. My future is bright.*

**601 - Being Yourself.** This is a number that relates to possible

marriage, commitments and devotions to a spiritual cause, or community. It could be taking vows to help with the needy or homeless, or to defend animal rights. In general 601 is a commitment to self, which in turn, is lived out in the world. *I commit to that which is in alignment with my true being.*

**602 - Undesirable Combinations.** This number is

represented by oppressive partnerships and liaisons. Joining or connecting with another, in any manner, can turn into something undesirable. 602 represents something that starts well, and ends in pain and loss. Be wary of anyone coming into your life, related to mergers or commitments. *I am whole unto myself.* Rainbow Moonstone.

**603 - Baby On Board.** This number has to do with

communications and broadcasting. It also has to do with additions and expansions to the family, such as a new child, grandchild, or pet. This is a highly fortunate number that predicts many blessings. Timing for this number can be September into October. *I am part of the larger whole. All blessings flow to me now.* Goose Animal Totem.

**604 - All Roads.** This number has to do with securities, and striking out on your own. Which path should you walk? The way of independence and possible risk, or the tried and true? Either way, 604 signals good fortune. *I am lucky, and all ways prosper me.*

**605 - Play Time.** This number asks you to look at what you

are neglecting in your life. This is not so much about responsibilities, but rather neglected enjoyment. Do you need more fun? Romance? Time with kids? Time with your pets, hobbies or getting out with friends? Or just time to yourself? 605 is the number of magic, and childhood dreams. It is a number of miracles and what makes life worth living. Hope. Pleasure. Enjoyment. Make these a priority, right now. In general, this is a good number for financial investments, such as art work, or objects to invest in, as well as charitable giving, that pays back later in karmic reward. *I am allowed to play, and enjoy my life. I find pleasure in living.*

**606 - Time Out.** 606 is about love. Where is it needed in your

life? It may be time for you to step back, and take stock of a situation. What is your purpose in it? Where can you bring more love? What is the spiritual purpose? This number is about viewing everything from a perspective of love. Your life becomes more beautiful, when you view things in this way. This is a number of luck, in finding peace and contentment. *Divine Love flows through me now.*

**607 - The Nodes.** This number speaks of your spiritual

purpose in being here. It is directly related to things that are easy to do, versus things that are unfamiliar and new. 607 says to realize that doing what is easy, just because you are good at it, is not necessarily the way. These are dead ends. Your opportunity, is to do what you've never done, and find purpose and pleasure from it. Do what is natural to your temperament, but is a path untried. A study of the North and South Nodes, in astrology, would be helpful in explaining this in more detail. With the new, you step into your power. This number is close in meaning to 47. *I walk a new path, bringing evolvement and fulfillment. I bravely step into the future.*

**608 - In The Money.** This is a number of immense karmic reward. It states that the individual will prosper, in almost all undertakings. This is particularly beneficial for finances, business ventures, positions of power and influence, advancement and returns on investments. All is as it should be, with 608. *Abundance flows to me, now. My goals are achieved.*

**609 - No Holds Barred.** This number has to do with things of the Earth, and their value. It represents success with nothing standing in the way. When you decide what it is you are after, this number delivers. *I am Divinely blessed. I have all I need.*

**610 - Monastery Habits.** 610 is related to past lives and carryovers into this life. You may have spent a previous life as a monk, or taken vows of celibacy. In this life, you are comfortable being alone, or have issues with aloneness. You may need your space to keep yourself centered, and retain your energy. Perhaps you are an empath. 610 is coming up, to let you know that you may have a helpmate coming, who will be complementary to your lifestyle. It is up to you, whether you want to receive this. Your life is on track, for your spiritual purpose. *I am always in the correct place, and have what is necessary for me.*

**611 - Spectator Inspects.** Words can make or break this situation, whether directed at yourself, or outward. Also, what others are saying to you, may not be the whole truth. You can get into trouble, by agreeing to something, or voicing your opinion. It is best to say nothing, and observe objectively. Does this have love as its basis, or are people feigning interest? Are the motivations connected to good intentions, or is there deception? *I quietly observe, and in doing so, receive all the information I need.* Ajoite.

**612 - Listen And Learn.** This number is related to pauses in life, and time periods for reflection before action. Your Guides have much information for you, and are asking you to open and receive. Your clairvoyant abilities are strong, as well as your ability for spiritual journeying to other dimensions, for healing. Whether or not you recognize these, you are being given much psychic information, at this time, in order to expand your current view about life, or a particular situation. Take the time to tune in. *I am in tune with my guidance. My psychic senses are open.*

**613 - Beginning Again.** This is a number of good luck, new relationships and the renewal of love. Reigniting old partnerships, and all new beginnings are connected to this number. Decide what you want, and it comes to you. All is possible, and your future awaits. *I am blessed in many ways. My future is filled with joy.*

**614 - Cooperative Connections.** This number says you have many positive connections, that lead to success. It is a matter of getting the word out, and letting others know what you need. It may be helpful to write down your goals, and the time frames you would like to see certain things happen. The Universe is willing to assist in making them a reality. You are surrounded with support, and cannot fail. *I am connected to a greater whole. I am blessed by all.*

**615 - Pleasure-Seeking.** This number has to do with beauty and enjoyment. It is a break, a vacation, or a time to enjoy that which is pleasing to you. Going to a movie, an art museum, a concert, or getting out of town is beneficial. Also air flights, air planes and jet-setting. A very positive number, and a sign of good luck. *I enjoy my life. I am able to take breaks, and see the world.*

**616 - Rediscovered Freedom.** This number has to do with abrupt endings, and major life changes. These are very positive, and for the best. You will be more empowered, and your load will be lightened, on the other side of these endings. This is a positive number of a new life, a new calling and coming into your own. *I am reborn in Spirit. As I release the past, I welcome new energies and ways of being.*

**617 - Bumps In The Road.** This number is setting you up for success, with some minor setbacks. Overall, what you are aiming to achieve, has been destined to be a win. Keep to the course, and you will definitely see happy results. *I am blessed with goodness, and lessons that help me grow.*

**618 - Appearances.** This number has to do with the trappings of surface value. It is idolizing beauty and looks. 618 says you have to act and look a certain way, in order to be accepted, and supported. It is basing things on exterior value, instead of what is inside. You will have to look deeper here, if you want to avoid the trap you are about to fall into. And the trap may look like a lovely oasis. *I am not fooled by outward appearances. I am shown the truth.* Lepidocrocite.

**619 - Binding Fears.** 619 says that if you hold on too tightly, you get nowhere. You want to escape from feelings of "not having", or losing control. The advice is to choose the freedom from not having to decide or act, at all. Allow Spirit to lead you, and the situation will resolve itself. Trust that no matter what happens, it is for the best. Spirit will never lead you wrong. Only the ego (fear) does that. *It is safe to release and let go. Only good can happen in this situation.*

**620 - Where I Belong.** 620 talks about things that are not alike, and trying to fit them together. The results can be loneliness, heartache or feeling abandoned. This number is about exiting abusive, or hurtful situations, and honoring your true value. Find like-minded people, who have your best interests at heart, and associate with them. If you don't believe you have value, or are undeserving, then hang out with supportive people who think you do. *I attract situations that uplift and support my true nature, as a Child of Source.* Wavellite.

**621 - Aim High.** Whatever you are considering, 621 says to aim for the highest. You are going to achieve it, so ask for the best and reach for the stars. This is another number of guaranteed success, so go ahead and shoot the arrow. *I achieve all I set out to do. I am blessed.*

**622 - Impossible Dreamer.** 622 says you are being unrealistic in what you are pursuing. The situation is not what it appears to be, and even though your intentions are pure, you are not surrounded by the same. Do not give your trust blindly. If you take over the reins, you will begin to see reality, free yourself, and find a happy conclusion. *I see clearly, the truth in all situations.*

**623 - Don't Sign.** This is a very lucky number, especially for

help and assistance, as long as you don't sign any contracts, or become obliged to someone else. Many want to assist you, but do not join forces, or owe these people, as that could prove to be a bad decision. Stick to what you know, and work toward your own goals. Accept help, but keep yourself free, and not held to any reciprocal obligation. Avoid commitments and negotiations. *I am free to do as I please. I am not beholden to anyone or anything.*

**624 - Love Affairs.** This may be the start of a new

relationship or friendship. Be sure not to give too much, at first, until this proves to be an equal partnership of give and take. Romantic interludes, and attractions to the opposite sex, are highlighted. Make sure that you are not giving up part of yourself, in order to be involved. Don't enter into anything that asks too much of you. There are people who are truly beneficial, and time may seem to stand still, when you meet them. Your connection is from outside of time. Soulmates, Twin Souls and the like, are featured. *I attract healthy and whole relationships.*

**625 - Happiness Earned.** This is a number of much-deserved

success. You have good luck coming to you, and should say yes to whatever you are involved in. *I appreciate my many gifts, and am grateful for my success.*

**626 - Sacrifices and Blessings.** 626 has to do with fertility and growth. Particularly in the areas of childbirth, family and finances. It alludes to having to juggle more than one thing. Perhaps you are having more children, or having to work two jobs. Maybe you are a single parent. Taking care of dependents, may mean sacrificing a relationship, or time. Wanting money, may mean sacrificing a relationship, or being able to have children. Where your focus is, is where the growth happens. *I know what is important to me. I find joy in living.* Guardian Angel Hahaiah.

**627 - Setting My Sights.** 627 steers you toward success, but only to the degree that you will allow success to come to you. Do not let lower-level desires get in the way, as this will block your good. Keep your eyes to the straight and narrow, and your success is assured. *I desire only the good, for myself and others. I am blessed in many ways.*

**628 - Merry-Go-Round.** You are reviewing the past, and deciding that you do not want to repeat the same mistakes, or attract the same type of person the next time around. You are looking for something new, or better than the current situation you find yourself in. Ask for help from Spirit, to be released from the continuing cycle of beginning, then having to start over. Forgive the past, and allow Spirit to take over. In this way, you can break these repetitive cycles. *I let go, and let flow.* Rue Herb.

**629 - Difficult Terrain.** This is a number of karmic burdens. It involves the areas of relationships and desires for power or prestige. Many battles and loss can happen with this number, due to hard lessons that need to be learned/experienced.

Eventually, you will exit this pattern, and find peace, but you must go through the discomfort first. Forgive whatever comes up, and all involved. *I ask Spirit for strength, in order to do what I must do. I forgive myself and others, and find peace.* Pyrope Garnet.

**630 - The Winning Point.** An excellent sign of victory in all undertakings. You can do anything you put your mind to accomplishing. *I am blessed. I achieve my desires.*

**631 - One Is Lonely.** This can be a reclusive, or lonely number. It suggests avoiding others, due to previous pain and heartache, or betrayals of trust. If you continue in this space of avoidance, you will only suffer, and not rebound, or move on from the trauma. Repair rifts, or heal the damage done to you, by trying again, and keeping your eyes open. What you think, you will attract, so don't pull in the same energy this time around. *I open myself to loving and trusting again. I trust myself, and that is what is most important.* Dragonfly Animal Totem.

**632 - Speaking Out**. Stand tall, and don't be afraid to speak your truth. What you ask for, comes to you. Speaking with love, will bring love and prosperity back to you. You can accomplish many things, by simply allowing love to flow through you, and speaking the truth, now. *I am love and truth. I am provided for, by an abundant Universe.*

**633 - Eternal Blessings.** A number of wisdom and enlightenment. Your ability to see things as they are, is bringing good fortune. Use what you know, and be a vehicle for Divine Love. *I celebrate the many benefits coming my way. I act with wisdom.*

**634 - Butterfly Emerging.** A number of karmic lessons learned, that ultimately brings about change for the better. You are morphing into a new life, with hidden talents. You have removed a layer of fear, and broken through an old cycle. This could be a lifestyle change, such as going vegetarian, but the possibilities are limitless. *I move into a new phase of love and light.*

**635 - Broadening Your Position.** 635 relates to expanding one's territory or environment. You need a place where you feel nurtured, and can relax. If someone is in your space making this difficult, you need to carve out an area to call your own. This can also relate to looking for land, building a home, or expanding your portfolio. This number is expansion in all areas, especially with your financial sector, status and ability to influence those under your responsibility. *I have room to grow. I reach my highest potential.*

**636 - Enjoyment of Life.** A reward number, that applies to all areas of your life. Enjoy the benefits and gifts that are headed your way. *I am thankful for all that is given to me, and I open myself up to receive with grace.*

**637- A Mystic Is Born.** Spiritual values are changing. You are being shown what is important in life. This may be through experience, or direct messages from your Guides. Being around others who share your values, will give much needed support. You view is getting ready to tilt on its axis, as a new perception is born. *I am truth. My life and my thoughts reflect this, now.*

**638 - Timeless Connection.** You may be receiving messages of hope and love from the other side, or talking with the dead and departed. Look for signs that deceased relatives may be sending you, to get your attention. Ask for help, from those you have lost. You may receive a vision, or visitation from Spirit. *No one is ever lost to me. I still feel the support of those I have loved and lost, with me always.*

**639 - Hidden Treasures.** Buried gifts, talents and abilities are coming to the surface. Good luck that seems hidden, is coming into the light of your consciousness. Good fortune is yours. *I am capable. I have all I need.*

**640 - Forest For The Trees.** You have tunnel vision. You must become more aware of who and what is around you, if you are to avoid being taken advantage of. You can create situations to your liking, but must first be more realistic, and get out of your own head. Good luck follows. *I am wide awake, and alert. I see what needs to be seen.*

**641 - Prize Catch.** This is a number of favors. Many step up to the plate to offer what you want, or need. The Angels are prodding you forward, and showing you the way. Happy partnerships are also highlighted. *I receive all blessings, with love and grace.*

**642 - Another Chance.** This number signals an improvement in relationships. It means taking a pause, to realize and be thankful for what you have, and give time to another, so that they can accomplish their own growth, as well. It relates to giving someone (or yourself), another chance, or allowing them to redeem themselves. At the very least, it asks you to forgive what has been done. *I create happy relationships with loved ones.*

**643 - Fail to Succeed.** This number says to take the time, to see clearly where you are headed, and carefully map out all strategies to get there. This number can warn of plans being upset, by unexpected changes. If you know change is coming, prepare for what comes after. Don't stop, simply because things don't seem to be turning out as originally hoped. There is a better way, and failing may be the way to finding it. *All experiences are leading me to my good.* Guardian Angel Vehuaiah.

**644 - Silver And Gold.** This number is connected to monetary gain, and gain through partnerships. Other people's money is finding its way to you, or they invest in your future. Investments are secure. You can accept these financial gifts, but stick to your own advice about where it goes, or how it is used. Group ventures are fortunate, as long as you are the one leading. *I am blessed with monetary abundance, and find financial freedom.*

**645 - Deceptive Attractions.** This number is talking about scruples, or the lack thereof, relating to situations or people you may be involved with, at this time. Realize that you may be being sold to, or being asked to sell yourself. Think deeply, about whether this is really worth it, in the long run. Ethics are something, that once lost, are hard to find again. Keep your actions aboveboard, and do what is right. It is okay to have what you want, just go about it in the correct way. *My soul is more important than temporary satisfactions. I always do what is right, and am rewarded in return.* Archangel Iah-Hel.

**646 - Long-term Possibilities.** This number talks about two

people building a solid foundation together. Both parties must be careful, not to let insecurities, possessiveness or control issues get in the way, of what could be a very beneficial partnership. If both are coming from a true space of centeredness and wholeness as individuals, the joining can be beautiful, with many depths. This number bodes well for long-term relationships. For business relationships, both parties must be confident, and have equal measure to bring to the table. If this is the case this can be a beneficial partnership based on trust. *I attract partnerships, that are holy, healthy and happy.*

**647 - Mission Of Peace.** This number is talking about a

spiritual vision for the future. You are motivated to bring peace and harmony to others, as well as share your love. This is why you are here. Your soul knows this, and if you are not yet aware of your purpose, you will be getting more information and experiences soon. This number may also have to do with moving, or traveling for spiritual purposes, such as volunteering for mission service, visiting a place of high vibration, or going to an event to meet other like-minded individuals. *I am dedicated to my purpose. I find joy in my path of service.*

**648 - Fear And Repression.** This is a difficult number, of

karmic obstacles. The heavy energy here, can bring on depression, listlessness, and frustration. The obstacles can be in the form of karmic relationships, setbacks, or just plain bad luck. A lot of these come out of the blue, and begin to affect your psyche. Doubt, fear and the anticipation of failure creeps in. These negative emotions, which essentially boil down to fear, are coming up for you to clear them. Do not let negative energies have or take over control, over your right to happiness. *I can overcome all things, as Source energy is within me.* Orange Calcite.

**649 - The Morning After.** This is an ominous number, relating to dangers, and bad omens. It is connected to endings of all kinds. The message of 649, is that some things cannot be avoided. If you can make it through the darkest times, the Sun will always rise. And your Sun will rise, after this dark period is over. Depending on your previous karma, and what you have done with the negative energies from 648, will depend on the severity of the circumstances with 649. Everything can be made easier by turning your life over to Spirit. *I am comforted through the darkest night. I am cleansed and given strength, to weather any storm. I have no fear, for the Sun will rise again.* Smoky Quartz.

**650 - Sincerely Yours.** 650 relates to messages of love, especially those that are written, such as love letters, emails or text. Good news is coming, and the way is clear. Communication is highlighted in all relationships. This is a time of happy messages, announcements and feelings. *I give and receive love, and am filled with joy.*

**651 - Contest Of Wills.** There is a lot of drive and energy with this number, which may call for a need for calmer space, where you can reflect, meditate or pray. Getting too caught up in the momentum can get you lost, and you will miss important things, mistakes can be made, or the situation comes to a standstill. 651 carries a lot of masculine force, and the energy of competitiveness. A calmer passive approach is needed, before the situation backfires. Otherwise, this is a highly dynamic time, where a grounded approach brings success. I act with foresight and wisdom. *My choices are based on the highest good, and I prosper, in return.*

**652 - Born Again.** Changes are coming, and life improves.

This number has to do with new chances, fresh starts and beginning again. These come quickly, as the movement with this number is swift and certain. Endings become beginnings. *My life is being reborn for the better.*

**653 - Migration.** This number is connected to 652, and

signifies movement forward, in a literal sense. Are you considering moving to a new location, or is this shift symbolic? 653 involves expansion, as well. Are you moving to a larger house because you are increasing the size of your family? Whatever you are heading toward, or moving into, it will be bigger and better. *All changes are for my highest good. I am blessed with what I need.*

**654 - Angel's Ears.** Trust that what you are putting out to the

Universe, is returning to you at the perfect time and in the perfect way. The angels have heard your request, and are assisting you in all ways. Anything is possible, if you have faith. 654 warns that trusting in anything of the world, to bring you happiness, or be your answer now, will be misleading. Trust only in a higher power, and follow the instruction you are given. *I am empowered by Spirit. Only my inner guidance knows the true path to true joy and prosperity, and I trust it to lead me, now.*

**655 - Objective Accomplished.** This is a symbol of the successful completion of goals. Aligning your intentions with spiritual truths and having generous intentions for all involved, will help you reach success. *I achieve my goals and desires. All are benefited by my efforts.*

**656 - Loving Life.** Know that whatever you are considering at this time, is going to be successful, as long as you are approaching it with loving intentions. Doing what you love, and sharing it with others, is the key to a happy life. *I can accomplish anything I set my mind to obtaining.*

**657 - Wise Sage.** This number has to do with conflicts and resolutions. You may need to seek out counsel or advice, in order to understand your current blocks and difficulties. Whatever is causing the trouble, outside help will get you a new perspective. Otherwise, things remain at a stalemate. *I am always given the help I need. All answers find me now.* Bornite.

**658 - At Your Command.** This number is material reward, good luck and a great deal of power. It represents ruling positions, being at the head of something and life going your way. Rejoice. It is an excellent sign that things are in your favor. *I give thanks that I have all I need. My every wish is provided for.*

**659 - Labels of Oppression.** This number has to do with your family lineage, ancestors, changing a surname and social classes. It deals with relationships between people, that have to do with labels of superiority or inferiority...that you are, what you are born into. Have faith in yourself, and do not label who you are, in connection with childhood beliefs imprinted on you. You are a powerful being, in your own right, and no label could ever define you. 659 also says you can break ties to patterns that are handed down through generations. It is time to end the cycles, and not pass them forward. *I am a Divine being. I am the light. I am love. There is nothing else.* Douglas Fir Essential Oil.

**660 - Pondering Peace.** This number has to do with the deeper realms of consciousness, and the unconscious mind. It would be wise to meditate, visualizing yourself merging with all. Open to receive guidance and information, in your meditations, and you will find the answers to all problems. What was hazy, is clear. *I immerse myself in the pool of consciousness, that joins all beings as one. I bless and honor my brothers.*

**661 - I Love Me.** This number has to do with love of self. This can also have to do with having a career in modeling, or doing something, where you are the focus. This can relate to being a public, or religious speaker, a teacher, an authority figure, or someone who is looked at and noticed. This is about respecting your physical body, and its limitations. If others are passing judgement, see yourself through the eyes of love. Good energies flow to you now. *I love and approve of myself. I am Divine Love made manifest.*

**662 - Lovely Love.** This number is about giving love, and letting its energy flow through you, in all communications. If your actions are based in love, there are no consequences. If your actions are based on selfish desires, you will most likely not be happy, in the long run. *I choose the light. Divine Love flows through me, now.* Morganite.

**663 - Wise Teachers.** You may encounter someone acting as a sort of guru - someone who comes in for you with a message, or guidance that helps you, and gets you on track. Much assistance is coming to you now, especially in the form of spiritual advisers, or those with the wisdom to help you. Training, hard work, and taking action, are suggested, as this number guarantees success. Especially in relationships with partners, family, the arts and business. *I am guided in all ventures and undertakings.*

**664 - Gimme A Break.** This number speaks of rigidity, and needing a change of scenery. Taking a small trip, a drive, or an extended vacation by yourself, will help you to loosen your grip on whatever is pushing, or driving you to over-do. Get out of the house, or go away by yourself, in order to refresh and clear your head. With a break, comes clarity and direction. *I am relaxed, and at peace. I let go, in order to avoid burn out, and wait for divine guidance to point the way.*

**665 - Loving Intent.** This number is directly connected to 662. *I choose to express love.*

**666 - Unmasking The Beast.** As with all numbers, this one can be used to promote good, or evil. 666 has been singled out, however, and become a symbol of the dark side and the devil. Some references state that "the number of the beast", was originally 616. Me personally, I don't care, because I don't choose to give power to dark forces, but rather circumvent their influence, turning all things to Love...by going within.

Anything created by ill intent, is not the true nature of reality. So, what is 666 about? 6 has to do with values, money and the material world. It is related to the planet Venus, and what we love. Therefore, we can say that a triple 6, is an overabundance of worldly influence, and a warning to get your values in place. Trusting in a world that is only going to change, and eventually claim you in death, is not a sure road to anything but misery of the soul. It can mean a great increase in finances and material reward, which is good, but at the cost of going down roads of emptiness and eventual depression. Robin Williams comes to mind, here, as someone who had the world in his hands, and was so depressed, he ended up committing suicide, when drugs, or alcohol failed to block out the pain. This number is a calling back to Source. To love. Unconditional and with the will to only bless one another. 666 warns of uncertainties, related to temptations that are not as they seem...darkness that appears to be the light (darkness always plays on your fear). Temptations that name the devil (other names here) as gods. What an empty existence, following such a trickster, as you could literally die tomorrow, or in the next 5 minutes. Because die, you will. And where is the devil, then? What did he really give you? Empty material objects. Fame and seeming power that imprisoned you. 666 says, "Don't be fooled!" There are many trying to lead you down the path of satisfying cravings, which are inherently related to your fear. Why let fear rule you, in the deceptive form of comfort, found in meaningless worldly power? Your satisfaction will be temporary and brief. 666 also says you have the remembrance of Divinity within you. That it is time to end this cycle of reincarnation and worshiping a world, that is really just pain, underneath all the enticing trappings. Every delight here, has a payment, a suffering, a punishment. You know this. Step forward, and deny the empty. Call forth your true power, in Spirit. The rest is creations of the lower mind. With inner knowing, all else will be added, as your every need will be supplied. *I am a Co-Creator, with Source. I cannot be a victim of the world I created, without my permission. My Sovereignty means I am at the mercy of no one. In creation, there is no lack.* Archangel Michael.

**667 - The Rapture.** This number is an awakening of the previous one. It is the Divine Revelation. You may have had an experience, that has shown you the true way, or will have a direct experience of higher love. This state is not describable in words, but can come about spontaneously, through seeking to become love. 667 is success in all undertakings. Good luck and a higher understanding, or awareness are promised. *I am a channel for love. I experience the bliss of higher love energies.*

**668 - Ground Control.** This number represents a battle between focusing on material, or spiritual life. Losing perspective, and getting completely immersed in power bids, materialism and agendas, will have a price. Something will be lost, that will be regretted, and recognized as having more value, once lost. 668 urges you to seek the spiritual meaning behind your everyday life, to understand what is truly important. *I am one with Divine Love, which always leads me to joy.* Golden Heliodor.

**669 - Sitting Pretty.** This is a number of complete worldly success. All goals are achieved. Extreme luck in all endeavors. *I am born under a lucky star. All comes to me now, in its perfect timing.*

**670 - Seeking Grace.** This number guarantees Divine help

from higher sources. You are in tune with nature, and Mother Earth. You can find comfort and clarity by being in a mountainous region, or at a higher altitude. It is also a number of travel, and going to see family, which is especially beneficial if they live on, or around mountains, streams, or lakes. The energies of these places will be very healing for you, and the ideas that come to you, in this solace, will be beneficial. *I find peace in nature's tranquility. I listen to the silence, and my questions are answered.*

**671 - Money Management.** This number calls for organizing

and increasing your personal finances. It is not related to another person that provides your finances, such as a spouse, benefactor, receiving child support, etc. It applies to income *generated* by you. You may need to be working in a different situation, doing something else, altering an aspect of your business, or just managing your income better. *I am responsible for myself. I take the time to care for my financial situation.* Yellow Sapphire.

**672 - An Empty World.** This number involves a choice of

the dark path, or the light. Your intuition is strong, and you know the correct way to go. Dark forces tempt you with material advantages, but the world cannot offer you everything; only temporary desires, that change with time, mixed with experiences of pain, hardship and eventual death. Choose life. Choose Spirit. Choose the light. *I am a child of light. I seek only the light, as all other paths are illusions, leading to pain.* Guardian Angel Mumiah.

**673 - Brotherhood Of Souls.** This is a number of compassion for others. It is a message to be aware of another person's needs, not just your own. Know that your decisions will affect many, so take other people into consideration, before acting. Opening your heart to those around you, and seeing everything as part of the whole, will help you feel true purpose in your life. *I recognize Divine Spirit in my brother. We are in this together.*

**674 - Natural Surroundings.** You need to go on a walk. Get outdoors. Put your feet in the dirt. Growing a garden, or feeling the energy of the Earth is very settling and renewing for you. A spiritual experience, or visitation could happen, while you meditate in nature. If you're needing answers about something, follow the above advice, and ask the nature spirits for assistance. Be sure to leave a small token or gift for them, in return. Then listen to what comes to you. If you cannot get outdoors, buy a few crystals or houseplants, and sit with them, or spend time re-potting, so you are touching the soil. *I am one with all of nature, and the Earth. Natural energies renew my Spirit.* Meteorite.

**675 - Lending An Ear.** This number represents not being listened to, or heard. Or you are not listening to your logic and reason. Someone may be keeping out important details. You are blindly going forward, and trusting in anything and anyone in a particular situation. Or your frustration is building, as those around you are letting your words and needs go in one ear, and out the other. *I am always heard. I listen, in return.* Frangipani Essential Oil.

**676 - Correct Choice.** This number is related to 666, and is the renewal of Spirit. It is being lifted up, and finding the true fulfillment of inner joy. 676 is also related to the manifestation of dreams and career pursuits, especially in the artistic fields. There is much joy in your reality, and creative ventures are born. Significant births are highlighted. *I choose the path of Spirit. My life is joyful and rewarding.*

677 - **Levels of Awareness.** This is a highly spiritual number of reward and accomplishment. You are ascending to higher levels of spiritual awareness. This number also suggests access to the Akashic Records, and exploring your record of where you have been. It may be time for a reading of your records, as you have entered another dimensional level of accomplishment. Meaning, you are bypassing certain unpleasant circumstances that are no longer necessary for you to experience. *I accept my spiritual purpose in being here. I am awake and aware, and my path is revealed to me now.*

**678** - **No Barriers.** Dreams are quickly put to a stop, as walls come up blocking the path, or direction in which you are headed. Know that there are reasons that your pursuits are being delayed. There are usually lessons to learn, or the timing is off. You will eventually succeed, however you must go through these obstacles, first. *I have faith, that my desires are coming to fruition. I walk the path, and do not stray from my course.* Azurite.

**679** - **Runaway Train.** This number relates to tender feelings and sensitivities. Someone may be walking all over yours, or you are feeling things much more deeply, as of late. Be careful of a tendency to railroad others, or disregard their feelings and opinions. 679 relates to trusting others blindly, and possibly getting hurt. *I honor my sensitivity. I see clearly what is there, and protect myself from unnecessary disrespect.* Guardian Angel Nith-Haiah.

**680 - Elemental Magic.** 680 is a number of spiritual and material reward. It is a good time to ask your Angels to help you manifest what you desire. Calling in the nature elementals of fire, air, earth and water, and learning to work with them, will help you perform miracles in your life. Your supply is increasing. *I am blessed with many gifts. I have the assistance of the Divine Creator's Heavenly Angels.*

**681 - Trust Your Gut.** 681 has to do with assimilation, and how you are processing things. Are you having trouble digesting what others are saying to you, or do you have actual digestive issues going on? It may be a sign to clean up your diet, or analyze for food allergies. Maybe you need a colonic cleanse. People with digestive issues tend to worry a lot. Are you worrying about every little thing, or is a situation consuming your thoughts? *I assimilate ideas, and life with ease. My worries melt away, as I trust Spirit is taking care of what is needed.* Rhodochrosite or dark pink stones.

**682 - Vanquishing Fear.** This number says that what seems to be starting out as a good thing, is actually set to fail. The nature of the situation is karmic, and set to occur on your path. Note that the seeming failure, is actually experience that expands your spiritual perspective. The Angels are working on the elimination of your fear. Healing will come after this phase, as well as hope and renewal. To make this transition as comfortable as possible, let Spirit guide your steps. Everything happens for a reason. *I see and accept the lessons, inherent in my* *current situation.* Cypress Essential Oil.

**683 - Reaching The World.** This number is related to promotions, reaching the heights of a profession, and having an influence on the masses, or whomever is in your circle. Your influence has a trickle down effect. You are a blessing for others, and they remember you, long after you are gone. Goals are achieved, with 683. *My life is in the hands of Spirit.*

**684 - Stay In The Boat.** 684 is antagonistic energies that increase by resisting them. Many troubles and problems can result, from a mixing of these energies. Think things through, act with caution, and find acceptance in your current situation. Stay in the moment. Looking at the future, or pushing too much will backfire. Relax and be in the flow. Staying in the boat, as it bumps into rocks, and eventually drifts around them, will keep you from injury. Trying to get in the water, and force the boat to go where you want, will get you nothing but lost efforts and pain. Don't swim against the current. *I remain in a watchful stance, as I am led forward, moment by moment. I trust that all will be well in the end.* Neroli Essential Oil.

**685 - Million Dollar Idea.** This number relates to a mind that works very efficiently, and thoughts that move quickly. With 685, many ideas are coming to you now, and they are definitely ones that are worth following through. This number is a ticket to success, and you should go forward, regardless of difficulties (as these are merely blessings in disguise). All is working in your favor. *I trust that I am blessed. Great joy and abundance are mine.*

**686 - Genetic Code.** 686 talks about cleansing your ancestral karma. Despite good fortune, there is still loss happening in your world. Performing a clearing on your DNA would be wise. This cleansing prevents your children, and many generations to come, from absorbing the pain of your ancestors. *I am love. Love is all.* Cedarwood Essential Oil.

**687 - Beauty & The Beast.** This number is about overcoming karmic challenges. Avoiding difficulties, or parts of yourself that you don't want to look at, will not make them go away. You will triumph in the end, if you will summon your courage and face yourself. What you *thought* you would see, is not quite as frightening as reality. *I am a beautiful Spirit. I let my light shine.* Crushed Thyme Leaves.

**688 - Safe Passage.** This number carries a warning, about dark side energies attempting to pull the wool over your eyes. You may be walking into a trap with many lures, and lies. Be wary of "too good to be true" promises, or of that niggling sense of unease in your gut. *I am safe. Spirit sees clearly, and I am guided to safety.* Guardian Angel Manakel.

**689 - Strained Nerves.** This number signifies the difficult energies of stress and anxiety, that could possibly be manifesting into back and shoulder pain. There are solutions to solving your problems, and this is simply becoming centered and letting emotional issues roll off your back. You don't need to take everything on. Let disturbances roll off like water. *I am in the present moment. All is well.* Variscite.

**690 -Lucky Ducky.** This number involves all forms of good fortune, collaboration, compensation and helping hands. Your efforts are noticed, and people genuinely like you, and want to help. *I give thanks for everyone in my life. My blessings are many.*

**691 - All Is Supplied.** Many changes are afoot, and these need not be a bad thing. Life is going to be new and different. People you need, are entering the picture, and taking on their new roles, and new situations are falling into place. *My life is changing for the better. I welcome the new, as all blesses me now.*

**692 - Hard For The Money.** This number has to do with working at nighttime, having a second job that you work in the evening, or a business you are starting on the side. It says there are increases in money, or appreciation from others. This cycle of extra effort won't last forever. Hope is on the horizon. Your hard work is rewarded. *My diligence pays off. I attract prosperity.* Donkey Animal Totem.

**693 - Unique Purpose.** You may have the gift of gab, or talents in specific areas, that others can't help but notice. Do what you are good at, because you will succeed. Everyone has an ability that is unique to them. Good fortune in all undertakings. *I celebrate my gifts from Source.*

**694 - Natural Course.** There may be storms going on right now, but the air will be clearing. Major change may need to happen first, in order for things to get better. In the meantime it can be frustrating, because despite your efforts, the situation runs its own direction. *I trust that all my needs are being provided for, and everything happens for the best.* Rhinoceros Animal Totem.

**695 - Loud And Clear.** This is a number of luck, and psychic abilities lead you to it. Intuitive information will not lead you wrong. Follow what you know, in your inner self, and all will be in your favor. *My inner voice speaks to me, and I am guided in all ways.*

**696 - Easy Street.** This is a number of material abundance, success in the arts and in all areas of life. Victories over health conditions, spiritual challenges and sibling rivalries. All is smoothed over, as not much can deter the momentum of 696. *I am blessed with freedom, and many opportunities for healing.*

**697 - Get Out The Map.** This number says a lot of energies, motivated in one direction, brings results. Whatever you desire to accomplish, can be achieved. Therefore, it is wise to consider the direction you're headed, first. Step back and take the time to determine whether this is the correct path for you, because you will arrive at the destination you decide on. You have the determination to get yourself there, so the way is assured. *I step forward with care and consideration. My way is sure.*

**698 - Trouble In Paradise.** For all intents and purposes, everything should be going smoothly, but there is interference. Karma is raising its ugly head, and causing issues. The overall meaning of this number, however, is good fortune and success, so any disturbance will be overcome. *All will be overcome. All is well.* Chicory Herb.

**699 - Benevolent Benefactors.** This is a highly fortunate number, especially in the areas of relationships with significant others, and anything to do with the arts, decorating, music and health industries. *I am assisted in all areas, and am grateful.*

**700 - As Above, So Below.** Achieving higher states. This number has a high spiritual vibration. It represents another dimension, where there is perfection, in the expression of love, harmony and peace. This number is asking you to bring some of that energy into your current situation. Know that you are becoming these vibrations. 700 says you have attained a high status, or the top of your game. It is a divine connection with the Angels, and higher energy beings. Many extrasensory abilities may be awakened, at this time, and more clarity and connection to all higher spiritual planes are open. *I am in Divine oneness with all. I am an agent of love and peace.*

**701 - Necessary Evils.** This number represents spiritual testing, to rid your soul of residue, from past lives, poor choices and previous mistakes, or bad judgment. It is not meant for you to suffer, but rather to work through this time, see the lessons, and move on. Work with the energies, and let go of that which needs to be released. Your energy and aura is being strengthened, by moving through difficulties. You are ever growing and ever evolving. *I am committed to my soul's purpose. I move through any seeming difficulties, knowing that all has a purpose.* Faden Quartz.

**702 - Reading The Leaves.** This number has to do with extreme manifestations of psychic and intuitive abilities. Like a blossoming flower, your psychic senses are heightened, at this time. Note that there will be challenges and tests, in using these abilities, as well as many things of which you are unaware, that can challenge you. It is for you to dedicate yourself, to honing your strengths, in whatever area is natural for you. Learn to use your abilities to your advantage, and for guidance. There are many at higher levels, who wish to assist you, and want you to trust and make decisions, from intuitive information, rather than the ego. Following your gut, brings success. *I open myself to the higher energies of love. As I release fear, my intuitive ability increases.*

**703 - Pirate's Booty.** This number has to do with harvests, abundance and bounty. You are, or will be rewarded for your efforts, equal to the energies that you put forth. The timing for this gain, is the month of October. *I enjoy the results of my efforts. I put forth love, and receive love in return.*

**704 - Seeing Is Believing.** This number suggests good luck with real estate, property, vacation property and anything that represents a secure, or sure thing. Investments in these areas, are well spent. Unions and partnerships are also beneficial with 704. This is a harmonious number of luck and situations moving in a positive direction. *I make wise decisions, based on logic, intuition and trustworthy information. I am set to succeed.*

**705 - Moments In Time.** 705 involves seeing the magic in ordinary life. It is time for you to stop, and take a closer look. The thoughts, visions and information that comes to you, when you take a pause, will be of great use for your future. *I slow down, and see the benefit of taking a break. I am guided in all things.*

**706 - Time For Change.** This number is about release, usually on a spiritual level. Many changes and endings are occurring, for your future benefit. These changes will bring more stability and security to your life. This may signify endings of certain relationships, changes in the way you do things, or in your belief system. *I accept the rhythms and flows of life. All change benefits me now.*

**707 - Lucky Sevens.** This number signifies quick and drastic growth in your spiritual life, possible improvement in health, and in your connections with other people. Your dreams can manifest, at this time, as body, mind and spirit are in alignment. This is a fortunate number for the future. *I am a powerful spiritual being. I am Divine Love.*

**708 - Allure Of Emptiness.** This number suggests the ego, or lower self abusing spiritual power, for selfish desires. You may be too caught up in materialism, and doing whatever is necessary to achieve your aims. Things will not be a bed of roses, though. However, the small calm voice of Spirit is also felt in you, so it is your choice whether you choose to listen. *My spiritual guidance never steers me wrong. I will have my needs met, without having to act out of fear or forcefulness.* Betta Fish Animal Totem.

**709 - Willing To Surrender.** Your desire or will is at odds with the will of Spirit. If you push your own ego agenda, you will possibly ruin your plans for the future. Trust in your inner Spirit, and choose to create only that which is alignment with Source. To do otherwise, will mean that you will have to learn this the hard way, usually through loss. *I align my will with Spirit. Everything works in my favor.* Mountain Lion Animal Totem.

**710 - Entry Fee.** This number is connected to 701, however, you can choose to overcome some of its hard energy, by aligning your intentions with the will of Spirit. *I am willing to forgive and surrender, so Spirit can lead me into the light.* Falcon Animal Totem.

**711 - Leaps in Consciousness.** Expansion, growth and realization is connected to 711. Seeing things as you have not seen them before. In some cases, reaching toward enlightenment, through discipline and spiritual practice. This number is connected to the higher level dimensions, and the beings that reside there. An immense spiritual shift, and connection is about to happen. *Higher knowledge is available to me now. I achieve and master all that I set out to do.*

**712 - Waiting At The Station.** This is a number of pauses, to consider your next move. It is a number of good fortune, and taking the time for contemplation before action. If the delay in time was not by your choice, know that it is for much needed evaluation. *I do not have to rush. My success is already waiting for me.*

**713 - Will Of The Father**. A number of strength, and power of control over a situation. 713 signifies power of the Word. Remember that all power comes from recognizing my own sovereignty, as a Divine Child of Source. *My will is at one with The Creator's. I am invulnerable.*

**714 - Write Now.** This is a number of communication. It may be time to reconnect with someone you've lost touch with, sit down and write that article or novel you've been thinking about, or undertake some writing or creative project. Lost communications are reconnected. *I allow creativity to flow through me, for the benefit of others.*

**715 - Staying the Course.** This number has to do with light and dark side energies. It has a bearing down effect, as if the darkness is battering your soul. Instead of one thing, three things seem to go wrong. Underneath these challenges, though, are successes. You can be accomplishing what you want, in a particular situation, if you focus on what is going right. Hold on to the good, and you will be given the means to handle the weight, that has settled over you. There may be deaths at this time, but just as often miracles. It seems that anything can happen with this energy, so the advice here is to laser point your focus onto that which is beneficial and working. 715 can assist you in much growth and progress, but just as easily turn and hand you pressures, stress and deadlines. Keep your focus. *I remain in a positive mind frame. Spirit eases my worries and burdens. All things are happening for my highest good now.* Benitoite.

**716 - Take the Next Step.** You have been on a long road, up until now, and it has been wearying at times. 716 is saying there is a light at the end of the tunnel, a situation is coming to an end, or relief is in sight. Resolution is certain, and good news awaits. Continue on, and persevere. Giving up now, would make all your former efforts wasted. Realize that only so much can be accomplished at any given time, and you must work within the parameters of the situation. Sometimes you cannot fix everything, or force things to happen. The time for readiness is coming, and your objectives will bear fruit. Just keep believing, and doing what you can. You will be rewarded for tenacity and patience. *I walk forward with confidence,* *knowing that all will eventually come to pass. Everything has its perfect timing, and all will be resolved successfully.* Labradorite.

**717 - The Door is Open.** This number signifies a turning point in your life. A chance to make a different choice (although many choices are available to you at this time). This means that there are actual choices to choose from now, whereas before there was no choice or option. Know that a situation is no longer stagnant. You are not trapped. Choose, or the choice will be made for you. The standstill is over. What seems like chaos or upset, will actually bring you more stability in the future. *I allow change to bring me what is necessary in my present situation. I trust that all is well, and only good finds me now.* Black Agate.

**718 - Power in Relationships.** The focus is on relationships, and your responsibilities to them. What relationship is this number referring to, or is it referring to how you treat yourself? How have you contributed to creating the situation as it is now? What type of relationship have you created? What type of partner or experiences have you attracted to yourself? These are questions to ask right now, as examination is called for, so you can evolve the situation. You are in control of whether this relationship is healthy or harmful. Have you convinced yourself otherwise? Have you given control to the other person, or an outside force? Taking responsibility for your part in it, is the only way to change things for the better. Always choose love, for yourself and others. *I attract healthy and harmonious relationships. As I love myself, my relations with others heal.* Azurite

**719 - Time Clock.** You may be feeling your age. Even if you are young, or consider yourself very old, you may be feeling a sense of the unsure, or time moving by too quickly. Maybe you feel you have not accomplished much. You are re-evaluating what you have done with your life. What do you value? What is important? What should you be doing with your remainder of your time here? These are all questions that are coming from a soul level, and your plans for the future should be laid now. It is time to think first, and then act. Good fortune follows. *There is always time for me to accomplish that which is necessary. I begin now, to live this day.* Sodalite.

**720 - Spirit Is Calling.** 720 is steering you toward your spiritual nature, beliefs and path. You must focus on your soul's mission for being here, in order resolve past, present and future issues of pain and difficulty. Become love, and learn what that is. Begin to see with the eyes of love. This is the only road for you. Without spiritual understanding, the world remains an empty place of pain and repetitions of the past. *I accept my divinity, and oneness with Spirit. I am much more than this world and this personality.*

**721 - Overcoming The Odds.** This is a number of high success. Perhaps winning, after overcoming many difficulties. Good luck arrives. It is up to you, what you do with it from here. Many gifts and opportunities are coming you way, in the forms of love, intuition, material goods and people. *I am blessed by Spirit.*

**722 - Prophetic Path.** A highly psychic number, 722 signals a time of increased awareness. You are experiencing much extrasensory development, input and stimulation. Use these for guidance, and trust yourself. Be careful not to have your head in the clouds, as it is just as important to maintain logic and other mind states as well. *I give thanks for my many abilities, opening up to me now.*

**723 - Special Delivery.** This is a time for stillness and

waiting, so that one can see the next move. You do not have to search, work, or stress to get what you need. Simply ask Spirit, and wait for the delivery. You will have assistance in all things. Gains and blessings. *My needs are always provided for, and I relax and trust the Universe to deliver in the perfect way.*

**724 - Peak Of The Mountain.** This is a powerful number of

success and good luck, in the areas of health, partnerships, and business. With 724, you will overcome and prosper. *I accept my personal power. I trust Spirit to bring me that, which I need.*

**725 - Abracadabra.** When you walk into a room, magic

happens. You can not go wrong with this number. All things are set to triumph. The past is gone, and you are now in the flow of creation. *I can make anything happen, through the wisdom of the One who sent me.*

**726 - Do not Despair**. There is always hope, and something

new. This number tells you to keep hope alive, and that any difficult situations will not be like this forever. It is a good time to connect with others, and reconnect with family members, with whom you may be estranged. This is a time for reconnecting, reunions and reminiscing. The past and future come together in the present. 726 is also saying it is a good time for traveling, especially if you are going to see family, or a friend. In business, it is a good time for negotiations, signing contracts and legal issues in general, as long as you read the fine print. *I celebrate my many connections. I open to networking with others, as Spirit works through all, for the highest good of all.* Spessartine Garnet.

727 - **Spiritual Evolution.** This number is related to 722.

Your prophetic vision is clear. Your spiritual path may be of upmost importance, at this time. Many transitions are happening, and you are evolving toward a higher state of consciousness. Much is revealed to you now. *I am clear, and see the higher purpose in what is happening.*

**728 - Impeded progress.** This number involves many

hardships to contend with, on your road to achievement. This is two steps forward, one step back. The obstacles come in many forms, and something will probably have to be given up, in order to proceed. You will reach your goals, however, if you will apply persistence, and always find the spiritual meaning behind appearances. *I am determined to succeed. All is being provided.* Geranium Essential Oil.

729 - **Amplified Energies.** This is the time for fast action.

Projects move along a lot quicker, or come to their conclusions. 729 is also signaling that the time has come for spiritual changes in your life. Things are vibrating and moving up to a higher level, and you are moving with it. You may notice body changes at this time, as your cells accelerate their vibration. It is also a time of fast healing, so whatever has been bothering you, can be healed, if you move with this energy. A clean diet can assist this, but most importantly, positive emotions and thoughts can clear out any negativity, and pave the way for a healthy happy future. *I allow the heightened energy to move through me, and lift me up into Divine healing. All things move and change quickly for the better.* Chrysoprase.

730 - **Within Reach.** You are the master of your fate.

Whatever happens at this time, is up to you. All things are possible, if you back them. Step up to the plate, and deliver your destiny. *I can create my life. I choose wisely.*

731 - **Body Care.** Pay attention to your health. It may be a

good time to update your look, do some body care, and notice how others view you. How do you come across? What message are you sending about yourself, based on how you take care of your appearance? Are you watching what you eat, exercising regularly and thinking positive? First impressions are especially important right now. Treat yourself. Take care of you, and do some pampering. *I care for myself and my appearance. I show up, polished and presentable, ready to take on the world.* Pink Tourmaline.

732 - **Divine Summons.** Your time is now. This is a wake up

call. You chose to suffer, but it is no longer necessary. Choose to let go of your need to punish yourself, because the time is at hand for your luck to change, to good fortune and spiritual blessings. *I am an innocent Child of the Creator. All is forgiven, as I accept my true identity.*

733 - **Garden Of The Gods.** See 742. *I create miracles, now.*

734 - **Gold Medal.** This is a spiritual number of earned good

luck, clarity and reward. Success in spiritual matters,

investments with buildings or land, and public-reach ventures. *I am successful, and give thanks that my decisions are sound.*

**735 - Be On Guard.** Analyze carefully, those that you associate with, and what their true motives are. Some people only do things for their own benefit, so don't be taken advantage of, or tricked into something that is not what you thought it was. If it is purely for fun, then say, "Yes". Anything else is probably a "no", right now. *I am awake and aware. I see all that I need to see.* Dark Purple-black Amethyst.

**736 - Old Is New.** This is a number of success, but it involves having to go back and learn an old lesson. One that you thought you were finished with, but is coming up to be cleared. It may be difficult, but know that you are finishing the final round of this, and much growth and good luck comes on the other side of it. *I move through situations with ease. All is well.* Clover Herb.

**737 - Serene Balance.** This can be a challenging time, with karmic repercussions. It is wise to keep your emotions calm. This can be done by using essential oils, crystals, meditation, visualization, or any other means of keeping emotional balance. *Only good can come of this situation.* Pink Petalite.

**738 - Ancestral Aeons.** You are completing the end of a very difficult karmic cycle, in the area of family and love relationships, or DNA inheritances. Karmic Saturn has had it out for you, in the previous number, 737, and it culminates with this number. Follow the advice for 737. *I maintain a centered outlook, knowing that all will be well. Difficulties are fading, and being replaced by joy and good luck.* Hemimorphite.

739 - **Sovereign Being.** 739 is a recognition of your divinity.

You are about to experience your true value. Joy and happiness are connected to this number, and it is the birth of all things positive. *I am the Light of Spirit. My true nature is joy.*

740 - **Starry Starry Night.** This number has to do with

expansive thoughts, which lead to questions, and the search for answers. You may have an interest, right now, in astrology, astronomy, star watching, UFOs or even your soul's other-planetary origins. Outer space calls, as well as inner space...fractals, science, the biology and makeup of things...you may be questioning your very existence, or why you are here. What is the purpose of it all? Where do I come from? This could take a literal form, such as searching for birth parents, thinking of adopting, finding missing persons, searching for someone, searching for a partner and the like. Getting to the bottom of things, and getting answers, is the energy of this number. You will be led to what you seek. *All answers are available to me now. I find peace in my search.*

741 - **Experience The Wonder.** This is a number of magical

or miracle type abilities, such as levitation, invisibility and suspending time. Open to miracles, because you are about to have yours. *I experience miracles, as my natural state of being.*

742 - **Sprouted Seedlings.** This number represents an

incredible new beginning, or a fresh start. Powerful energies are at play for new life and prosperity. *I am naturally lucky.*

743 - **Cat Out Of The Bag.** Keep your plans to yourself. If you

speak about them, other people will sabotage you, either directly or unconsciously. Stay quiet and continue on, and you will accomplish your goals. *I protect my creations, until the time is right.*

**744 - Puppeteer.** This number represents heavy ties, or

control from others. People close to you may be energetically corded to you. These attachments, or cords create vacuums for them to continue to suck energy from you, and send their negative emotions to you. These need to be removed. Perform a cord removal on yourself, by running your hands over your aura (including under your feet and above your head) to feel for the energetic ties of others. Pull these out from both ends, as if pulling out a plug. Have your angels carry off the cords, and then fill the remaining area with the light of Spirit. *I am free from all unwanted attachments and invasions. I am powerful and impenetrable.* Palo Santo Oil.

**745 - Making Senseless.** Your rational mind is trying to

control the situation, instead of letting things flow toward their natural destination. When we are over-rational, it usually has its basis in fear. What are you afraid of...afraid to lose? Face it, and release its hold on you now, so that the situation can grow to its full potential. All will not be lost. *I am willing to allow Spirit to lead me. I trust a higher power to make my decisions.* Elemi Essential Oil.

**746 - Practical Progress.** What you start will grow bigger,

with more opportunity, more growth, progress, outlets, income and the like. You must be realistic about your goals, though, if you are to succeed. *I am grounded and explore the facts, before acting.*

**747 - Skullduggery.** This number suggests challenges, and hidden agendas. People are not speaking their true motives, dishonesty is a possibility, there are disruptions and information can be misleading. Use your inner intuition, to ascertain what is true or false. *I am open and aware of who and what is around me, at all times. Spirit always protects me, as I place my trust completely in my own inner knowing.* Guardian Angel Reiyel.

**748 - Burdens Lifted.** It has been challenging, but things are going to be alright. In fact, this number is saying much better days are nearly here, and the Sun is rising over that hill you are climbing. Things do not have to continue, as they have been. You now have choices, that you may not have had before. Ask for guidance. *I give thanks for the many gifts Spirit has given me. I find relief for my troubles.*

**749 - In God's Hands.** This number relates to the outcome of 747. From here, one has learned to trust in the comfort of Spirit, alone. *I rest in the hands of the Creator. All is well.*

**750 - The Hermit.** 750 says you may be looking for some alone time, or a focusing on the self. The message is to not listen to society, or those that would seek to influence you, out of expectation, but rather to find your own voice. This requires time alone, getting to know you. Get out of the energy fields of other people, turn off your cell phone and other distractions, at regular alone-time intervals. The wisdom is within you. You will find it. *My inner voice speaks to me clearly, and guides the way.*

**751 - Burn the Letters.** This would be a good time to write down your goals, wishes and needs on a piece of paper. Address it to Source. Be willing to allow the changes, that will be required, if you receive these desires. Then, as an act of faith, that what you asked for (or something better), will be given, burn the paper, throw it away, or put it away from your eyes (maybe to read at a later date), so that you can be assisted with these things in the perfect way. *I let go, and let flow.*

**752 - Teach Me.** This is a number of the "power of the Word". It is about relaying your message to the world, whether this be through writing, speaking, or teaching, you are here to share your visions and perceptions with others. To be an example to others, by how you live your life, how you relate with people, how you speak, how you act, and the choices you make. *I am the truth. Love flows through me, for the benefit of all.*

**753 - Have And Have Not.** This number says you think you need other people, or what they have in order to get what you want. It is a belief in lack, and having to "take" or "get". What do you think you cannot have? Spirit never deprives you. Sometimes things are simply not in our script, or kept from us, because Spirit can see the whole time line, past/present/future, and is making the best decision for you, and everyone involved. Trust that you are where you are supposed to be, and have what you are supposed to have. This number may also mean someone is jealous of what you have. You should not feel guilty, for your good fortune, because it is in your life script to have it, otherwise you would not. *I have everything I need. There is no lack.* Imperial Topaz.

**754 - Wild Goose Chase.** This number contains disruptive energies, that can take you in circles. Trying to chase, or attain something, will lead to its destruction. This can be a positive number, if one is willing to go with the flow, and drop personal agendas. *I place my trust in Spirit. I am guided forward, toward the best possible outcomes.* Patchouli Essential Oil.

**755 - Reinvent Yourself.** You are the determining factor in what will happen with your life. Will you live for the good of others, or will you choose to think only of yourself? You will get back what you give. Take actions that you can be proud of, and be remembered for your good will towards others. The blessings can be many, with 755, but it is up to you. Remember, as you bless, you are blessed. *I act for the highest good of all.*

**756 - Here Kitty Kitty.** It may be a good time for an animal companion, or to take more time with your pets. Their energy can calm you, and assist in your overall health and well-being. If you can't have a pet, watch animal videos, visit a petting zoo, or an animal sanctuary. This is a number of good fortune, and a happier home life. *I honor all life. We are all here on a journey to grow and learn love, together.*

**757 - Sun's Path.** This number says to just "be". Radiate happiness. Break the ice with others, by smiling. Walk with a bounce in your step. Listen to music, if that helps lift your Spirit. Fake it till you make it. The end result with 757 is joy, so take your first steps on that road, now. Focus on this, and everything else you are wanting will follow. The timing for this number is late July or early August. *I am filled with joy, abundance and health. I am at peace.*

**758 - Pain, Pain, Go Away.** Your reality is at war with your daydreams. Escapism leads to loss and the like, as a result of not paying attention to what needs to be addressed. There may have been much pain in your life, but burying it will not make it go away. It will raise its ugly head, at some point. Facing your pain in steps that you can handle, and learning ways to heal it, will enable you to move beyond it and enjoy your life more fully. Ask the Angels to send you the answers. *I am honorable and brave, as I heal the past with forgiveness.* Bergamot Oil.

**759 - High Honors.** This is a number of accomplishment, and recognition for your efforts. Its message for you is good luck and the reaching of goals. *I accomplish that, which I set out to do.*

**760 - Blast Off.** See 706. *I am moving into a new and better future, of joy and fulfillment.*

**761 - R & D.** This number says that if you are in poor health, your situation should be improving. Answers can be found, through research. Much assistance is available, and good luck follows. *I seek, and always find.*

**762 - Shadows.** This number has to do with things that happen in stillness, or at night. This can also mean a lack of light, or the darkness calling. Are you getting visitations, or feeling an ominous presence, or pressure on your chest in the evenings? Are you spending time in low vibrational level nighttime activities, or environments? This number says to reexamine all of your motives, and find your area of weakness.

What is it you fear? You are attracting to yourself, energies that reflect this. *I find my inner strength, and fear nothing, as my soul is my stronghold.* Agrimony Herb.

**763 - Whistle While You Work.** All lasting achievements in the physical world, come from spiritual strength. Whatever you do create, will not completely satisfy you, because your true fulfillment, is in Spirit. You will be led back to finding your life purpose. What is it all for? This is a number of joy, but more so in the spiritual sense. *I find joy in living a life of purpose.*

**764 - Abundance For All.** This is a number of worldly success, and financial gain. The warning is to be careful not to forget others, in your quest to succeed. Wish the same for everyone. *I am blessed by Heaven. I am thankful for all I have.*

**765 - Back In Time.** This number can mean covering old ground, and revisiting old memories and lessons from the past. People from your past, could be showing up at this time, or you may hear from someone you haven't seen in awhile. Possibly, this person is from a past life, and you may feel like you know them, even though this is your first meeting. You may be getting intuitive information, and sensing something coming. Your past revisits you, if you haven't let go of it, and brings unresolved issues into your future. These can be positive or negative experiences. *I honor all my relationships, and learn from them.*

**766 - In The Hands Of Fate**. This is a fortunate number for relationships, physical health, emotional balance, making positive first impressions, and abundance. Success is in the palm of my hand. Everything in my life is changing for the better. *Divine signs are guiding me every step of the way. I have all that I need.*

767 - **Streak Of Luck.** This is a number of good luck and gain, through spiritual pursuits, partnerships and the material world. All is in alignment for your good fortune. *I am blessed by Spirit. I give thanks for the many gifts, coming to me now.*

768 - **Full House.** A number of worldly gain and prosperity. An auspicious sign. *I am blessed with abundance.*

769 - **Moderation In All Things.** This number is signaling it is a time to have some fun. Let loose, but watch excess. Exert self-control. It is a time of temptations, and getting lost. Stick to the principles and the ethics that you would wish yourself to live by, and say "no" when it is appropriate. Do take time to relax for a bit, and enjoy what you have. What feels good, *really* feels good right now, but again, self-control is called for, so that one's objectives are not lost. Enjoy, in moderation. But enjoy. *I let loose and allow myself play time and enjoyment. I stay in control of my mind, heart and intentions, not giving my power away to anyone else, or losing myself in the process.* Purple Fluorite.

770 - **Globe-trotting.** This is a number of manifestation, and calling your dreams into being. Luck in partnerships, children, creative projects and travel is highlighted. *My dreams are manifesting at the perfect time.*

771 - **Guilty Conscience.** You are not meant to suffer, but

this does not mean you should be seeking easy escapes from it. Instead, face the demons inside. What do you feel guilty about, and why? What is the underlying negative feeling that needs to be released? Karma can come in a blessing form, instead of suffering - it is just a flip of the switch. Do some inner work, by finding books, teachers and the like, that can help you to overcome the illusions of the ego mind and release the guilt. Archangel Anael, planetary teacher, presides over this number. *I am a child of Source. My true nature is innocence and love.* Rose Flower or Oil.

772 - **Born To Live.** This is a number of endings that lead to new blessings. All that is happening, is for the highest good. Situations turn in your favor. *I am always in the right place, at the right time.*

773 - **All Is Provided.** A number of good fortune in many areas. Family, spiritual and financial sectors are blessed by heaven. Our wish is your command, is connected to this number. *I am at one, with the presence of my true inner self.* Archangel Sariel.

774 - **Transcendence.** Put aside differences, and realize your good is upon you. The Angels say, "Open your eyes." Fulfillment and blessings are on their way. Don't block what is yours, with petty emotions, or doubt. Archangel Zagzagael is connected to this number, one of the Angels Of Glory. *I am lifted up, in glory.*

775 - **Exalted Blessings.** Your Spirit is being lifted up. All is made new. This is a number of the highest blessings, wisdom

and hope for the future. All good things come with 775. *I am filled with the Light of Spirit. Love leads the way.*

776 - **Dream a Little.** Dreams and visions are strong. Pay

attention to your day dreams, night dreams and any inspirations you are getting at this time. They have messages for you about your true nature, and what will make you happy. They are important, and what gives your life purpose. *I dream a happy dream of a future time, that is closer to my reach, every day. My visions become a reality.*

777 - **Jackpot.** The triple seven is an extremely lucky number.

It suggests winnings at games of chance. It also represents the higher levels of consciousness, closest to that of Source.777 represents Angels of the highest dimensions, and transcending conscious thought. It is Divine perfect love. It is outside of the world, and therefore uplifts this plane of existence. It represents the purity and innocence of Spirit. 777 says you have been blessed by Spirit. Your soul is ascending in this lifetime, and the return home to Spirit is assured. *I am aware of my Divinity. Divine Love flows through me.*

778 - **Play It Safe.** This is a warning number of deceit,

betrayal and underhanded dealings. Watch your back. All is not as it seems. *I am always protected. Everything works out for the best.* Sandstone.

779 - **A Leg Up.** This is highly fortunate number of assistance

from spiritual guides, religious authorities, CEOs, business associates, investors and benefactors. Good luck overcomes all hardship. *I am assisted every step of the way. I have all I need.*

**780 - Dark Side Of The Moon.** There are many difficulties to contend with, and dark forces have "targeted" you, so to speak. Proceeding with caution, and using protective measures is called for, especially relating to other people, other people's money, and legal issues. *Spirit leads me out of the darkness. I am surrounded with love and protection.* African Green Garnet.

**781 - Lean on Me.** Conflict arises, if one is set on selfish motives, and ignores the needs of others. You must look to your right, look to your left, and look behind you. This number suggests you may have only been looking in front of you...of what you need to beat, of who you need to climb over, or get around. This number tells you to look behind...who you left behind...who has got your back, or has been assisting you...Who is flanking you with support. These people are not your competition, but your brothers in the game of life. Support them, and you get where you need to go, peacefully and with satisfaction. Things get easier when you give your brother a much needed helping hand. All these things shall be added unto you. *I give thanks that my brothers are with me. We love and support each other, knowing that we all will get where we are going. There is enough for everyone.* Red Spinel.

**782 - Beggar's Due.** This is a number of conflict and loss. The issues must be worked through, in order for the soul's agenda to be accomplished. You can be easily deceived by others, and be pushed to make choices that are not what is best, but rather what you *think* is best for you. If you choose love, no matter what, you will find the way. The looming mountain will become a valley of peace. This number says that you, or your life, will be a lesson and a blessing for those that follow. *I am* *willing to choose love. I am love. Love is all there is.* Padparascha Sapphire

**783 - Shaping Destiny.** See 789. The variation, is that you will have more assistance and luck, to reward your efforts. *I call upon the Angels for assistance, during challenging times. All roads are leading to my victory.* Archangel Sachiel (Zachiel, Tzadkiel) for correct action.

**784 - Irreverent Relations.** 784 talks of karmic troubles, that resolve themselves in the end. The problems may be coming from family members, or partners. You are being taken for granted, or put upon. You deserve to be treated with respect, just as you give respect. Take a stand for yourself, or eliminate contact with those who treat you with unloving intent. In this way, happiness can be found. *I am worthy of love. I honor and respect myself.* Bay Laurel Essential Oil.

**785 - All or Nothing.** There is power in this number, if one knows how to use it. It is time to go for it, full force. Don't hold anything back. Put everything you have into what you are doing. No half measures. Only by committing fully, will you accomplish what you are seeking. Rid yourself of doubt, feelings of insecurity or not being good enough, and give your full attention, confidence, and will to making your dreams happen. *I gather together the full forces of my being, and push forward into success. Nothing can stop me, as I am one with the true genius of my Spirit nature.* Tsavorite.

**786 - Feeling The Burn.** There may be difficulties at this time, but you have the forbearance to get through them. People or situations may be agitating you, but know that these challenges are helping you grow as a person. As you meet the challenges, the eventual luck of this number kicks in. *I go with the flow, understanding that life goes in cycles.* Ruby Zoisite.

787 - **Quicksand.** You could be in danger of being pulled into

something that is not for your benefit, but rather your downfall. You could be leading yourself into this trap, by your inability to control your desires, or to say "no", and mean it. Analyze to see if your actions are from fear, guilt, or the desire to escape a situation, person, or emotion. If so, they are the wrong actions to take. Don't allow yourself to become so distracted, that you cannot see the truth any longer. *My mind is focused on Spirit. I attract only people and situations that help me stay on my path.* Celandine Herb. Sprinkle as a border.

788 - **Piercing The Veil**. You are at odds with yourself. The

battle is within, not outside of you. Meditation, prayer, or silent observation will be beneficial at this time. Good luck arrives, after a battle with fear. *I am courage and strength. I am divinely guided.* Pink Himalayan Quartz.

789 - **Diamond in the Rough.** This number takes great

strength and fortitude, to overcome its difficulties. If you are in for the long haul, and hang tight, things will work out in the end. You will be rewarded for your efforts, in spiritual and material gifts from Spirit. In peace of mind. You have many gifts to give to this world. Many may be jealous, want what you have, or wish you ill in some way. You have been blessed, but have been given many difficulties to attend with, to develop your tenacity and strength of Spirit. You are being refined, like a diamond. Cut into a shape to reveal your brilliance and your true inner beauty. Try to roll with these testing times, and do not succumb to the pressure. You are being molded into a superhuman. *I allow myself to be molded and shaped into my true being. I am a powerful light worker, here to evolve my soul.* Black Opal.

**790 - Caravan Of Time.** This number signals endings, that

begin a new cycle. Resisting change will make this number difficult. Know that you are rising from the ashes, into something better. Give it time, and allow what is unfolding, to reveal itself. Holding on to the past, will prevent you from moving forward, and will only cause loss and pain. *I willingly allow myself to be led by Spirit. All things renew themselves, when I trust solely in my inner truth.* Spider Animal Totem.

**791 - Booby Traps.** Your goals are at odds with your true

spiritual path. There are many conflicting energies with this number. It would be best to release your will to Spirit, and be guided through the difficulties. *I am Divinely guided every step of the way.* Guardian Angel Anauel

**792 - Start The Ball Rolling.** You have been stationary for

too long, and this number brings some much needed energy. Be ready for change, because it can be positive, and what is needed. Spiritual goals are achieved, and you may be reaching a new level of insight. *I move forward with confidence and grace. All is revealed to me at the perfect time.*

**793 - Time for a Trip.** This is a good time to take a

shamanism workshop, or anything connected to journeying in a spiritual sense. 793 promises that the information gained during inner travels, will be of benefit to your future. This number is a good omen. *I heal all the inner parts of myself, and clear the way for a bright future.*

794 - **Nest Eggs.** This is a number of monetary gain, security, new growth, and travel. It is a good time to take action, and build up your reserves. Success and good fortune arrive on your doorstep. *I am blessed with many gifts.*

795 - **Cup Runneth Over.** This is a number of success, and overcoming all odds. Anything can happen. *I call forth that which I need. All is supplied from an abundant Universe.*

796 - **Off Kilter.** There is a lack of balance between body, mind and Spirit. Are you living your truth? Are you practicing nutritional eating habits, positive thinking and self-love? This number speaks of excess, and the desires of the lower nature. It is important to heal our childhood wounds, as well as all levels of ourselves, and keep them in balance. *I am healthy, whole and happy. I have all that I need.* Feldspar.

797 - **Ask And It Is Given.** You are coming to the end of more than one cycle, in your life. 797 says that much progress has been made, and now it is for you to decide what is the next step for you. This is a fortunate number of success, in worldly, or spiritual goals. *I am ready for success.*

798 - **Arms Of The Angels.** Throughout the difficulties connected to this number, you are always supported by Spirit. You can rest on the wings of your Angels, knowing that they will catch you if you fall. You also have much support around you, in the form of friends, associates, family and even

strangers. All come to support you at this time, with 798. You cannot fail. Even if you believe on some level, and in some small or large way that you are a failure, it is not true. You are so much bigger than this personality you have chosen to be in this lifetime. You are expansiveness, connected to a vast support system of loving intervention. Move forward with grace, knowing that all of your efforts are rewarded, and you are kept safe in Spirit. *There is no issue too small or large, that has not been resolved in Spirit. I trust, that in all situations of darkness and pain, recovery and loss, or in joyful celebration, I am always enveloped in the security of love.* Golden Healer Quartz.

**799 - Seventh Heaven.** You have learned many lessons, and

now your focus is clear and concise. You know what you want, and you understand that life is about spiritual lessons and growth. You are receiving much assistance from Angels, Spirit Guides and Guardian Angels. Your purpose is clear. *I live the life I was meant to live.*

**800 - High Achiever.** This number suggests mastery over the

physical plane, bringing high levels of achievement. You can rise to any position, and make what you want, happen, in the material world. You are connected to Angelic beings on higher levels of manifestation energies. Riches and wealth, can be indicated, as 800 represents symbols of power, and resides over the visible and concrete world. *I attract all that I need. I use my Source-given power, wisely.*

**801 - Get What You Give.** This number warns of selfishness,

self-aggrandizement and the pursuit of power, for power's sake. It is a warning, not to act rashly, or in the interest of only self. There will be a backlash. Follow the ways of Spirit. This will mean going completely outside of what you are being drawn toward. Spirit will lead the way. *I see the thread of unity that connects us all. I honor my brothers, and ask for the highest good, for all involved.* Turkey Animal Totem.

**802 - Parent Trap.** Are you cultivating nurturing

relationships with those you live with, or close family members? In particular, this number is relating to parents and children (or pets). Possibly there are issues with one member being suffocating or overbearing, or maybe there is a lack of affection and appreciation. This number is signaling you to pay close attention to your home life, and heal the problems, rifts, or issues that are being ignored, because of lack of money, energy, or time. Make your foundations strong. If you live alone, honor yourself, and treat yourself with love and respect. *I give and receive love, easily and effortlessly. I enjoy my home, and the loving support I feel when I am there.* Yellow Opal.

**803 - We Are The World.** This number is lucky, if you

choose to honor and respect other people's opinions and contributions. Everyone's viewpoint has validity. *I value everyone, as my brothers in Spirit. The will of Source, be done.*

**804 - Choices To Be Made.** This number says you have

reached a point of resolution and choice. Your karmic wheel can turn in either direction, meaning you are at a place of neutrality. Good, or unfortunate karma will come up, at this time, based on what you create for yourself. Take time to meditate on your actions, and ask to be given wisdom and direction, in each moment. Your future is in your hands, and not the hands of fate. *I walk the path to love. Spirit guides my steps.*

**805 - Clean Slate.** This number is connected to the one before it. You have assistance from your Guides. Many miracles can happen, if you choose the way of Spirit. This may mean remaining unattached to outcomes, and willingly letting go of that which needs to leave your life. You have the power of choice. *I refrain from all error, by joining my will with Spirit. Miracles become natural for me.*

**806 - Manna from heaven.** There have been opportunities offered to you, or there is a major opportunity about to be offered. 135 speaks of monetary gain, in the form of a new job, more clients for your business, recognition that brings in a raise, a promotion, or anything that increases your cash flow. This number also refers to powerful people that control your finances, or directly influence your money, such as a boss, a business partner, a buyer, a spouse or someone that supplies your income. *My good is coming to me now.*

**807 - Dark Or Light.** This is a number of spiritual challenges, and taking sides. There is a battle being undertaken, for your soul. You have a choice to make, between pursuit of materialism, or commitment to your spiritual path. If you stay grounded, awake and aware, you will make the correct choice. *I always make the best choice, for the salvation of my soul.* Lizard Animal Totem.

**808 - Colliding Karmas.** This is a number of difficulties, and hard karma. Another lifetime is merging together with this one. In order for you to proceed in your growth, there may be loss, as the situation was set up, to bring about a painful experience. There were wrong choices made, and the loss will be the correcting of them. You may not be aware of what these choices were, or the overall grand scheme of things. Fate is having its way. There is a doorway out, however, if you will listen to Spirit, and follow what you are given. This karma, however difficult, is coming to an end in this lifetime. Do your best to get through whatever the challenges are, and know that on the other side of it, is hope and joy. *I am fully aware of the present moment. In it, are all things possible.* Wasp Animal Totem.

**809 - Mid-Life Crisis.** This number is connected to the

previous, and is the moment of truth. It is the actual clash of the difficulty, and suggests that you are coming through to the end of it. There is still the doorway out, and you can be freed, on the other side of this. No matter how bad things are, you *will* have peace again. *I trust that all is working according to the Divine Plan. I keep to the course, set for me by Spirit. Only goodness and truth lie before me, comfort me.* Vanilla Essential Oil.

**810 - Commitment.** This number is here to challenge you, to

overcome barriers and outdated beliefs. You can rise above, and move out of difficulties, if you are willing to put in the effort, and stick to it. This is a push forward, from the Universe, to keep going. Don't give up. Don't give in. Don't take the easy way out, of inaction. It is a calling to pull together, and unite. Accept help. A way to your goals exists. Just reach for it, and most importantly, commit to it. Think about the word commit, and what it means. It involves unwavering resolve, and action. And that is when the magic can happen. Reach for the stars, because you can overcome everything in the process...soon there will only be the stars, getting closer to you, as you will have conquered the world. *I commit to my dreams fully and completely, and am willing to do all that is necessary to make them happen. I accept help along the way, with a grateful heart, and I enjoy the journey.* Guardian Angel Daniel.

**811 - Show Down.** This number is a joining of extremes. 811 is often manipulated by dark side energies, but can also be a wake-up call to the light. Choosing to use the 811 energies for light, can bring much reward, and spiritual growth. The benefits of this number, relate to gifts of the Earth, as well as your overall destiny. There will be something to give up, but it will be what was not good for you anyway. You stand to gain much more, if you hold to the light, and cast out the darkness. *I am a child of Source. By choosing the light, I become the light of salvation for the Earth.* Antelope Animal Totem.

**812 - Detached Observation.** This number is challenging you to overcome what you are seeing/perceiving, in order to evolve and break the cycle of reincarnation and death. It asks, that you forgive, in a higher form, so that your lessons will be alleviated. This is not a working off of karma, so much as it is a tolerating, and forgiving of it. As you disassociate, and detach from these worldly trials, the less they have a hold on your future. It is self-mastery, that is asked for here...a detached, observant and forgiving mindset. The world is transitory. 812 is a sign that you have chosen a difficult path, in whatever you are undertaking. Realize that there will be obstacles and possible difficulties, that you can do nothing about. If is for you to keep on, keeping on. There is a higher purpose for what you are going through, so relax and try to make yourself comfortable for now. Detachment is the key. *I let go and let Spirit guide me through all seemingly dangerous* *waters. I am always in constant supply of the life-giving streams of Source.* Dalmation Jasper.

**813 - Power Emerging.** This signifies a time to stop and

observe. You are realizing the purpose behind many of the things that have happened to you recently. Or you have an inner knowing, that what is happening, needs to happen. This number implies incredible strength, and the ability to go forward with your life, in new and different ways. No longer will you make the same mistakes. You move beyond this circumstance, and find power and fortitude to continue into your new life. *I am well-guided, and find my way. All is available to me now.*

**814 - All Systems Go.** This is a number of good luck and

rewards. As old energies die away, new opportunities, new starts, creative business or marketing ideas and new beginnings are coming out of the blue. Your presence is powerful, and affects others. *I am reborn in Spirit. All is working in my favor.*

**815 - Love Me, Love Me.** If you are looking to move ahead, or

improve your reputation, then this number is saying that it is possible. Know that you can sway and win approval, but be careful that this is not at the expense of your own self-respect. The people you are dealing with, at this time, may require submission or subservience of you. This may be subtle or extreme, but either way it is the same. Think, rather, that you would do well without this person's influence or support. 815 says you think you need, what is outside of yourself. This is not so. If you will let go of dependency, you will have what you want. There's no reason to rely on anyone else, other than Spirit. *I take care of me, for I have everything I need.* Zebra Stone.

**816 - Shroud Of Darkness.** 816 warns of overindulgence,

greed, selfishness and addiction. If you have acted in the interest of any of these dark temptations, you will end up with problems and loss. By helping others, and acting on their behalf, as well as your own, you are helped in return. It's the difference between being trapped, or freed. *I choose the light of Spirit. It is my true identity.* Ussingite.

**817 - My Only Hope.** This number speaks of failed efforts,

that are karmic in nature. There is much conflict with this number, and though you try, and put much effort in, you keep experiencing setbacks. There is a light at the end of the tunnel, and asking for signs will help you through adversity. Heed any warnings you are given, and act immediately. Don't wait to fix a problem, or to exit a sinking ship. *I am given clear guidance. I always know the correct action to take.* Guardian Angel Achaia.

**818 - Eyes On The Prize.** This number has to do with

monetary gains, sporting events and anything involving competition. It is a race to the finish. Success comes with material goals, but may be at the cost of a few friendships, or your peace of mind. *I have everything I need. I do not have to force my supply. All comes to me in the right timing.* Sheep Animal Totem.

**819 - Shaking Foundation.** A period of happiness, is being

disturbed. You have had a running streak of luck in some area, or have experienced good karma, and disruptions are cropping up. These endings, or obstacles are part of the normal cycle of life, and will lead you into understanding deeper layers of why you are here. *All is well. I give thanks for my ongoing good.* Katydid Animal Totem.

**820 - Child Of Light.** Difficulties from childhood come to the surface, to be healed. There were betrayals that destroyed trust, and these are playing out in your present. Either those around you are proving untrustworthy, or your trust in yourself is in question. Have faith! You are not who you were told you were. Your identity is not a reflection of how you were treated. Your worth is greater than rubies. Building back your self respect and sense of worthiness, should be your priority now. Cast out those demons from the past, that would tell you otherwise. *I am a child of Source energy. I remain in innocence of Spirit. This cannot be changed...and certainly not by a world that lives in illusions of fear.* Sandalwood Essential Oil.

**821 - Hot Water.** Your words can get you into trouble. Many can be hurt by what you say, as well as by what you decide to do. Therefore, it is best to avoid situations that you know could be harmful to the other person, or other people. Focusing on your own life, and living it, will prevent you from causing others unnecessary pain and damage. You could permanently sever the ties you have with these people, by continuing on your present path. Instead focus on you, and what you need to work out in yourself, before involving others, or bringing them into your situation. *I heal myself, so that I am a blessing to all.* Green Tourmaline.

**822 - Fool's Paradise.** This is a number of warnings. Heavy karma is related to a 822. If the advice for 821 was not followed, 822 is the result. This is a number of pain, loss, disappointment and suffering. This may be you, or someone that you have hurt, by not saying no to a situation that you should have. It also symbolizes walking blindly into a situation, and someone or something pays the price. The advice is to ask for guidance from your Angels. Forgiveness apologies and healing are needed. *I choose to end karmic cycles with myself and others. Spirit guides me to the higher path of Grace.* Guardian Angel Sitael.

**823 - Foul Play.** There is success with this number, but

someone gets hurt in the process. Be aware of how your plans can negatively affect others, and realize that what we reap, we will eventually sow. Therefore, do not pursue anything, that has the potential to harm another, unless this is beyond your control. In all other ways, 823 is a number of good fortune and material success. *My actions are for the highest good of all, and I am blessed in return.*

**824 - Road To Riches.** This number has a very similar

meaning to 823. *I act with love, and my blessings return to me, in exact proportion to my actions.*

**825 - Deals With The Devil.** This is a number of triumph

over adversity, but there is the energy of those who would drag you down, and draw you to the darkness. These are dead energies, of greed-driven desire and temptation. Analyze carefully, those you are interacting with, and any deals you are thinking of entering. There are higher joys with 825, and someone seeks to take these away from you. *I am always protected by Spirit. I call forth my Guardian Angels of Divine Love, and am filled with the love and light of Spirit.* Guardian Angel Chevakiah.

**826 - High Stakes.** If you are considering entering into any partnerships, at this time, the advice is to steer clear. There is double karma, with this number, and you're walking a treacherous road. Emotional, and/or financial betrayal is possible. All is not as it seems. If you find yourself in this situation, spend some time in quiet contemplation, and ask your Soul for advice on how to proceed. In general, 826 says to be aware, and act with extreme caution. *I am always protected by Spirit. I focus on my relationship with myself, and I have all that I need.* Yellow Apatite.

**827 - Painful Predicament.** 827 is the immersion into the conflict from 826. You are in the midst of troubles, but there is an end in sight. The cause of the situation is karmic in nature, but you will come out on the other side, and not all will be lost. In general, 827 warns of seeming success, with hidden undercurrents of duplicity. *I trust that Spirit sees me through all things. My way is made easy, and my burdens are light.* Rainbow Aura Quartz.

**828 - Divine Decree.** 828 has to do with extreme difficulty, depression and loss. Anxiety and stress can be alleviated, by following the small still voice within. This oppressive energy must be dealt with, but do not let it take over your life. A lot of the energies and interactions are from previous lives, and are playing out now, in a continuing pattern. The idea is to break the pattern, forgive, and focus on the sparks of hope and brightness in the other areas of your life. This too shall pass. *I have the strength of Christ within me. I can overcome all obstacles, with faith in the Divine.* Beryllonite

**829 - Clear The Way.** There is much hostile energy with 829.

Warnings come, in the areas of partnerships and income, such as betrayals, dishonesty and loss, but you are also receiving clarity on the situation, as well. Don't ignore the facts, or the signs being given. Clear guidance can lead you out of the dangers. *I receive clear guidance from the my inner self. All is well.* White Agate.

**830 - Familiar Roads.** You have been down this road before.

Situations that are cropping up at this time, have an air of familiarity about them, and you are wise enough now, to not repeat old mistakes. Avoid speaking your thoughts, or trying to explain. You cannot change others, or situations, but you can avoid getting involved. Old reasons are no longer valid, as wisdom has been gained. *I see from a higher plane of awareness. My choices are for the good of all. I use my power wisely.*

**831 - Up And At 'Em.** This number has an air of loneliness

about it, and you could be spending too much time alone. Stalling or hiding from life, can lead to depression or listlessness. It is time to make a plan, set goals and start living the life that is waiting for you. Ask your Guides for reassurance and direction. *I am filled with energy, and motivation. I create a happy life.* Guardian Angel Elemiah

**832 - Ball Of Fire.** This is an extremely fortunate number of

goodwill, success and assistance. You have the wherewithal to get the job done, and are set to succeed. *My life is blessed. All works in my favor for the highest good.*

**833 - Niagara Falls.** 833 has to do with utilizing your skills wisely, in terms of investing, finances, saving, spending and the like. It has to do with the monetary world, but also the wealth of wisdom and knowledge coming to you at this time, in areas of your spiritual growth. Trust the information that you are receiving. The word "wealth" has many meanings, and can apply to many areas of your life. Timing is spring into summer. *I am grateful. I tap into the vast wealth of information and knowledge, that is within me.*

**834 - Movers and Shakers.** This number is talking about car issues, or possible issues with transportation. Being able to get somewhere, or be where you need to be. It would be advised to make sure you get your car checked, or review travel itineraries very carefully. Also, 834 speaks about issues with our need for control. A car represents power - the power to get somewhere, have a job, pick up groceries or make things happen in our world. It signifies movement. If we are stagnant, and holding on to control in certain situations in our life, movement will be forced on us. Sometimes this movement will tear down what has been constructed, or what you are holding on to. Do not resist change. *I let go, and allow life to bring me what I need.* Obsidian.

**835 - Tree in the Road.** This number suggests obstacles that stand in the way. Sometimes these are represented by you, karma being played out with other people, or the situation is not beneficial. This is the feeling of being stuck between a rock and a hard place. Something is going to muck up the situation, and goals cannot be met at this time. The advice is to pay attention, to what is happening. Forgive and bless what blocks you, whether that is your own defeating attitudes or patterns, or someone else's. Ultimately, it all reflects back to you. Sometimes you are being protected from making a bad decision, or continuing with a course of action, that is not for the best. So, with that in mind, bless what is seemingly standing in the way, so that the next step to take will be clear. *I acknowledge that all things are for my highest good, and I allow the truth to come to me now.* Kaolinite.

**836 - Race To The Finish.** There is good luck with this number, but the energies of Saturn are making sure you learn lessons first. Your drive, or willpower seems to be blocked at every turn. This can create frustration and angst. The advice, is not to force anything, but rather examine the issues at hand. What are the fears, that are pushing you toward a certain outcome? Finding understanding of the situation, and what is going on, will help you move through it. *I have understanding, and Divine clarity.* Hematite.

**837 - Crux Of The Matter.** You are at a turning point, where you can decide to make things more difficult for yourself, or move through the difficulties, learn and grow. Examine your true intentions. If they are aboveboard and pure, then you have the understanding that there are lessons to learn. 837 is related to 836, in many ways. Karmic circumstances are coming up, at this time, to be released. *I move through all situations, with ease. Spirit is my guide.* Anthophyllite.

**838 - Sealed Lips.** This number is related to the two before it, and describes the situation, as it has progressed to its culmination. Release is at hand. There may be some losses, and others could possibly be hurt. It is not a time to speak your mind, or to speak up at all. Learn the lessons, and move with what is happening at this time. *I am led through the darkness, into the light.* Auralite.

**839 - Trinities.** This number suggests conflict in a relationship, such as a love triangle, or 3 people at work, 3 friends, etc., or even issues from your childhood of the mom/dad/child relationship, that you have brought forward into your adult life. There are old pains that have carried over into your present relationships, either with others, or how you treat yourself. If you are in some kind of conflict triangle, then see how each person's roles relate back to your own childhood and parent issues. You may be running the same patterns, just in different forms. Bless all involved, even if this may seem like the hardest thing to do, and keep blessing them until you feel the situation shift. Either you will resolve the conflict, or be removed from the situation. *I observe how things are connected to me in threes, and I strive for balance and healing in all areas of my life.* Archangel Jeliel.

**840 - Be Nice To Yourself.** Release your Spirit, and set yourself free. Unbind yourself from worries, obligations and deadlines. You are in need of downtime and relaxation, as well as not holding yourself to such strict standards. Cut you a break. Are you as hard on others, as you are on yourself? If so, learn to be kinder, and forgive your perceived shortcomings. Your vision of you, is not really you, but a made up creation of unrealistic expectations and beliefs. As you begin to loosen your grip, everything flows easier, and problems take care of themselves. Life may seem to be pushing you to keep up, and get a handle on everything and everyone, but it is really just you doing this to yourself. *I release unrealistic expectations of perfection, and realize that all is in its right place. I flow through life* *with ease.*

**841 - Five Stars.** Good luck, good karma and spiraling to a number one position...841 promises good fortune in all undertakings. You can overcome any obstacle. *I have fortitude and grace on my side. The Angels bless and assist me in all ventures.*

**842 - Fishing For Problems.** A number of financial and material success, but with some difficulty. There is the energy of loss with 842, which should otherwise be a positive number. Be careful of hurting someone, or getting hurt. Weigh carefully, the benefits in pursuing a matter, if pain and loss could be the result. *I am raised up in Spirit, and act in accordance with the will of Source.* Nutmeg.

**843 – The Soul's Fortress.** Aligning with dark forces, may bring temporary success, but this will usually landslide into a physical and spiritual prison. Regardless of how the world may see your situation, this is a serious warning, that all may not be a bed of roses. Say "no" to whatever you are being offered, even if it is a "dream come true". Energies of evil intent are spotlighting you, and playing upon your fear-inspired weaknesses and desires. Align yourself with the light. Let Spirit take over the reins, right now. *My soul is one with Source. Source is love. Therefore, I am one with love, and all good things. I cannot be harmed.* Black Tourmaline.

**844 - Separation Of Past & Present.** There is a lot of karmic energy escalating with this number. You have two past lives, overlapping with this one. The energies may be bringing the situation to a sudden ending. The advice is to understand your role in the karmic pattern, to prevent this from happening. The timing for this, could be mid-to-late summer. A past life regression may also be helpful. *I see clearly, and release my patterns of fear, control and belief in lack.* Cerussite.

**845 - Keep Walking.** Walk the straight and narrow, because the path ahead is limited in its access. You must be paying attention and stick to the plan, stay on course, and not miss the signs. Rewards can be found if you stay to the task, and don't let emotions cloud your thinking. Focus your thoughts and move in one direction only. All will fall into place, as you find yourself in the right place at the right time. Doors will open for you, if you laser point your vision. All will unfold in front of you, if you leave distractions behind and continue on. *I know what I want, and confidently walk in that direction. All things come to me now, as I keep my eye on the prize.*

**846 - Bow Out Gracefully.** This number has similar energy, to 486. The difference is, that you have more of a choice, as your intentions will determine the outcome. *I choose the path, of the highest good for all.*

**847 - Light Of Morning.** This may be a difficult and trying time, but the sun will rise on a new day. Read 748. *Spirit moves me through difficulties, with ease.*

**848 - Protect Your Investments.** This number is signaling a time to get your finances in order. Do you need to increase your income, to meet demands? Do you need a different way to earn your money? This number also asks you to consider your investments, or lack thereof, and their efficacy. Have you been properly handling things...contributing to savings, investing, paying on debt? Spending, after these are taken care of, and controlling your spending is also a consideration. Is someone or something interfering with your income and livelihood? *I am always in Divine Supply, and manage it wisely.* Buffalo Totem.

**849 - Brute Force.** It will take all of your focus and energy, to get through possible difficulties related to this number, but rise above, you shall. The energies can be violent or hostile in nature, but 849 says you will conquer the challenges. Try to remember that any hardships, at this time, are related to past karma, and does not determine your future. *I trust in my inner knowing, alone, to deliver me from adversity.* Girasol Opal.

**850 - Cream Of The Crop.** You are being rewarded the very best, as your karmic due. This number has to do with shaving down one's options, to pick the finest choice. All good is coming to you now, in the areas of love, family life and money. *Divine goodness is mine to reap.*

**851 - Self Knows Best.** It is best to act alone, with this number. There can be much success, if you follow your own advice, and what you know. Monetary gains, and creative accomplishments are possible. *I celebrate my good fortune, and act with the wisdom of Spirit.*

**852 - Siren's Call.** 852 suggests dangerous waters. Alligators are swimming at the edge of the water, just underneath the surface. There is definitely a chance of injury and loss, and you must be awake and aware, of the lure and temptation to enter the water. Anything tempting, or "too-good-to-be-true", is just that. Indulging in fantasies, desires, or letting the lower nature rule, leads to danger and deception, and is basically a trap. *I align my mind and my intentions, with Spirit. I deny the temptations of the ego.* Tiger Iron.

**853 - Your True Source.** This number suggests much

increase and productivity, in the areas of finances, investments and relationships. There is a warning, however, that ego desires and fears could destroy your progress. Greed, or the fear of loss (which causes you to hang on too tightly), is likened to holding something delicate in your hand. If you squeeze too tightly, you will crush it. Understand that your needs are being provided for, and reject fear, and all feelings of doubt and lack. *I am of Source. All comes from within, as needed.* Brecciated Jasper.

**854 - Peace Is The Way.** This number is related to 486, but

says, that on the other side of the difficulties, will come peace. This number relates more to money, home life and spiritual challenges. *I ask for assistance from my Guides, and my answers come quickly and clearly.*

**855 - Anxiety Of Mind.** This number says that you are

getting too caught up in something, and are neglecting what is important. There can be much success, but this good fortune could cost you peace of mind. Hard work is producing results, but you must have balance in your affairs. Being all work, and no play, leads to burnout and depression. *I approach life, from a balanced and centered viewpoint. There is no need to rush. Everything happens in its perfect timing.* Nuummite.

**856 - Successful Prototype.** There are oppressive energies with this number, but overall it is a sign of good fortune, and coming out on top. Daily routines and rituals, are also highlighted. Becoming more organized, or finding ways to make your daily life more productive, brings success. To avoid the downside of this number, always follow your intuitive guidance. *I am sensitive to the needs of those around me, and find ways for everyone to benefit.*

**857 - Self-Sabotage.** This number has to do with old issues from the past, that relate to fear and lack. In particular, the lack of love, leading to problems with self-image, self-esteem and self value. 857 has a lot of energy behind it, but you pull the rug out from under yourself, by not feeling worthy, or ready for success. Whether this relates to another person, business, or a creative venture, you are your own worst enemy. A lot of these negative feelings sprang from your childhood, but also from various relationships with dysfunctional people. Taking a higher view of your life, and looking at it from a spiritual perspective, will help to heal your issues, or at least overcome their influence. Having a spiritual reason for living, is necessary, in order to move beyond the old wounds. *I am a child of the light. I am a precious creation.* Guardian Angel Lelahel.

**858 - Top Of The Line.** 858 suggests that you have conquered previous karmic cycles, and the overcoming of these, brings reward. This number is connected to communications at large, and massive growth in the areas of finances, investments and business. It also relates to magical relationships with soulmates, and those of like-mind. Overall an extremely fortuitous number. *I am blessed with the abundance of the Universe.*

**859 - Difficult Decisions.** See number 589. The current problems are due to neglect. *I am a child of the light, and I call this light forth in myself, now.* Blizzard Stone.

**860 - Well-To-Do.** Love and money come together with this number. Magic can happen, and what you have been waiting for, is upon you. The wish you made on that lucky star is granted. Receive your good fortune, and know that all situations are coming to successful resolutions. *I rejoice in my good luck. Prosperity flows to me, now.*

**861 - Green Eyed Monster.** This number can harbor resentment or jealousies, as well as a vindictive mindset. Usually what we see in others, reflects what we think we lack. Searching for acceptance, or justification from others, will only lead to being deceived. Stand tall, knowing that you are a child of Source, and do not need to search outside of yourself for value. *My needs are already fulfilled. All is provided for.* Eudialyte.

**862 - Thoughts Become Things.** Negative emotions may be making you sick (or you could already be physically sick), if you ignore them. If you are not accustomed to looking at your emotional state, these may be a hidden, or habitual emotions, of which you are unaware. It is for you to acknowledge how you are feeling, and take steps to change negative feelings.

These will manifest over time, into an unhealthy body, if left unchecked. It is also wise to keep in mind, that destructive emotional states, usually originate with negative thinking patterns. Take time to look up various affirmations, that can change the way you think. *I am happy, healthy and whole.* Guardian Angel Seheiah.

**863 - Young & Old.** If you have elderly parents, they could be needing your care. Spending time with the elderly, or young children helps you keep your perspective. You need to get outside of your routine, to alter your viewpoint. Being with the very young, or someone much older than you will help you remember where you are from, and where you are going. It has a grounding effect. Take responsibility for those that love you. *I love and accept those that are on this path with me, and I honor their needs. My way is clear. As I give, I receive.*

**864 - Troubled Waters.** Related to 846. *My life is calm and free of conflict. All is well.* Pumice.

**865 - Sensitivity.** This number has a lot of positive energy behind it, with minor concerns regarding emotional setbacks or pain. Overall, though, 865 is good luck and new beginnings. Childbirth or small children, new creative projects or pets are related to 865. *I choose wisely, and ask for the highest good, for all.* Guardian Angel Miniel.

**866 - Fruit of the Earth.** This number is saying it may be a good time to garden, and eating more fruit, may also be helpful. Strawberries, watermelon and apples in particular. Flushing out the system, fasting and detoxifying are recommended. A clear mind and body, always helps one succeed. *I enjoy perfect health.* Gray Pearl.

**867 - Dreams Come True.** What you dream for yourself is

being delayed, by the demands of daily life and old karma. It is like going to an unfulfilling job, daydreaming about going home, and looking at the clock to see your day has only just gotten started. You will reach what you are desiring and aiming for, so don't give up. *My dreams are being fulfilled in their perfect timing, and in their perfect way.*

**868 - Take The Leap.** This is a number of faith being

rewarded. It is positive karma, that signifies taking a journey, or going in a direction you have not gone before. If you are considering taking a risk, now is the time to do it. Jump. *I trust in Spirit. I have all I need.*

**869 - Practice Love.** Love is the answer to your problems, at

this time. There are many dangers and dark roads, and you may have given in to selfish wants, desires, petty jealousies, anger or other negative energies, that don't serve you. Entertaining these, will get you more of the same. Acting out of a higher love vibration, will bring you into love and happiness. Then, the guaranteed assistance you receive, will be aboveboard and in your best interest. *I choose love, as that is my soul's lesson in this lifetime.* Avalonite.

**870 - Fictitious Enemies.** This number is a challenge, to

overcome dark influences, and control your thinking. An easy way to do this, is to turn your thoughts over to Spirit. Put your Higher Soul in charge of what goes on in your mind. Taking the easy way out, or using your will to force a situation to work in your favor, does not bring satisfaction. The opposite effect happens, as what you put out rebounds back to you, multiplied. If you try to control, you are controlled. If you wish ill, you receive ill, and so on. *I honor myself and others. We are part of the same family in Spirit.* Ocean Jasper.

**871 - Cave Dweller.** Something serious or devastating has happened, and you want to run away, or hide. Perhaps this is just a general feeling of ongoing depression, or pain. The idea of living in a cave may appeal. At times, we do need alone time to rejuvenate, and refuel our own energy supply. In this case, being alone would be unhealthy, and not the answer. Maybe you have already been holed up and alone. It is time to take a step out, don't isolate yourself, make a phone call, repair a rift with someone, reach out and make amends, or make new friends. This number could also mean that you are avoiding someone, or some aspect of yourself. It is time to face things, and heal. *I reach out with gratitude to those around me, knowing I am always safe and protected with Divine Love. Sharing this gift of love with others, helps me heal, and rewards me with the same.* Lavender, dried flowers.

**872 - White Flag.** 872 is a call from your soul. Surrender to your inner knowing. Open your heart, look within, and know that you are supported and uplifted. You cannot fail, because Source is one with you. This number can be challenging, as it is tempting to give up control of your life, to an outside power. Surrendering to your inner self, is not sacrifice. Your true will is for you to experience love, joy and peace. All things that represent these three, will be given to you, if you will allow your soul to lead the way. *I am in in alignment, and at one with my true nature, which is Divine.* Datolite.

**873- Take the Lead.** This number signifies a leadership position, but it has to be on your terms, or you are not happy. This relates to leadership in a business, a group, a cause, a relationship, family, friendship, etc. You are being called to steer the ship. You may have to think about more than yourself, and do it, for the sake of the mission or the other person(s). You have the clear head, and the vision to lead the way. You have the answers at this time. *I step into my true mission in life, and allow all that wishes to manifest through me from Spirit, do so now.* Granite.

**874 - Making Room.** 874 says to do a blessing on your home and/or work space. Bless those that live, or work there. Clear out what is not serving you, or cluttering the space, and welcome in what is trying to reach you...whether symbolic or literal. Give thanks for all that is being given to you at this time, no matter how small or miniscule. *I open to the new, and clear the way for my good, now.* Blue Hackmanite (for its high sulphur content). As this stone may be hard to find, a combination of Sodalite and Sulphur can be substituted.

**875 - Getting To Get.** This number represents you giving selflessly in a situation. The problem is, there is an imbalance, and you are over-giving, while getting very little back. There is a warning of becoming drained, or depleted of all your energy, over time. Your intentions are coming from a pure place, and the situation may have started out being very fulfilling, but examine closely what is really going on, behind-the-scenes. Are you being respected, or respecting yourself? The solution here is to draw boundaries of what you will and won't do, and stick to them. *I open myself to giving and receiving.* Aqua Aura.

**876 - Brush It Off.** It is a powerful time to reach out to others, and connect with old friends...friendships relationships, business associates, relatives, or those with whom you have lost contact. This is a time for reconnecting, and new beginnings. Doing things differently. This is not a time however, for repeating painful, or harmful situations with those who caused suffering. Heal your past and present, with forgiveness. *I release and let go of all painful memories, that live in my mind. The past is over. A new future awaits.* Hedenbergite.

**877 - Feeling At Home.** This is a number that has to do with home life, and where you are living. Are there issues at home? 877 is asking you to find, or create harmony in your living space. This may be with others, or in the actual look and decor of your home. Where you reside, is your place to rejuvenate your energy, and recharge. Are you homeless at the moment? What are your feelings about your home life? Healing is needed. It may be something as simple as giving yourself a special place in the home, that is decorated just for you, or something as complex as healing a relationship that is causing issues. Is the mortgage too high? In any case, if all areas of your home life are in harmony, 877 is a sign that a new addition is coming to the home, and more security. *I am safe, comfortable and at peace, in my home.* Glendonite.

**878 - Head On.** This number talks about karmic issues in relationships, and wanting to hide, or avoid a certain person, or confrontation. This is not necessarily a negative number, but more a number of avoidance. What are you running from, or not wanting to look at? Success comes, by being around the people you love with open honesty. Issues can be healed, if you will face them head on. The choice is yours. *I bravely face others, with honesty, an open heart and the desire to heal.* Erythrite, wash hand after use (as it contains arsenic), or wrap in a cloth.

**879 - Up to The Next Level.** This number is talking about

completion. There is a cycle that you have been in for a very long time, and it is coming to an end. You are full circle, and must examine what has gone before, in order to initiate a higher and better phase. This number says better things are coming, if you will recognize and complete your former lessons. Usually the lesson is in a general sense, and applies to all areas of your life. There may be one area that seems to stand out. 879 usually signals an emotional issue, related to fear. 879 asks, "What is it you fear?" If you can answer this, you have solved a large part of the equation, and can clear the air for a fresh cycle to begin. *I recognize when fear is playing a hand in my life, and release it as an impostor. The only truth is love.* Chrysanthemum Stone.

**880 - More Than We Believe.** See 808. Progress through

karma is made, if one allows Spirit to lead. *I am Divinely guided, and protected. There is no lack or pain. These are illusions of the mind.*

**881 - Mission Accomplished.** This is a number of success in

the financial and material realm. 881 is a powerhouse number that packs a punch. If you have set a goal for yourself, get ready to skyrocket to number one. It is your karmic destiny to succeed. You are flying on the wings of fate, traveling as far as your imagination will allow. *As a Divine Co-Creator, I supply my every need. I rejoice in my good fortune.*

**882 - The Ruler.** This is a number about claiming your power

in personal relationships. This may be your child, spouse, parent, employee, boss, client etc. Claiming your power, does not mean that you hold power over someone else, or take away their power. It means respect, and not draining the other person. If you decide to be in a relationship...which means taking your attention away from taking care of yourself, and giving some of that to the other person...then you need to be receiving the same, in return. Otherwise, one party is weakened from giving away their energy and power, and the other becomes "the ruler". They, in a sense, begin to own you. This is imbalance. Honoring another person's right to their own power, is respect. This is crucial in any relationship. But first comes self-respect. *I maintain respect for myself, and therefore respect others, in turn. I am a balanced, whole and free individual, in my own right.* Trigonic Quartz .

**883 - Community.** This number is a sign, that it is a good

idea for you to become involved in groups, to start a group, teach, join a workshop, or interact and network with others in a group. This could be something that you do from home, or online, such as a social media group, master mind group, or something that you create locally in your community. It could also be a support group for help with personal issues, business, or other areas where group input, assistance and support is needed. This number involves connecting with like-minded individuals. Groups can help motivate and increase the energy of any goal, bringing it into manifestation. We all need each other, as we do nothing alone. *I reach out to others, and our energies unite. We are stronger together than apart.* White Pearl.

**884 - Victim Of Fate.** Your needs get sacrificed for others, or something gets taken away, like your time, your money, or your peace of mind, so that someone else can benefit. There is uneven give and take. The other side of this number, is the benefit of having done this cycle in the past, and now it is over...you have learned from it, and no longer allow this energy in your life. *I accept my life lessons. I trust that everything happens for a Divine Purpose.* Kammererite.

**885 - Brand Spanking Good.** This number is one of renewal, after heartache and difficulty. Things are turning around, and good news is on the way. There is another piece to the story, that has not come into play yet, but know that you may see an increase in finances, receive recognition, a change in your reputation, or others opinions of you. All new things can happen at this time. *I move from fear, discouragement and pain, and realize that all things are renewed in this moment, if I but ask.*

**886 - Bliss.** Harmony and beauty rule here...the harmonies of words, such as poetry, beautiful music, or a tastefully decorated home or work space. Whatever assists in your balance is called for, to rejuvenate your inner creative self, and spark desire in your expressions. You need stirring up. You need excitement, a muse, or stimulation. You need your soul stirred. Allow the rhythms of beauty to bring you a sense of wholeness, joy and ecstasy. These will carry over into your life. If something is going to make you feel good, now is the time to spend the money on it, or say yes to luxuries. *I surround myself with expressions of beauty, joy and love. I am a channel for these, and they unfold in me every day.*

**887 - Addicted To Love**. This is a culmination number,

meaning you have reached a certain degree of spiritual growth, and now face a new level of fear. This is a challenge to overcome your addictions, which is really an addiction to fear. Spirit says, if you would deny the fear, and the seeming terrible consequences it promises, illusory painful outcomes would disappear. Fear is the stranger here. Is there anything that Spirit could not overcome, remove, or heal? It is in fear, that belief is formed. You will experience that which you believe, or will remain in a state of waiting for that which you fear to manifest. Either way, you are trapped in a state where miracles cannot reach you. Turn your fears over to Spirit. Turn your addictions, which are escape mechanisms from fear (which hides or masks itself as misery, depression, anger, grief etc.) over to Spirit, as well. 887 says you can do this now...take the first step, or maybe you have begun this process already. It is for you to continue. What are you addicted to, and what do you fear? They go hand in hand, in many ways. *I am a being of Divine Love. I am one with Spirit. In reality, there is no fear.* Emerald.

**888 - Build Your Nest.** This is a number of wealth-building

and growth. 888 suggests that you should utilize the information available to you, to invest, or take action with your money. It is said that this number brings great riches however, this may be symbolic of many things. There are riches in terms of loving relationships, advancement in career, a highly developed skill set, riches of the Soul, those in your pocket-book and riches in the areas of wisdom and knowledge. The advice is to take as much time investing in your connection to Divine Love, as you do the material world. Otherwise, one can be caught up with the power, inherent in this number, and be led astray. Remember 88 is used as the number of satan(see end chapter). Don't give energy to a false power. Deny dark forces. *I am blessed and enjoy unlimited abundance.*

**889 - Honoring Feelings.** This number has to do with

feelings of anger, hurt and resentment, that is usually with another person, but spiritually has to do with your anger at yourself. These are feelings that have been with you a long time, perhaps buried or denied. The indignation seems to fuel you toward accomplishment, but many may be hurt in the process. Originally, this anger stems from you getting hurt, probably repeatedly, and turning that hurt into anger for survival. It is harming you long term. Anger management, healing, spiritual studies and techniques may be required for you to let this go. You must also forgive yourself for what you did, or didn't do in your life, and how you hold resentment for your mistakes. A dramatic healing is called for, as this cleansing may take some time. *I understand that everything has its purpose, and happens for a reason. I am at peace with myself, my life and with others.* Papagoite.

**890 - A Master In The Making.** You are becoming what was

suggested in number 89. Powerful energies are leading you toward your destiny. Allow Spirit to bring you to your joy. *I am a child of destiny. I allow Source to determine what is best.*

**891 - Writing On The Wall.** There are many growth

opportunities coming, and you need to discern between opportunity and challenge, so that you can decide the best path available to you. It may be time to explore methods of divination, guidance in meditation and other ways of discerning your future, so that you can be prepared. This would be a good time to study tarot, or get a tarot card reading. *I open to my natural psychic abilities, and trust that the information I receive is correct, and for my highest good.*

**892 - Light At The End.** This number is challenging you to

get through difficulties, and say no when necessary. Things are coming to a head, and the way out is being shown. Finish up unfinished business, and take the exit you see in front of you. Things will be looking up, and you will be rewarded, when this karmic time is over. *I am flanked by support from my Angels. All is working out, as it should.* Chabazite.

**893 - Deep Six The Past.** A great amount of energy and focus

needs to be spent on the underlying meanings behind difficulties. This can help you get through current problems. 893 also says that you need to be getting more rest and sleep, in order to accomplish, that which needs to be done. If a situation is difficult, 893 says you can turn it around. Let others know you care, and heal what needs to be healed. Forgive the past, so it does not become the future. Whatever you feel right now, is magnified. *I am a Divine Being, in an illusory body. My abilities and purpose are far beyond this incarnation, and how it defines me.* Oregon Opal.

**894 - Breaking The Bonds.** This number is connected to

relations with other people. Some of your relationships are amazingly supportive, but you are also surrounded by the opposite extreme. This number says to be prepared for betrayals, upsets and dishonesty. There may be relationships that are dying off, and this is what is meant to happen. Either they were not what you thought, or you did not come honestly to the situation. Some of these endings may come unexpectedly, and be the biggest surprise. Realize that this is unfinished karmic business from past lives, and let happen, what will happen. Forgive. Release. Let go. *I let go, so that the new can come in.* Rhyolite.

**895 - Freedom From Oppression.** Related to 589, but things are in state of change. *All is working out for the best. I welcome positive changes.* Carnelian.

**896 - At All Costs.** This is similar to 869, however dark motivations are strong, and you are in need of following the advice for 869. Success is assured. *Love is my true identity. As a loving being, I have all I need, when I give it to others as well.* Archangel Cahetel.

**897 - Haste Makes Waste.** This number represents a time of frustrations and lessons. Even though things may seem meaningless, everything has been for a reason. Meditating on this, is advised. Spending time in this type of reflection, will give you a larger viewpoint, and enable you to see the higher purpose. Better times are coming. *I find that still silent place within me. All answers come to me now.* Dendritic Agate.

**898 - Path of the Soul.** This is the time to take a pause, and shift your focus. Recognize who you truly are, and what you came here for, so the opportunity to complete your soul's journey does not pass you by. All is provided, when one is on their true path. It may seem like you are giving something up, by letting go of the wheel, but in actuality, you are allowing yourself to experience the peace of knowing that all works out for the best. The challenge is for you to explore yourself, and why you are here. *I focus my thoughts on what is truly important in life. I look within to my inner self and listen to my heart.* Melikaria

**899 - Love & Compassion.** This number has the color pink

attached to it. 899 means that you are in need comfort, and to be in a lighter love energy, such as the color pink suggests. It may help to visualize this color, or carry a pink crystal. You are in need of gentleness, compassion and self-love. 899 suggests being kind to yourself, and eliminating contact with those who are unkind, or disrespectful. It also says that you may be removed from situations such as this. Be aware of your health, whether that is physically, mentally, emotionally or spiritually. There may be illness at one of these energetic levels, or the possibility of sickness. These afflictions, come about from abuse, or mistreatment by self or others. Thoughts and emotions bring this negativity about through manifestation. A cleansing is needed, and a reconnection with your spiritual higher self. Be kind to you; you are all you have. *I love and honor myself, and treat myself with gentleness and respect.* Pink Danburite.

**900 - Rocket Man.** 900 symbolizes an incredible energy surge

of motivation with focus. Previous patterns and cycles have been completed, and major accomplishment has been achieved. Physical energy levels improve. You may be ready to pass on what you have learned to others, or move into a new sector of your life. New interests and skills come to the forefront. Your options are open. Good luck is yours. Claim it. *I am opening to a new cycle in my life, of love, fulfillment, inspiration and abundance.*

**901 - Trailblazer.** This number symbolizes a fresh start, into new territory. 901 is a number of Source. This is the Divine in all things. You are connecting with Divine energies, and finding your true center. The answer here is to listen to the voice within, and your success is assured. Realize that everyone around you may have messages for you, and to "listen", not to the words themselves, but the message for you alone, in what they are saying. They are part of you, and are one with you. It is time to trust and stand out on your own. Take the lead. Take the leap. Move forward, even if there is no path that can be seen, you are blazing a new one. *Good luck and good fortune finds me now.*

**902 - Diligence.** This number talks about energies that are not in harmony, but not necessarily unfortunate. You have vision and drive, at this time. Everyone around you has a purpose and a message for you. If you do not act rashly, you will understand what that is. Patience. All good things come to those who stay calm. This is also a number of merging. You are being asked to join together with those you are interacting with, and come to a common ground. Find agreement. Mend fences. Forgive the past. Reunite and renew those relationships that have gone to the wayside, or have been a cause of anguish. Repair partnerships with others. Find peace and common ground. You are in this together. Work together. Allow for differences. Partners who are spiritually compatible, could be entering your life now. *I am always blessed. I do not need to push or force, to have what is mine. Timing is everything.*

**903 - Unplug.** Time for a break! Slow down and take some time out, to get a different perspective, and come back recharged and energized. This is a positive number of strong guidance, assistance and good luck. 903 is merging with the energies of Spirit, in creation and action. It is the type of action that has to do with thinking and speaking. You must say your truth. You must ask for that which you desire from Source. You must understand that your thoughts, emotions and will must all be in alignment. The thoughts must be creative, the emotions must be still, and the will must surrender. Then Spirit can lead you gently and definitely toward your goals. *I am at peace with my world. I find rest in Spirit.*

**904 - Fried Circuits.** This number has to do with electrical energies. These can be electricity, appliances, computers, radio waves, or the energy between two people. (As I write this, the smoke alarm just started going off.) It also has to do with the electrical energy of the body. We are electric beings, and our brain is a transmitter and receiver. This number suggests a warning of issues with something electrical, or health related issues of the brain or nervous system. It may also suggest your nerves are fried, or over-strained. Recharge, take a rest or do what is necessary to make a change. 904 also says build a stable foundation under that which you are trying to create. If it is a healthy relationship, a business, a painting, or whatever, you must proceed from the ground up. Make sure all your ducks are in a row, and all details have been accounted for, as organization must come before success. It is beneficial to be conservative right now, but not too conservative. It is time to read the fine print, and make sure you are on solid ground before continuing. *I am calm and centered. All is well in my world.* Campbellite.

**905 - On The Move.** 905 energy is alive! This is movement, freedom and lack of constriction. 905 is telling you to open up to the wind in the trees. Hear nature calling you to be free, to choose, to live. It may be a good time for you to be in nature as much as possible, or to bring it into your home. Five is saying travel if you can, or let your mind roam. Daydream. This is how ideas are born. Release the past. Let go of the old, outworn and outdated, and move forward. This includes old patterns of thinking. Money is coming. This is a number of miracles. What is it you need? Ask the Angels for help, and you will receive what is the best for all involved. *Miracles come to me naturally.* Archangel Hamied, of the Christ Light.

**906 - Family Lineage.** This number is related to family, including your ancestors and descendants. There is a strong line of support, and you are here to pass on a new legacy of love. Examining DNA patterns, or seeking shamanic help to work through ancestral patterns, will bring many shifts and blessings. This is a number of assistance on many levels, inherited talents and utilizing your gifts. Ordinary life, can turn extraordinary. It is also a time to be peaceful. Are you meditating, giving time for spiritual pursuits, breathing, doing yoga, taking a bath, creating art, or anything that calms your Spirit and clears your mind? Make peace with family, friends and those with whom you are having difficulties with; bridge troubled waters, and lay down the hatchet. Let go. Let Flow. Let yourself be freed of all that would upset you in this moment right now, and join with your brothers in the light of oneness and togetherness. *I honor my heritage, and bless the world with my unique gifts.*

**907 - Selective Seeing.** You are in a transition. There may be sudden shifts, or the need to let go of what you are afraid to release. Because of this, you may not be seeing things for how they actually are. 907 says it is time to find an alone space, where you can take a few minutes each day to be yourself. Let go of judgments. No one is around to argue or criticize. Just be you. Sing, laugh, cry, or do whatever you want to do, that you have been denying yourself...that others have been seeming to deny you. Take time for you. Stop the train, if the majority of your day is spent doing for others. Carve out time just for you, every day. Get alone, even if that means leaving town to do so. Delve within yourself, and discover who you are, why you are here and where you want to be. There is nothing to fear. You are Spirit, not the ego-self that appears to be here. Your "sins" don't exist outside of this place. *My way is made easy, and my burdens are light. There is nothing to fear.* Aurora Borealis Stone.

**908 - Law Of The Land.** There is a higher karmic purpose, in what is happening. You may have legal issues going on, or some conflict that needs resolution. Your ability to be optimistic, may become difficult, but know that there is healing and gain, when you break free of this situation. Ask yourself some questions. What is your greatness? What are you great at doing, being, creating? Who are you? It is time for you to pay attention to your personal power, and just how immense your Spirit is. You are so much more than your identity, or name. You are a vast Spiritual Being. You deserve respect, care, love and abundance. This number is saying it is time to allow this, and set your boundaries. Determine how far another is allowed to cross. Determine how you will be treated. Step into your power, and go for your dreams. 908 says they are about to come true, or will come true. They may need you to put in the work, first. *I ask for clarity and guidance. All is working out in my favor.* Archangel Nemmamiah.

**909 - Back to School.** You are in a learning phase. Spiritual studies, going back to school, and universities are highlighted with 909. You are expanding your knowledge with this number, whether this means going to a trade school, taking continuing education, job training, business masterminding, reading books and educational materials, attending seminars or workshops, or enhancing and expanding your spiritual knowledge, understanding and viewpoint. *I willingly learn my lessons, and expand my influence.*

**910 - Snooze You Looze.** The future is up to you! Your life is in your hands. Motivation increases. Remember that everything reflects back to you, so what you give out, you get back. Choose the higher path, and see the results fall into your hands. *I create a future of love, abundance and benefit for all.*

**911 - Telegram.** This number has to do with messages, and information coming through for change. (Even though this number is recognized in the US for a tragic event, the numbers of a month and day are interpreted a little differently.) 911 relates to messages through the mail, or by other means, that bring good news. Change is coming for the better. *Good news is coming to me now.*

**912 - Under The Surface.** This is a number of separation, and the return to wholeness. Deep-seated emotional issues rise to the surface, to be released. Hidden parts of yourself, become known. All that you have tried to escape, seems harmless, when seen in the light of day. Your perspectives are shifting, and you are sensing the cohesive oneness of all beings. If you are not experiencing this, then it would be wise to meditate, or find time alone for contemplation. You are in the midst of a massive healing shift. Soul growth and finding peace within, are imminent. *I am at one with all. I am at peace.*

**913 - Mayday.** News is coming, regarding some kind of loss.

Know that what is best, in the overall grand scheme of things, is happening now. All change is what is meant to happen, or what is necessary. *I am guided, protected and comforted at all times. What I need, will find me.* Strombolite.

**914 - Mindful Prose.** 914 is, in general, an extremely lucky

number. It suggests that you may be good at poetry, or should try your skill writing lines, or song lyrics. It may also suggest picking up a book on poetry, but writing your own, can be an exercise for getting in touch with your deeper self. Sometimes poetry writing can lead to channeling. It is a good time to memorize an affirmation, or a quote that is meaningful to you. Even better, write your own. Making it rhyme helps you remember it. Also, this number is talking about your memory. Remembering details is important, as well as remembering people and who they are, for later reference. Increase your memory skills to enhance your mental capabilities. *My mind is a clear channel. I have access to all memories, as needed.*

**915 - Double The Pleasure.** Your talents and abilities are

magnified, and people are noticing you. What you ask for is given, and the path seems golden. You seem to be getting twice what you asked for, and good luck abounds. *I give thanks for the blessings that fall into my lap, everyday, in a perfect way.*

**916 - Step Lightly.** 916 has a spiritual lesson, and a strong warning. Delays, setbacks and destruction can come about, through exerting your power, or anyone holding theirs over you. You must proceed with caution, and keep your eyes open. Keeping the peace with others is crucial. Come from an inner place of unselfishness, rather than ego. Do not let fears push you into positions and places in life, where you could have a lot to lose. Don't force others to show their hand, or bend to your will. In turn, don't let others have too much control over you, that would put them in a position to cause serious or irreparable harm. *I accept that all is in its perfect place, and has its perfect timing. I do not feel the need to force issues, or allow myself to be bullied, as all is unfolding in its own way.* Bear Animal Totem.

**917 - Savings Account.** This number is connected to 916, and says that there is healing and hope for the future. 917 says money, and good fortune are coming. Healing the past, and having money to save or invest is assured. A massage or energy work would be helpful, at this time. *I have a brighter future, coming to me now. Abundance is mine.*

**918 - Waning & Waxing.** Frustration can build, as what you want to happen is getting delayed. The change of the moon cycle may bring things into the light. What has been hidden or kept from sight, is revealed. Psychic abilities are at an all time high. *I am led by Spirit. All things happen in their correct timing.* Peach Moonstone.

**919 - Glory Hallelujah.** Your highest purpose is being born.

Whatever you are here to do in the world, is beginning to manifest, or amping up to a new level of actuality. Happiness is yours. A beautiful blessing finds its way to you. If this represents the birth of a child, it may be twins. *I am doubly blessed, and give thanks for the good coming to me now.*

**920 - Psychic Guidance.** Intuition is very strong right now.

Rely on your natural psychic senses. Follow the gut feelings, nudges, dreams, or information you are receiving at this time, even if it may seem illogical. It is also a good time to explore methods of divination, if you are interested in tarot, runes, astrology etc. Answers and correct guidance come through intuitive channels, that may not be easy to explain to others, but 920 is urging you to pay attention. *I am a psychic being. My abilities are strong and accurate, and Spirit guides me correctly.*

**921 - On The Brink.** This is the calm before the "born".

Success is on its way. Take this time to prepare for it, and think it through, all the way. Do what needs to be done, to anticipate getting what you want. Be in a state of expectation. *I welcome the good, that is finding me now.*

**922 - Excitable Emotions.** This number says that things may

be very sensitive, or it could be an emotional time. 922 also says that things could happen suddenly, or unexpectedly that cause emotional reactions. Depending on the situation, these emotions could be celebratory, or sorrowful. Feelings are heightened, and you will be overly reactionary to what is going on. Try to stay in a calm, centered space, so that you are prepared for whatever is going to happen, and can act accordingly. If you are tuned in, you will sense when these surprises or changes are coming, ahead of time, and can prepare. *I am calm and centered. All is well.* Amazonite.

**923 - Guaranteed Results.** You cannot lose, with this number. Success in any undertaking is yours. Allow it to be. *I trust in an abundant Universe.*

**924 - Night Shift.** There may be roads that are not wise to follow. Earthly ego desires, bring no meaning to your life. Spending time getting in touch with the seasons, and the natural rhythms of the Earth, however, would be beneficial. Using magnets or resetting your natural biological clock, gives you more energy and improves your mood and sleep cycle. Going to bed early can help. There is much interference, and dark energies trying to pull you off your path. They could possibly be what is disrupting your sleep, or causing the problems, you are now experiencing. *I am a child of the Earth. I experience great joy, aligning myself with natural rhythms.* Mochi Marbles.

**925 - Yogi Dreams.** Spiritual pursuits are highlighted. Higher education or studies into unknown, or hidden mysteries is beneficial. Your beliefs are being re-aligned. This number is auspicious for the future. *I am a being of light. Spirit moves through me, guiding my way.*

**926 - Defining Territory.** You need space, or alone time.

Others are encroaching on your space, ruining your concentration, distracting you, or interfering with your ability to stay emotionally balanced, and get things done. You need an area you can call your own, to recharge your battery, or get a different perspective. Maybe its just some peace and quiet that is needed. The reverse side of 261, is you are afraid of being alone, or hanging on to someone too tightly, and need to find out who you are, by yourself. *I have a right to my own space. I take the time to care for me.* Panda Animal Totem. (As I am editing this, the date is 9/26, and a man is talking so loud, I cannot concentrate.)

**927 - The Adept.** This is a number of reward and

achievement. You are mastering many levels of yourself, including your Earthly life, your emotions and your psychic awareness. Much luck is associated with 927. You are ending many cycles, and moving into becoming the expert. *I am skilled to accomplish all that I need. I reap the benefits of my efforts, now.*

**928 - Shipshape.** You are being forced to value yourself, and

overcome fear. Hard experiences, or lessons are aimed at this very thing. As you overcome the past, your strength, confidence and self-respect increases. You may have had many restarts, or stops and starts. This is changing, as new energies of joy are entering, and success is assured. *I love and respect myself. I do not need to seek it from others. I am whole.* Nebula Stone.

**929 - Divine Plan.** Your spirituality needs to be the central focus of your life. You have a message for the world, and something to teach. This may be in a literal sense, or in your daily interactions with others. This is a lucky number of drive and intuition, a powerful combination. *All has purpose in my life. Nothing happens by accident.*

**930 - Key To The Universe.** You have all you need to create whatever you intend, as well as the wisdom to exit this plane of existence, and its reincarnation cycle. You are the key to yourself. You can choose to take any doorway. All is available to you. All choice remains with you. What is it going to be? *I am the master of myself.*

**931 - Illusory Separation.** This is a number of possible loneliness and isolation. The individual may be cut off from contact with others, in a literal sense, or there is someone that you are unable to contact. This isolation and separation is not healthy. The tendency is to withdraw into oneself, as a reaction to rejection, or hide. Opening one's energy to reaching out, solves dilemmas. This number also relates to the illusory separation we perceive between each other. It is a good time to meditate, and connect with the oneness of all beings. This will assist and enrich your life. *I am in communion with all.* Amblygonite.

**932 - Eskimo Buys Ice.** This is a fortunate number in all areas, but particularly in the fields of communication, business, finance and sales. Success comes, because you have mastered a certain level, and are putting in the hours to make it happen. All roads are paved with gold. *I am one with success.*

**933 - Supply And Command.** See 932. Assistance is given in all enterprises. *Prosperity is my natural inheritance.*

**934 - Love Others As Yourself.** 934 may be rooted in your past relationships with siblings, parents or partners, and patterns that carry over. Whether you were taught to love yourself or not, 934 says to remove harmful relationships that may be in your present life. You must choose you, and to learn to love you requires eliminating negative and abusive influence. Otherwise you could sabotage what you have built, so far in your life, as well as destroy solid foundations that lead to many benefits. Honor those that have gone before, and choose love. *All living beings are my family. I am part of the larger whole.* Columbine Flower.

**935 - Claim Your Rights.** This is a number, of breaking free of illusions, relationships and anything else that is holding you back, from being who you really are. Freedom *should not* come with a price. Exiting something that was unhealthy, usually costs you to get involved in the first place, and will have a fee (usually quite costly) to leave. You do not have to earn, or deserve freedom. It is your natural right, that has been stolen from you. Ultimately, it is those "in charge" who control the system. No one is in charge of you. *I honor myself, and all people, as having their own right to freedom. I break all contracts, negotiations, initiations, agreements and anything I agreed to anywhere, at any time in the past, as null and void. This is a free will Universe.* Cacoxenite.

**936 - Front Of The Line.** You live a life of harmony and abundance. All is flowing as it should, and all efforts are rewarded. *I receive all that I need. My blessings overflow, to share with others.*

**937 - Green Man.** A trip to the mountains, or some place where you can get away from troubles, would be very beneficial for you at this time. Just as thunderstorms and rain bring in a fresh new energy, being out in the elements, renews your spirit. This is a fortunate number for speculation, career changes, and all new undertakings. *My Spirit is one with my mind. All is as it should be.*

**938 - Turning Point.** This is a spiritual challenge number, asking you to make a choice between your spiritual path, and your own personal agenda. When you choose your higher path, you realize you can have both. There is no lack, although we have been programmed to believe this. In Spirit, we have all...we are our larger selves, not the small part that incarnated as a personality. You are so much larger than what you are doing in this world. Now is the time to make the choice, and your choice will affect your future, from this point forward. *My Higher Self guides me on my path. My will is one with the Divine.* Herderite.

**939 - No Doubt About It.** This is a successful number of gain, promotion and attainment. All ventures expand and grow larger. Channeling skills may become apparent, or grow clearer. *I attune my energies to higher channels of wisdom, light and love.*

**940 - Counterbalance.** This number warns of dangers and possible endings. Be prepared for a radical shift. Know that when things are out of balance, the Universe tries to right itself. You may not have realized that this equilibrium was off, but in the higher perspective of our lives, all is happening for a reason. If it is time for someone close to leave this plane, ask for the comfort and guidance of your Guardian Angels. Difficulty can be bypassed, or handled easier when we calm the mind, and attune ourselves to Spirit and inner guidance. *I am safe in the loving arms of Spirit. Everything is happening for a higher purpose, and I trust this, whether or not I can see the end result.* Archangel Haniel.

**941 - Signs Of The End.** This number is a sign that things may be coming to an abrupt end. You may have felt this for some time, but now it is happening, and is out of your hands. 941 is saying that there will be healing, and renewal, when this is over. You may need to cleanse the body, take extra care of your back and spine, and take herbs to purify the blood. *I flow with life, and allow that which is passing, to go.* Snowflake Obsidian.

**942 - Gimme, Gimme!** This is a number of desires not being met. It can bring up many negative emotions and influences. You may be tempted into jealousy or wanting what another has, and what you think you do not have. The danger is, this can also lead to unnecessary spending, getting in debt and indulging in what is not good for you, because you have an inner feeling of being deprived, or neglected. These are traps.

True Spirit is abundance. *I trust that Spirit brings me everything I need, at the perfect time.* Serandite.

**943 - Claim Your Rights.** See 935. *I am free from all repression, and anything or anyone who tries to interfere with my spiritual destiny.* Vulture Animal Totem.

**944 - Me Time.** This number represents the struggle between doing what you need to do, and the sacrifices that everyday life and others demand of you. This number has to do with family obligations, work obligations and the daily requirements of life in general. 944 says that you are getting caught up, and possibly losing yourself, in a situation, or in another person(s). Quiet time is needed. Even if this is only five minutes, where you can sit and evaluate. Much of your time is spent doing things that you don't want to do, and not enough time spent pursuing your dreams, or finding joy in living. This number signals that it is crucial for you to carve out time for yourself. *I honor and love myself. My life is mine to live.* Orange Calcite.

**945 - Judge Not, Lest ye be Judged.** This number has a message about judgment. Either you are judging others, are associating with judgmental people, or being unfairly judged. This activity, or energy, has the effect, of hindering the person passing judgment. When we demean, or criticize others, we attract that energy back to ourselves, because we are all essentially one Spirit. If you find that you are the judge, release this tendency to place blame or denounce, as it causes harm to others and yourself. You may have self-esteem issues, but tearing down another, will not lift you up. If you are the victim, bless those that curse you. 945 could also be talking about a situation, where your judgment is off, or you are not assessing it correctly. Lift yourself up, into the higher energy of Spirit, and bless those around you, and you will be blessed. *I am one with all. I mind my business, and let Spirit handle the rest.* Bronzite.

**946 - Weight of the World.** 946 is a sign that you are

experiencing large amounts of stress in your life. It could be manifesting as headaches, inflammation in the body, digestive issues, sinus conditions, or other issues. These conditions could possibly be caused by burdens that you carry, from day-to-day. The stress is taking its toll, and it is time to address the issues that are causing you to react. The solution, is to first meditate, ask Spirit for assistance, and then make a list of what is essential and not essential in your life. Anything that is related to another person's drama, is not yours, and you have the right to say no. You have a right to live your life, without their chaos and demands, interfering with what is important for you to accomplish. Create your boundaries, and stick to your guns. *I live a life of beauty and peace. I sail through life easily and effortlessly. My burdens are lifted, and all is taken care of for me by Spirit.* Azumar.

**947 - Captivity.** You are doing what is necessary to maintain

the status quo and keep the peace. This number warns of giving up your own needs, and bending to the will of others, in order to maintain a situation. If this is short term, then that is fine. On a long term basis, this is damaging to you, and keeping you from walking a free path. It would be best to remove yourself from a situation that requires you to constantly deny who you are, your needs, or to make large sacrifices, over a long period of time. You are a master in your own right. You are here to overcome the illusion of being imprisoned, or owned by anyone. *I am a Divine Child of the Universe, with my own path and destiny. I allow myself to follow that path, now.* Cuprite.

**948 - You, The Jailor.** This number has a feeling of being imprisoned, or trapped by something. You may be in a situation or state, of being tied to unwanted commitments. Is something tying you down? Are you trapping yourself in a situation that seems impossible to get out of, or overbearing and heavy? What is weighing on you? 948 says there are choices you can make, to get yourself out of this feeling, or literally out of your situation. You have to realize, that you chose on some level, to be where you are. By accepting it, instead of fighting against it, you can now choose differently, and start the process toward actual change. *I am free in Spirit. All things can be made anew.* Celandine Root.

**949 - Mirror of The Psyche.** This number is talking about deep inner needs, fears and issues that reside in our unconscious. Your fears are running your life. Delve into your psyche, and examine where these fears stem from...some may be from past lives, some from your very earliest moments as an infant, and many will be from childhood up to age seven. These fears are repeating patterns, and exploring any of these sources will help you eliminate their hold on you. 949 also asks you to explore your connection to all of life, and all things, and to understand that your world is a mirror, reflecting back, either of your choice for fear, or your alignment with your Higher Self. *I am comfortable exploring all aspects of myself. There is nothing to fear.* Cavansite.

**950 - Golden Vein.** 950 is a number of the energies of manifestation. What are you trying to create for your life? This number is a sign to call it forth. Creativity is strong, and hobbies and creative projects can grow into something more, if given the right attention and focus. *My life is filled with miracles.*

**951 - Full Speed Ahead.** You would be good in positions of authority, or leading others. Everyone is lined up to assist you. Changes can happen very quickly. Be wary in decisions, making sure that other people's intentions are pure. *I am assisted on all levels. My blessings are many.*

**952 - Nervous Nellie.** You may have restless thoughts, as your mind flits quickly from topic to topic. Ideas may flow abundantly, at this time. You may feel unsettled, itching to make something happen. There are slight nudges, coming to you from your intuition. Follow these, and all will turn out well. Your fiery nature must be tempered. Calm your mind, and flow with the current. Beliefs and viewpoints may be turned upside down. Overall, this is a number of positive energy. *I am at one with my higher purpose, and flow through situations with ease.*

**953 - Worldly Woes.** There may be disturbing things happening in the world, at this time. You may be listening to too much negativity in your environment, or in your news sources. It may be time to change to only positive news for awhile, or don't listen at all. The weight of the world, triggers you to feel anger, or sorrow from negative news, that seemingly keeps you powerless. Your powerlessness couldn't be further from the truth. Focusing on what is going right in the world, and joining with, and supporting others that are doing the same, is how you can find peace. Remember that words can quickly tear down what has taken years to build. Focus on the good, and emphasize what you want more of, not what is bringing you down. *I am powerful, and create change, with the positive energies of joy, courage and love.* Wavellite.

**954 - Mother and Child.** This number relates to past love relationships; in particular the mother figure. It is about repeating patterns from childhood, in current relationships. How are you being the mother, or a version of your own mother, in your current relationships? Or, are you choosing a partner, associate or friendship with someone who is similar to your mother? Did you lack a mother figure, or had a mother who was unavailable, or absent most of the time, causing you to seek nurturing through others? Looking at relationships through a higher perspective, can help you evaluate where possible problems are stemming from, and decide how you can heal a situation. The key is to realize your patterns, and the hole, or lack that you think is inside you that needs to be filled. We all have these wounds, but 954 is signaling that yours have come to the forefront in your current situations, and it is time to alter the patterns. *I am no longer a wounded child. I'm a child of Spirit, and am nurtured and comforted. I have all that I need.* Blue lace agate.

**955 - Winning Blueprint.** You cannot fail. This number catapults you into the high ranks of achievement. You can actualize anything you want, with 955. Miracles are waiting to happen, if you call them forth in the proper way. Reaching the top of the heap, is all but guaranteed. Movement and change is quick, like lightning. Instant results. *What I desire and need, finds me now, easily and effortlessly.*

956 - **Walking Gently.** This number has to do with endings.

It is an ending of a relationship, or two opposing ideas. This is usually positive in nature. It means that what you are seeking to break ties with, was not good for you, or is not good for your future. Opposition is stepping aside, and letting you move forward. Be careful what you say, and do not let anger color your words. Allow this shift and change to happen as smoothly as possible, without adding further upset or problems. *I am one with the flow of life.* Brazilianite.

957 - **Fabled Friends.** If you are interested in fairies, elves and

nature elementals, this is a good time to explore and connect with these beings. 957 suggests exploration and adventure into unknown territory. It is a time for you to open your mind to things you would not normally believe in. Connecting with the magical realms around you, heightens your awareness of the life force. All that is invisible, is being revealed. *I am surrounded by support from the invisible realms.*

958 - **Lock Down.** 958 means a hard stop to proceedings.

There is interference. If this is relating to finances, you are having to rein them in, and take control of spending. Or, you have a lot of resources, but this situation is telling you not to share or expend them now. This is not the time to squander, but rather protect and preserve what you have. There may be shakeups to your foundation, so you must stand firm. *I preserve what I have. I am grounded, and alert to the signs around me, and I wait for the appropriate timing.* Cinnabar.

**959 - A New York Minute.** This is a number of drive,

willpower and magic. You have a brilliant mind. What you envision, succeeds. You have the golden touch. Energies pick up, and bring in abundance with great speed. *My visions come true. I manifest what I need, with ease.*

**960** - This number has to do with the attraction of opposites.

Differences create a more unified whole. It is related to romantic partnerships, or any pairing that complements each other, whether that be in a skill set, temperaments, or helpful viewpoints. Good luck comes in pairs. This is a number of enjoyment and pleasure. *I live a fulfilling life of enjoyment, pleasure and happy experiences.*

**961 - The Visionary.** This number has to do with messages

from Spirit. Your Spirit Guides, your Angels and the Universe, are speaking to you, at this time. You are receiving information, either in dreams, visions, ideas or feelings. It is for you to follow through on these hunches, especially if they have a "right" feeling to them. Know that you are being given the information to solve, or heal any conflicts that arise. Do not be tempted to decide for yourself, but listen to your higher guidance. *I have all I need to succeed.* Lavender Quartz.

**962 - Soul Family.** This number has to do with children. Did

you lose a child or a loved one? Did someone close to you lose theirs? This is also a sign of childbirth and renewal. What has been taken, is being restored. Know that a child is never lost, as they continue to be with you in Spirit, or may come back in the body of someone else close to you...possibly another birth. They are part of the Divine plan with you, and together you agreed to play out certain scenarios (even painful ones) together, for higher purposes you may not be able to see, right now. Our soul knows its mission, and you must trust that all is happening, for the higher plan. We are all children of the Universe. As adults, we are still insecure little kids, still looking for that connection to love. If someone around you is calling out for love, then give it to them. 962 is also a message that your pets may need attention. *I am one with all in Spirit, and cannot be separate.* Unakite.

**963 - Put It In Writing.** This is a positive number of extreme success. The only thing that can hold you back, is negative thinking. 963 says it is a good time for writing, such as journaling, or writing that article or novel you've been thinking about. *My dreams are my reality.*

**964 - A Clean Sweep.** 964 is telling you, it is time to clear the clutter. What is cluttering up your life? Negative thoughts? A messy home? Friends that aren't supportive, or drag you into drama? A codependent relationship? 964 says to clear the space. Release old energy that is stagnating, and holding you back. Clean, clear and bless what is leaving. New situations, people, adventures and blessings are coming your way, once you make some room for them. *I live an uncluttered life. My mind is in harmony with my surroundings.* Prasiolite.

**965 - Check It Off.** There may be many things happening at once. There is a lot of input, stimulation and distraction, and trying to do too many things, can leave you ineffective. You are making progress, however, but you need to find a way out of the whirlwind. Delegating tasks, and eliminating that which is not immediately necessary, will help to scale back on the endless to-do list, that confronts you every day. You must prioritize, pick your battles, and get your life back into an organized orderly state. *I take care of my own needs first, and am able to say no, to that which is not truly necessary.* Silver Gray Druzy Agate.

**966 - Door Prize.** This is a fortunate number of harmonious circumstances, and winning at the game of life. Positive communications and relationships with kindred spirits are highlighted. *I attract loving relationships. I am healthy, happy and holy.*

**967 - Home Sweet Home.** This number has to do with your home life. Are there issues going on with the physical structure of the house, or does something need to be checked, that would normally be routine maintenance? There are warnings of losing a loved one, or possible problems with the actual home. Updating your home, or making your surroundings more comfortable and cozy, will help ease tension, and provide a place of healing for you. Feng Shui could help with this, as well as use of color. Create a place of peace, to calm volatile relationships with those who live with you. *I have order and peace in my home. Source is my support and comfort.* Apache Tear.

**968 - Can You Hear Me Now?** Are people listening to you?

Are you speaking with their interests at heart, or are you too focused on self, and what you want to say? This is a message to listen to your communication style, and how you relate with others. It may be a sign that you need to learn to listen. On the other side of this coin, it means that others may not be listening to you. Your needs are not being heard, and you are talking to the wall. Usually these two manifestations of ignoring someone else and their viewpoint, or your message not being heard, are connected. Meaning, if you are not being listened to, chances are, you are not listening. In another sense, if you are trying to get a message across to others, they are not getting it, or will not follow through with what you desire. Eventually, you will break through this block. *I bring myself to the present moment, and focus on that which is in front of me. I am all ears.* Aquamarine.

**969 - Cloud Nine.** This number is related to 966, and

connected to past life relationships that are karmically rewarding in this life. 969 is a fortuitous number of good luck and fortunate dealings with others. *I give thanks for my good fortune. All is working in my favor.*

**970 - Sequestered Sanctuary.** This number talks about

privacy. If you are working on a project, or trying to get anything accomplished, you need privacy. Keep your creations away from the prying eyes of others. Do not let them in on your secrets, or your plans. You can let others know about what you are creating or building, after it is finished, and has been released. Working alone, or in quiet private spaces is recommended. No matter what the situation, keep your secrets. Remove yourself from the influence of others, so that you can hear the quiet voice within. *I am at peace, and have the space to do what is necessary. I hear the still quiet voice within.*

**971 - Draining Life Force.** This number has to do with chaotic energies. There are many things outside of you, that are taking, or draining your energy. Are you spending too much time around technology, and being locked in to the computer, or phone? Are energy vampires around you? Something, or someone is sucking you dry. There is too much stimulation. Getting somewhere peaceful and quiet, and turning the world off, would be highly beneficial for you right now. *I find my inner sense of peace and calm, and let the rest go.* Gem Silica, or another light blue, or green stone.

**972 - The Dreamer Dreams.** This number could mean dissatisfaction with where you are, or what you have accomplished, and may lead to daydreaming, or wanting to be free of constrictions placed on you by others. You might have big plans, but feel unable to accomplish them, other than to dream. 972 is saying that Spirit is working with you, at this time, asking you to examine why you are where you are. What is mirroring the situation? When you can answer this, you will be led to the meaningfulness you seek. Many like-minded friends can be found along the way. The decision lies with you, and the Universe is waiting for you to take a step toward what you want...even if that is just making a decision. *I trust my visions, and make plans accordingly.*

**973 - Godly Goodies.** This is a number of unexpected circumstances, such as the birth of a baby, or a symbolic birth, such as an invention of yours, or a better way of doing things. It promises happy endings and success. *I give thanks for the many gifts I am given.*

**974 - Expect Miracles.** Good karma is coming to you. You can welcome it, by not resisting, criticizing or judging anyone. Place these negative mindsets aside. Abundance in many forms can reach you, if you will hold your hands out to receive it, with gratitude. All the blessings may not be apparent initially, so stay open. What comes in now, will pay off later. Gratitude will bring in more waves of blessings. *Everything is for my highest good. All is happening for a reason.*

**975 - Sit Back And Relax.** 975 suggests a lot of energies going on, and it may be time to open up your psychic senses, for understanding about what is happening. Things tend to be in a state of chaos, so you may want to wait until the dust settles, and just sit and watch, in the meantime. Not a time for action. *I sit calmly, in the middle of the storm, and await my answers.*

**976 - A New Form.** You may have on your rose-colored glasses, having hope in a certain situation, that is in fact ending. It is time for you to accept what needs to end, and let it go. Save your dreams and your heart for another day. Protect your sensitivities and soft areas. Keep hold of your dreams, and what they are leading you toward. Let go of old dreams that you put your energy into, whether this is a project, or a person. Hope never dies, just the old forms. Paint a new picture on the canvas of your future. *I face my future, with confidence and love. All is well.* Dravite (Brown Tourmaline).

**977 - Divine Placement.** This is a message that you are being directed by fate. You are where you need to be, when you need to be there. There are higher purposes at work here, and you are on the correct path. Whatever happens will be remembered afterward. Your deeds, intentions, creations and input will live on. This may affect one person, or many. *I am at the right place, at the right time. I accept whatever is happening, because I know it is for the best.*

**978 - Breaking Through The Ceiling.** The number 978 speaks of opposites, and the light and dark forces, that fight for humanity. On one side, there are those forces, trying to keep us from freeing ourselves from the trap of reincarnation. On the other side of the coin, there are those beings who wish to help others to ascend from this reality...those who wish to break the ceiling of restriction and repression that has been put over us. This is a time of choosing sides. Which side are you on, the light or the dark? Will you take the higher path, and stand in the middle - a space of neutrality? For in this space, neither side is recognized, and true unity can be found. Transcendence can be yours. In a more worldly sense, 978 talks about situations where others are taking sides. It would be wise for you to take the middle ground, and remain neutral. *I stand firm. I'm able to see all sides of any situation, and I stand on middle ground, uniting all as one.* Atlantian Quartz.

**979 - Spiritual Destiny.** You are here to overcome all karma, and go home. You have become a master of your reality, and as such are wise in the ways of the world. New spiritual information is coming to you, and your viewpoints on how the Universe works, may be shifting drastically. What you thought was your existence, is expanded as new information is entrusted to you. Blessings flow, and spiritual awareness is heightened. *I unite with the vastness of my Spirit, and am at one with the Universe.*

**980 - Child of Destiny.** This is a number of destiny. 980

suggests that you are in the hands of fate, and being guided to where you are going. You may not get every single thing you want, but there will be reward, for a job well done. You get what you asked for, whether you asked in this life, or the previous one. You are at the mercy of this fate, so to speak, but you are in good hands. Life can be bountiful. The future and the outcome are already set, however, so you will have to let the situation play out as it will. There is no use fighting fate. Just enjoy the journey. *I am a child of fate. All of life is working in my favor.* Rose Quartz.

**981 - Nobility and Honor.** This number has a promise of

advancement, with the warnings of aggression. If you are forcing issues, or pushing forward with hostility, or demands, then the victory of this number can backfire. 981 is a number of elevation and reaching one's desires, but the tendency to fight, lash out, or beat an opponent, is the type of energy that will begin your descent. If you oppose, you meet with opposition. What you put out into the world, gets mirrored back to you. This number asks you to take the high road, and go toward your dreams and desires with a hopeful, grateful and balanced perspective. Honor and bless those that have helped you thus far. Give thanks for the assistance you have been given, to reach new heights of achievement. *We do nothing alone. I am grateful and honored for the blessings bestowed upon me.* K2 Stone.

**982 - Weighing The Cost.** This number is about pleasure, particularly when shared with someone else. It is found in love relationships, but also with money, which can buy material pleasures. This number asks you to examine what you are seeking. What are you going to have to give up, in order to have the pleasure you seek? If it is a relationship with a partner, pet, child etc., what is the cost to you? Is there an imbalance of power in the giving and receiving? If you wish for money to buy possessions, that give a temporary, or even fleeting pleasure, what is the overall cost to you outside the monetary amount? For example if you are charging an item, and will have high interest to pay later it may not be worth the cost. Reassess your needs. *I go to the stillness within, and find immense peace and joyful ecstasy, where all my needs are met.* Amethyst.

**983 - Reckless.** Do you feel stifled, or frustrated? The warning here is to watch the temptation to say whatever you want, with no filter. Use self-control. Go ahead and speak your mind, but think it through before opening your mouth. Slow down, have patience, and you will find success. *I act and speak from a space of wisdom and control. I bring love into all my ventures.* Blue-green Kyanite.

**984 - Dark Before Dawn.** 984 has to do with issues of the soul, where beliefs are challenged, and life seems to be dragging you down. You may be facing difficult aspects in yourself, or your deepest fear is being brought to the surface, and playing out in a myriad of ways. Remember, the darkness is an illusion, no matter how real it may seem. You can turn troubles around, by following the guidance of your higher self. *I am made in the image of the Divine. Love is my only reality.*

Merlinite.

**985 - The Dance of Fear.** You are moving into a new phase in the karmic wheel. 985 is not the release from this karma, but a bearing down, that implies one has to address certain lessons, in order to proceed on the journey of life. These lessons, are the keys to reuniting with Spirit, Source, the Divine. The foundation has been built, and now the hard work continues. The release of fear is a layered process, and 985 says you are beginning this cycle. Usually, you will go through experiences, that help you release these layers. Understanding the fear, is not enough. Along with challenges, this cycle also brings with it, a focus on security, and the wisdom that nothing is secure, outside of Spirit. Learn to place your trust in the only place that it will be safeguarded, unless you entrust it to Spirit. *I honor my lessons, and submit to the experiences I chose. I am becoming whole again with Spirit, and my higher nature.* Tenorite.

**986 - Childhood Innocence.** This number relates to beauty, in the sense of purity and innocence. This type of energy applies to children. It is time to let go of issues from your childhood, and not repeat those with your own children, or those with whom you come in contact. These contracts are sacred. There needs to be a realization that children are their own persons. They came in with their own destiny, and should be treated with respect. In a related sense, this number is also applied to animals, as they keep their childlike innocence throughout their life. Respect those that are under your control, or responsibility. Learn from what they have to teach you. Bring that impeccability into your relations with others, and with yourself. Treat all with respect, and you will begin to experience inner joy expanding within you. *I respect* *and honor the innocence in others, and in all life. I see innocence and purity everywhere I look.* Guardian Angel Muriel.

**987 - Patient Progress.** This is a number of insight and

clarity. You may need to examine the current situation you find yourself in, and determine what your intentions are, as well as how you are giving up parts of yourself to it. This can be a beneficial number, if you are coming from your center, and not denying your needs. Surrender to Spirit, and let yourself be led. Wait for your guidance, and do not rush things. Wait. Proceed. Wait. Proceed. *I see clearly, and act with Spirit.* Hackamite.

**988 - Releasing Grief.** This number implies painful

circumstances, and possibly drastic endings that have occurred recently, or have happened some time ago, but are still with you energetically. 988 suggests that this is a time of hard work, focus and diligence. One must continue to focus on the task at hand. This includes your daily life, and what is going on, but it includes chipping away at old painful experiences, and learning to transform them into memories, instead of open wounds. It does not mean that you forget what happened, but that you learn to let go of its hold on your present. This means acknowledging the blessings that you now have, and moving step-by-step into a future, where you are no longer a victim of the past. Spirit does have many new, positive and enjoyable experiences for you, but you must work through and clear the karma of these experiences, first. Analyze your thoughts, and take steps to heal. *I choose to stay in the present moment. All things are renewing themselves.* Lava Stone.

**989 - Hamster Wheel.** This is a number of re-learning

lessons. It represents a pattern you are stuck in, and repeating. Mistakes will be repeated, in some other form, until you disconnect yourself energetically from this pattern. *I release the past, so that I can be free.* Rutilated Quartz.

**990 - Finish Line.** This is a powerful number of physical

energy, change, and accomplishment. You have mastered many things, and are at the pinnacle of enlightenment. 990 also says it is time to be more aware of the Earth. Sending loving energies can help heal the planet, as well as taking action to save the environment...the trees, animals, and our clean air and water supply. You have much influence, and the Earth could use your help. *I use my energy wisely. I act from the messages I receive from Spirit.*

**991 - On a Dream and a Smile.** Success is yours! Smile! If

something has happened and you don't feel like smiling, doing it anyway will help you shift your energies. A smile will win miles of success...a good attitude in your situation, guarantees things turn in your favor. People feel good around you, and are ready to buy what you are selling. *I have all I need to succeed. Joy brings more joy, and reasons to celebrate.*

**992 -A Gentle Hand.** This is a number of opposite forces, that

do not necessarily oppose, but balance. Different energies can work together in your favor. If you balance drive and force, with emotional sensitivity, all can work in harmony. Meaning, don't step on someone's sensitive feelings, because you can't restrain yourself. Work with others, and understand the needs of both sides of the situation. Luck comes through effort. *I have wisdom to understand what needs to be done. I act with kindness and prudence.*

**993 - First Class.** You need a vacation, or a change of scenery.

Long distance trips are highlighted. If you cannot travel in a literal sense, it is important for you to take some time to daydream yourself somewhere else. Put up pictures of locations you would like to go to, or take a vacation in your mind. Let it wander. Talking with others in far away locales, opening your business to become a more global one, and studying foreign cultures also apply, and bring good luck. You need to broaden your horizons. You have been too rigid or stagnant. *I allow myself some movement, as I break out of old patterns that are holding me back. Life changes for the better, because I change my routine.* Green Garnet.

**994 - Getting it Done.** This number relates to

procrastination, or avoiding doing what needs to be done. This usually happens, when you have given your power away to someone else. You are a dynamic person. You can accomplish great things. If someone has made you believe otherwise, either currently, or in the past, reaffirm your greatness, and send back to them their negative beliefs. Call back your energy you gave away to them. This is not to be done in contact with them, but in your mind. *I have confidence in my own ability to finish things. I do this, because it makes my life better.* Blue Aventurine.

**995 - Magic & Miracles.** See 959. The same energy applies. I

have the willpower to make anything happen. *All works in my favor.*

**996 - Peacemaker.** You ascend to greatness, with 996. This is the number of peace on Earth. The lion lies down with the lamb. Your spiritual journey has been an eventful one, and now you are coming to a sense of inner peace. You have a job to do in the world, and it is the title of this number. *I am the bridge between worlds, people and nations. There is no one my Spirit cannot reach.*

**997 - Fine Tuned Instrument.** You have conquered the ego, and lower natures. Your soul is moving toward ascension. You are fine-tuning your purpose, and where your path leads from here. Trust your vision as your mind is clear, and your judgment pure. *I find my path home. My way leads to glory and Universal Love.*

**998 - Wanting For Nothing.** This is a number of duality. It represents temptation, the lure of materialism and keeping up the status-quo, as opposed to spiritual focus and growth. Therefore, it reflects success in the mundane world, but at a cost. The lesson to learn, is when we pursue our spiritual path, all things are added unto us. If you're on the *true* path, there is no lack. If you are being required to give something up, this is not true spirituality. Another way to look at the meaning of this number, is monetary reward, or climbing the ladder of society's expectations, but having a price to pay. This price could be a loss of a spiritual belief system, so that when one comes to the end of their life, the pursuit of money, or success is meaningless. *I walk the path of my spiritual journey, knowing that I want for nothing.* Bismuth.

**999 - The Entryway.** This is the door to other worlds. 999 is the ultimate completion. You have finished your karma, and may move on if you wish. There is nothing held back with this number. Movement forward is guaranteed. You have mastered the self and the lower nature. The Angels applaud you. Your destiny lies in your purpose, that was defined in number 997. The Angels are calling you home. *I have completed my mission, and my path is clear. Where I go from here, is revealed to me now.*

**1000 - Lead The People.** This is the energy of the Sun, and

this solar system. You are a master. 1000 says you are authentic...who you say you are...and others see this, and follow, or trust you. This is the highest leadership position, and represents one who leads with grace, for the good of all. Do not be afraid to take the lead, or take the advice of those who are displaying these qualities. *I am a natural leader. I know the way.*

# Chapter Two:

# Beyond 1000

In this chapter, I get a little more in depth, on the energies of a few significant numbers beyond 1000.

## The Number 1111; 11:11

Following is an excerpt from my book, "5 Numbers of Destiny", where I introduced some of the energy meaning of the 11:11:

***11:11, 33 & Other Mysterious Numbers***

*You may have heard of the "11:11" phenomenon, which started in the early 90s, where large numbers of people have been noticing 11:11 everywhere they look. In addition to the 11:11, many people are frequently seeing other number patterns, such as "1234", "11:33", "12:12" or "1333", and so on. There is a lot of speculation, as to what these coincidental number sequences mean. It is believed that the "11:11", "1:11" or "11", is considered a doorway to a higher vibration of evolution, as the Earth moves into this more* *enlightened frequency. Synchronicities are related to this shift. I see the 11:11 as two doorways, representing the "battle" between light and dark, or good and bad. I feel that these energy doorways have opened up, and people are being given a choice which door they are going to take. Are you going to side with the light, and choose to allow your soul to evolve spiritually, or are you going to get sucked into the dark side, and remain stuck in the false power and suffering of an illusory world? These doorways can also be likened to choosing the Creative Self or the ego. (Some are of the belief that this evolvement opportunity will take us into a 5$^{th}$ dimensional reality.) There is a major fight, or last ditch effort happening right now, by those that would see us held back, to keep people in the darkness of ignorance, pain, anger, grief and suffering. A fight for souls, or the age-old battle between the light and the dark. It may be a time to make your choice. I also view the 11:11 as a doorway, for many souls to enter and exit, during this time of accelerated evolution. The 11:11, for me, is also a revolving doorway, meaning that cycles come and go. We evolve, then devolve, in an endless loop. Some see 11:11 as a divine alignment timing, for Twin Flames to reunite. A lot of these noticeable number repetitions and combinations relate to the sacred geometry of the universe. These numbers are markers along the way, of synchronous happenings and alignments. It is also thought that we are in a type of matrix computer program, similar to the ideas in the movie, "The Matrix". Number repetitions and serendipities are information about where we are in the matrix hologram. It is the very confinement of this program, that makes the choice for evolution, as mentioned above, necessary. In a nutshell, realize that the energies of such numbers* *as "33", "13" etc., represent the light side, and have positive messages, but are also being used by the dark side to trap, enslave and ensnare. Your intention and choice to evolve, or not to evolve will decide their influence on you, good or ill. This is a world of duality. While 11:11 has many positive connotations in the "New Age" movement, if you are a realist, you will have to consider the other side of things as well.*

*In the early 90's, Solara authored a book "11:11: Inside the Doorway". It fueled an awareness of the 11:11 phenomenon, and made it an organized movement. The premise purported to be a welcoming, of a spiritual shift for humanity. The 11:11 doorway was bringing in an age of peace. The sign that it was here, was backed up by the amazing coincidence, that people from all different walks of life seemed to be noticing the numbers 11:11, showing up everywhere they looked. And they are still seeing it today. The date of this "11:11 doorway" opening was 1/11/92. I was shopping in a new age bookstore, when Solara's book first came out, and I bought it. I was searching for truth, and yes, I was seeing 11:11 everywhere (starting for me in 1988-89). Over the years, though, something didn't feel quite right about the idealistic visions of this number sequence meaning. She had forgotten to mention the other half of the equation. (See the following section, 11, 3333, 7777, 8888)*

## The Numbers 11, 3333, 7777, 8888

These are also related to any repetitions of 1, 3, 7 or 8, such as 33, 77, 888 etc. I will start with the meaning of the number 333, which is related to ancient Egyptian religion, some of whose practices have been brought back to life in more recent times, by a man named Aleister Crowley. (Some say he was influenced by Illuminati agendas, but I choose not to give attention to, or go into my opinions on this matter.). Briefly, Aleister Crowley was an Occultist and Magician, born in 1875, who created his Law of Thelema, and practiced many rituals that were essentially, in my opinion black magic. His original focus was to overcome his ego and lower self, but that got lost in the mix of unrelated belief systems he meshed together, in which his personal journey became one of satanism, drug use, ritualistic sacrifice (what these involved, I don't wish to know...although he has made mention of the use of young boys used for sacrifice, in one of his books) and the taking over of his body by demons (he ended up in a mental institution). It is amazing to me, the number of people that want to follow the teachings of this man, since satan, lucifer etc. will always betray you in the end...the prince of darkness...is the prince of betrayal, so come on...why would you choose this path? Anyhow, I'm getting sidetracked...the number 333 is the name of the demon choronzon (I spelled that with a small "C" deliberately, as ultimately these beings are not of Source, and therefore, not real, except in the matrix construct...which is also not real. So they are unreal in unreality. I include satan, lucifer etc. with this.) If one is seeking enlightenment or returning to Source, he is the last great obstacle one must face to overcome the hold this world (matrix) has on one's soul. He represents obsessive desire, inconsistency, change and chaos, which is the epitome of this world, and the opposite of Source, or a peaceful state. choronzon has been seen in a positive light by some occultists, because he helps cast one's intentions outward to manifest personal desires (aka "black magic" no matter how it may seem, otherwise). This 333 demon, choronzon relates to the number 11. In the Qabalah Tree of Life, 11 means the Sphere of Daath. Daath is the Abyss (this world/matrix), where one enters the "Black" or "Dark Night of the Soul", where one is trapped in the mental state of the demon choronzon.

I believe the 11:11 is a doorway that opened for dark forces to enter, in alarming numbers. Their higher purpose (of which they are unaware) is to challenge us, and move us forward on our spiritual growth. For us, it is time to choose sides, or leave the planet if one cannot handle the energies. I believe this is why we have so much chaos in the world, as I see and participate in the battle of light and dark, currently being fought at extreme levels. On a positive side, it is the challenge we face right now, and an opportunity to overcome our egos. Demons will always teach a lesson, and unwittingly help us advance on our spiritual journey, if we stay on the path, and don't get sucked down by them. One can see many of the metaphysical, or new age teachers, like Wayne Dyer and Doreen Virtue, switching their teaching focus toward the overcoming of the ego, as taught in books like "A Course in Miracles", "Be Here Now" etc.

We are constantly deceived by dark forces. Solara (see 11:11) was doing rituals to open the doorway, believing she was assisting the good, when rituals in their very nature make it very easy for dark forces to do their work. In my healing work, when I remove a dark entity, I am given its name, if I ask. It is very interesting that when I go to Google the name, all that comes up are names of video games, tv shows and movie titles. These dark entity names are being used in media to hide themselves, so one cannot search for truth about them. I had to go to search page 5, or beyond, before I started finding information.

11, 333, 77 and 88 are numbers relating to satan, however, they can also be used for their exact polar opposite purposes of spiritual evolution:

11 is the number of magic or "magick", or any form thereof, and is wisely warned about in Chaldean Numerology. If one uses this number for higher purposes, it can be a number of mastery, such as in Pythagorean Numerology. 333 - As stated, represents the demon choronzon. This number has a light side, as well. 77 is the name of the goat on the altar - the devil in satanic worship, and also the 77 names of the devil. Funny that a double 7, to me, is good luck, and spiritual growth. 88 relates to the Illuminati. 8 is a number of power, related to the planet Saturn, which is the goat god and related to the world of false hopes and fake power. It also has its higher purpose, in karmic growth, lessons, and learning of the true power, that is Divine Love. As dark side chooses dates with these numbers, for certain rituals and actions, look for combinations of them, in noteworthy chaotic events in our world. Are you noticing the splitting off, between light and dark, in our world?

## Other Numbers

**1010** - This number represents choices, related to the 11:11, and the 12:12.

**1113** - "13" is another favorite of the dark side, since it is a number of power, however, as mentioned previously, the only true power is Divine Love. All others are forms of false gods, with transient fading agendas. Therefore, the combination of 11 and 13, is a lesson in the correct use of power. All greed, lust, desire etc. are lower forms of energy, that originate in a belief in lack. Since this world is a place of lack, putting our faith in it, and attempting to gain power over it, is pointless. All comes from the Father.

**1133** - Relates to dark side influence, and the opportunity to utilize wisdom, to choose love. It is the choice to overcome the ego self, and go home to Source.

**1188** - This number is used by the illuminati. Regardless of what their "mystery" agenda actually is, please send out love to all in the Universe, if you see this number.

**1333** - See the numbers that are related in this chapter: 1313, 333 and 1113.

**1212** - This is a number of mastery. You are reaching a level, where you can actually conquer karma. The results of your choices now, will be extreme. If you choose love, you will reap reward. If you choose hate, you find yourself in the lower vibrations of suffering and victimhood. This is a doorway home, that is coming up for you to choose.

**1234** - This is a number of accepting your power to choose.

For in choice alone, do we decide our fate. It is also a sign that things are moving toward their fated direction. All is lining up. Things move quickly, and your intentions are heard by Spirit.

**1313** - This is a doubling of the 13, and a very powerful

number of overcoming the karmic cycle. See also 1113.

**1488** - This is a number used by white supremists, (remember,

dark side does not get to own these numbers) and therefore, I ask that if you see this number, send love out to all in the Universe. This adds to 21, the conquering of the world, and its ego hold on us.

**2020** - This is the grand awakening of souls, and the exit

points to go home. It is more in a Universal sense, and a movement, that is coming.

**3333** - This number is related to different levels of fallen

angels and demons, as well as their opposite counterparts, that represent the wisdom of Source. Both seek to have influence on your path. The lower vibrations seek ownership of your soul, trapping you here, and the higher vibrations uplift you to the realization of the One Spirit that you are, which is part of us all. In a general sense, 3333 is a number of extreme luck.

**4314** - I write this number for a friend, who requested it. It signifies a life lived with many challenges and lessons. This may also relate to a temporary phase one is going through. These can be related to painful deaths of loved ones, that you will have to go through, at some point in your life, or other major lessons of hardship, depression and the like. It does not mean that your life solely consists of pain, or that you are meant to suffer. You are capable of overcoming these difficulties, and have the gift of prophecy. If this gift is developed, and nurtured, you will have the ability to see beyond the veils of this worldly illusion, and overcome the lower self. You will be guided. Your purpose here is not to suffer, but to let go of your belief that you need to. Choose joy. Choose love. Choose kindness toward self, and learn that this is what Source desires for you, as well. Then you will find it from others.

# ABOUT THE AUTHOR

Anmarie Uber's interest in the metaphysical field has continued, throughout most of her life. She had her first remembered contact with the other side, at age three, and an insatiable passion, throughout childhood, for ghosts, UFOs and anything paranormal. Anmarie began exploring astrology and numerology at age 16, and tarot, yoga, massage, nutrition, palmistry, crystal healing, Feng Shui, energy healing, and the philosophy of reincarnation at age 21. Her ongoing quest for spiritual truth has been all-consuming, and has many times taken precedence over personal needs, or worldly goals. What she has found, is that many belief systems can be roads to nowhere...another program to be sifted through. Although Anmarie has studied and lived countless spiritual and religious ideologies, the last five years of her life have been the most challenging, as the pressure to keep humanity down is increasing. Anmarie believes in finding the humor in difficult situations, letting go of needing to suffer, by living out "punishment" karma, and having faith in yourself. We are all programmed beings, trying to awaken. And awakening to your true Self, as the source of your creations, is the most important accomplishment in life. Her website is anmarieuber.com

If you liked this book, please consider leaving a review!

You can find Anmarie Uber on Facebook, Youtube and Patreon!

Learn how to neutralize patterns of poverty, infidelity, sickness, and other roles we replay in life, that keep us from happiness and fulfillment. We all have at least one difficult area that we struggle with...what is yours? This book explains where these patterns originate, and teaches you how to awaken, and remove them from your future life.

## "Cheat Sheet: How to Name Your Business using Chaldean Numerology"

***Get your FREE COPY here:***

anmarieuber.com

*Interested in learning how to erase difficult karma, and experience a life of abundance? Check out Anmarie's book on Chaldean Numerology:*

**Available through most retailers.**

CPSIA information can be obtained
at www.ICGtesting.com
Printed in the USA
BVHW061602030522
635996BV00032B/2377

9 781393 737773